SOFTWARE FOR SPATIAL ECONOMETRICAL ANALYSIS
Operation Manual of GeoDa、GeoDaSpace and PySAL

空间计量分析软件
GeoDa、GeoDaSpace 和 PySAL 操作手册

沈体雁　于瀚辰　曹巍韡　何泓浩 / 编著

北京大学出版社
PEKING UNIVERSITY PRESS

图书在版编目(CIP)数据

空间计量分析软件：GeoDa、GeoDaSpace 和 PySAL 操作手册 / 沈体雁等编著. —北京：北京大学出版社，2019.11

ISBN 978-7-301-30456-3

Ⅰ.①空⋯　Ⅱ.①沈⋯　Ⅲ.①区位经济学—计量经济学—应用软件—研究生—教材　Ⅳ.①F224.0-39

中国版本图书馆 CIP 数据核字(2019)第 084301 号

书　　名	空间计量分析软件：GeoDa、GeoDaSpace 和 PySAL 操作手册 KONGJIAN JILIANG FENXI RUANJIAN：GeoDa、GeoDaSpace HE PySAL CAOZUO SHOUCE
著作责任者	沈体雁　于瀚辰　曹巍巍　何泓浩　编著
责任编辑	任京雪　徐　冰
标准书号	ISBN 978-7-301-30456-3
出版发行	北京大学出版社
地　　址	北京市海淀区成府路 205 号　100871
网　　址	http://www.pup.cn
电子信箱	em@pup.cn　QQ：552063295
新浪微博	@北京大学出版社　@北京大学出版社经管图书
电　　话	邮购部 010-62752015　发行部 010-62750672　编辑部 010-62752926
印 刷 者	河北滦县鑫华书刊印刷厂
经 销 者	新华书店 787 毫米×1092 毫米　16 开本　18 印张　257 千字 2019 年 11 月第 1 版　2019 年 11 月第 1 次印刷
定　　价	39.00 元

未经许可，不得以任何方式复制或抄袭本书之部分或全部内容。
版权所有，侵权必究
举报电话：010-62752024　电子信箱：fd@pup.pku.edu.cn
图书如有印装质量问题，请与出版部联系，电话：010-62756370

序

自 2010 年我们编著出版《空间计量经济学》(第一版)以来,在国内外学者的共同推动下,空间计量经济学在中国的发展取得了长足的进步。这主要体现在三个方面:

第一,中国空间计量经济学的教学体系初步形成。"空间计量经济学"作为一门正式的本科生或研究生课程,被列入经济学、地理学、管理学、规划学等专业的课程体系和学科建设计划。据不完全统计,北京大学、中国社会科学院大学、中国人民大学、武汉大学、华东理工大学、上海师范大学、暨南大学、山东大学、郑州大学、厦门大学、中南财经政法大学、江西财经大学、青岛科技大学等高校已经开设"空间计量经济学"课程。与此同时,空间计量经济学暑期学校、专题讲座和各类培训如火如荼地开展,已成燎原之势。2016—2019 年,北京大学与中国区域科学协会等单位连续举办了四届北京大学研究生暑期学校"空间计量经济学前沿"活动,空间计量经济学的创始人之一、美国国家科学院院士、美国芝加哥大学卢克·安索林(Luc Anselin)教授,地理加权回归模型(GWR)的提出者、美国国家科学院院士和英国社会科学院院士、美国亚利桑那州立大学斯提沃特·福瑟林汉姆(Stewart Fotheringham)教授以及国内外著名空间计量经济学家、学者在暑期学校授课,共有 1 000 余名来自国内外各高等院校的青年学者和学生参加了学习和研讨,极大地推动了空间计量经济学在中国的发展。伴随人才培养和教学工作的需要,国内已有十余本空间计量经济学方面的教材和专著(包括译著)相继出版;部分大学的经济学、商学、公共管理学、地理学、规划学等院系已开始招收和培养空间计量经济学方向的硕士和博士研究生;空间计量经济学师资队伍建设也受到有关院系领导的重视,能够开设"空间计量经济学"课程的教师十分紧俏。可以说,到目前为止,中国已经初步形成比较系统的本土化的空间计量经济学教学体系。

第二,中国空间计量经济学理论、方法与应用研究成果丰硕,进步喜人。一方面,空间计量经济学在一些前沿理论与方法的研究上取得了若干标志性成果。北京大学虞吉海教授在面板数据最大似然估计的一致性证明、动态面板模型的拟最大似然估计、空间单位根与伪回归等领域取得了重要突破,香港中文大学黄波教授的团队提出了时空地理加权回归模型(GTWR),我们团队的于瀚辰博士采用广义加性模型等技术解决了多尺度地理加权回归(MGWR)的统计推断问题。这些研究成果进一步拓展了空间回归和地理加权回归等主流空间计量经济学模型的设定、估计、检验和统计推断,完善了空间计量经济学理论与方法。另一方面,空间计量经济学在人文社会科学领域的应用广度与深度不断拓展,推动了人文社会科学的空间化、定量化和综合化,成为空间综合人文学与社会科学发展的重要学科基础。应用空间计量经济学理论与方法分析和解决中国城市与区域发展的现实问题,提出和验证中国城市与区域发展的特征事实、理论范式与科学规律,是中国空间计量经济学的主要任务。近年来,空间计量经济学在各个领域的应用研究及发表的学术论文数量呈几何级数式增长,空间计量分析与地理信息系统正在成为对城市与区域问题展开实证研究的两项必备技能。总体上,中国空间计量经济学领域的科学研究呈现出以应用研究为主、理论与应用研究并进,论文发表数量剧增、学术研究质量不断提升,部分领域进入国际前沿、整体研究水平尚需进一步提高的发展局面。

第三,中国空间计量经济学研究社区已经形成。学术社区的形成是学科成熟的重要标志。过去十年,中国空间计量经济学领域的学术交流和国际合作日渐繁荣,国内学者、学生与国外的学术联系日渐紧密,一些青年学者和学生通过留学、访学和暑期学校等多种形式深度参与国际顶尖学者的研究工作,逐渐步入空间计量经济学理论与方法研究的前沿阵地。中国区域科学协会、中国地理学会等学术组织成立了空间计量经济学方面的专业委员会,推动空间计量经济学在中国的发展,广大学者和学生通过各种"线上""线下"的学术交流活动日益密切地组织起来,有关空间计量经济学的各种公益性甚至商业性的讲座、论坛、培训等活动在城市与区域研究这个"小花园"里如雨后春笋般层出不穷,分外耀眼。可以非常欣慰地讲,在包括安索林院士和福瑟林汉姆院士在内的国际著名空间计量经济学家的持续支持下,通过包括北京大学在内的国内众多高等院校、科研机构、学术团体和广大学者、学生的共同努力,中国空间计量经济学的发展经历了从"星星之火"到"燎原之势"的"黄金十年"。可以预期,随着中国科技创新从以"跟跑"为主逐步向更多领域的"并跑""领跑"转变,未来十年中国空间计量经济学也将从国际空间计量经济学"俱乐部"的"跟跑者"发展为"并跑者",并向局部领域的"领跑者"迈进。

为了尽可能地反映和吸纳空间计量经济学理论与方法的新进展,回应广大读者系统学习空间计量经济学知识与技能的需求,在北京大学出版社的支持下,我们决定对

《空间计量经济学》(第一版)进行大幅修改与调整,重新编写和出版《空间计量经济学》(第二版)。与此同时,为了便于读者在学习和理解第二版中出现的诸多概念术语、理论模型、推导解析、数学公式的过程中,也能够学会各种主流空间计量经济学软件的操作和使用方法,掌握开展空间计量分析和实证研究的技能,我们同步编写了《空间计量分析软件:GeoDa、GeoDaSpace 和 PySAL 操作手册》《空间计量分析软件:R 语言操作手册》《空间计量分析软件:GWR 和 MGWR 操作手册》三本实用性、操作性、手册性导向的工具书,并配有相应的课件和教辅材料,供师生们教学所用。

上述一本教科书、三本软件操作手册的"1+3"教材体系是北京大学空间计量经济学研究团队过去十余年教学科研经验的总结,也是对长期关心与支持我们工作的各位老师、同学的回应和回报。这套教材可以用作"空间计量经济学""空间数据科学""地理信息系统""空间分析与模拟""地统计学"等课程的教材,也可以作为经济学、管理学、地理学、规划学、人口学、城市与区域科学等领域的教师、学生与实际工作者学习和研究空间计量经济学的参考书,更是在时空大数据时代普及和推广空间计量分析的科普书。

本书是以安索林院士撰写的 *Modern Spatial Econometrics in Practice:A Guide to GeoDa, GeoDaSpace and PySAL* 一书为基础,通过搜集、整理、编译和中国化安索林院士团队所发布的有关 GeoDa 软件的各种资料编写而成的。整个编写工作由安索林院士团队的核心成员——美国芝加哥大学空间数据科学研究中心的李迅博士指导,由北京大学研究团队的于瀚辰、曹巍巍、何泓浩、吕永强、谭丽等同学历时四年共同完成,我负责对全书进行谋划组织、审阅修改和校对,并撰写序和导论等内容。GeoDa 软件家族包括基于图形用户界面的空间计量分析软件 GeoDa 和 GeoDaSpace,以及基于 Python 语言的空间计量分析开源类库——PySAL 等软件,是目前世界上最流行的空间计量分析软件之一,截至 2018 年年底,已在全球 50 多个国家拥有超过 27 万个用户。随着安索林院士团队将 GeoDa 软件进一步模块化、互联网化、移动化和大数据化的研发计划的实施,可以预期,GeoDa 软件家族的用户群体将进一步扩大,软件的使用场景将进一步丰富,软件的运行效率和用户体验将进一步改进,基于核心模块的各种增值软件将不断涌现,因此 GeoDa 软件家族无疑是当前最具有发展潜力和最值得读者学习的空间计量经济学软件之一。本书采用案例研究、软件截图、操作说明等形式,为 GeoDa 软件学习者提供简单明了、直观易学的操作指南,上篇介绍了 GeoDa 和 GeoDaSpace 的地理可视化、探索性空间数据分析、空间权重的创建与操作、空间滞后模型和空间误差模型的建立与估计等空间计量分析功能,下篇介绍了PySAL的数据读入和导出、空间权重矩阵的创建和操作、空间数据分析、各种空间回归模型的建立与估计、空间动力学分析等功能。

在本书即将出版之时,我要衷心地感谢两位空间计量经济学的重要创始人——安索林院士和福瑟林汉姆院士,感谢他们在过去四年中持续不断地指导和支持北京大学空间计量经济学研究团队的工作,使我们的教学、科研和人才培养能够迅速地对接国际前沿,走入理论、方法与应用研究良性循环的道路,成为空间计量经济学在中国发展的重要枢纽和重镇。感谢北京大学研究生暑期学校"空间计量经济学前沿"项目的支持单位和主办单位——北京大学研究生院、中国区域科学协会、中国地理学会、中国地理信息系统产业协会等单位,以及过去四年持续支持我们暑期学校的授课老师们、参加或推荐人员参加我们暑期学校的来自全国各高校的老师和同学们。大家共同的努力使得我们的暑期学校已经成为空间计量经济学学习和交流的重要平台,成为与大师"亲密接触"和"面对面"交流的"人性化"场所,成为激发学习兴趣、启发创新智慧、鼓励年轻人走向空间计量经济学研究生涯的灵动空间。感谢北京大学政府管理学院的领导和老师们,特别是我所在的城市与区域管理系的杨开忠教授、李国平教授、陆军教授、薛领教授、张波副教授、孙铁山副教授和刘伦助理教授。感谢北京大学出版社的林君秀主任、刘京编辑和任京雪编辑,没有她们的鼓励和敦促,本书是难以如期出版的。

我们深知空间计量经济学理论、方法与应用背后隐藏着深刻的关于"空间"的哲学命题、科学道理和技术创新"奇点",揭示"空间之谜"仍将是一条漫长的知识探索道路。本书难免存在许多谬误之处,恳请读者在阅读学习过程中给予批评指正,我们将在今后的工作中进行修正。希望中国空间计量经济学迎来与国际同行"并跑"的新的"黄金十年"!

沈体雁

2019年10月18日

导　　论

　　空间计量经济学是对空间经济系统进行计量分析的经济学科；是以区域科学和空间经济理论为基础，以计量分析和地理计算为手段，以处理空间数据所特有的"空间效应"为核心，研究区域科学或空间经济模型的设定、估计、假设检验、预测和应用的理论与方法体系；是区域科学、计量经济学和地理计算科学的交叉学科。自 Paelinck and Klaassen(1979)首次提出和创立空间计量经济学以来，经过四十年的发展，空间计量经济学已经成为一门具有比较完善的理论、方法与工具的新兴学科，成为从事空间政治经济分析和空间人文社会科学研究的重要基础学科。

　　随着现代信息技术的不断进步，作为理论与方法的显性化载体与支撑性平台，特定学科领域软件工具的研究开发已经成为学科进步的重要驱动力和核心标志。与空间计量理论与方法的进步相辅相成，空间计量分析软件的研发取得了长足的进步。到目前为止，空间计量经济学领域已经出现的主流的空间计量分析软件包括：GeoDa 软件家族、R 语言、Metalab、GWR 和 ARCGIS 等。本书旨在采用具体案例和操作说明等形式，具体而翔实地介绍由美国芝加哥大学卢克·安索林院士领衔研究开发的 GeoDa 空间计量分析软件家族，包括 GeoDa、GeoDaSpace 和 PySAL 三个软件包。全书共 22 章，分为上下两篇。其中，上篇 11 章，即第 1 章至 11 章，介绍基于图形用户界面的空间计量分析软件：GeoDa 和 GeoDaSpace；下篇 11 章，即第 12 章至 22 章，介绍基于 Python 的空间计量分析库：PySAL。导论部分，主要介绍三个方面的内容，包括安索林院士及其 GeoDa 软件家族的基本情况、本书案例数据集说明和有关术语说明。

1. GeoDa 软件家族

　　GeoDa 软件家族由安索林院士及其团队在美国国家自然科学基金、美国空间社会科学研究中心和美国加州大学圣芭芭拉分校、亚利桑那州立大学、芝加哥大学等高校的支持下研究开发和发布使用的空间计量分析软件工具。2002 年，安索林院士团队发布第一个版本的 GeoDa 软件，截至 2018 年 9 月，该软件在全球 50 多个国家拥有 27 万多个用户,成为最流行的空间计量软件之一。本书介绍的软件版本是 GeoDa1.12.1.161。

GeoDa 软件的主创人安索林院士目前是美国芝加哥大学社会学部教授、空间数据科学研究中心主任,美国国家科学院院士、美国艺术与科学院院士,地理信息科学专业大学联盟会士,Walter Isard 主席。作为世界著名的空间计量和空间分析专家,以及空间计量经济学的重要奠基人之一,安索林院士长期从事空间计量经济学理论和方法的教学、研究和社会服务工作,在空间数据的探索性分析、可视化、建模及其开源软件研发等领域进行了开创性工作。他将先进的空间经济分析理论与方法应用于城市与区域、环境与自然资源经济学、房地产经济学、创新经济学、犯罪学、公共卫生、选举、国际关系等空间社会科学研究领域,取得了丰富的创新性成果,产生了广泛的影响,成为横跨信息科学技术(特别是地理信息科学技术和时空大数据科学)和人文社会科学两大领域的世界顶尖学者,由此获得了 Walter Isard 奖(2005)和 William Alonso 纪念奖(2006)等众多奖项。

迄今为止,安索林院士已经发表 150 余篇学术论文,出版了多本专著和文集。其中,1988 年出版的专著 *Spatial Econometrics: Methods and Models* 已成为在该领域的经典著作,被引用次数超过 9 000 次。他也被世界权威规划杂志和 Google 学术多次评为被引用次数最多的规划学者,总被引用次数接近 50 000 次。通过这些工作,他将早期尚处于边缘地位并且缺乏空间分析软件的空间计量经济学方法论推向了计量经济学的主流,同时也为地理信息科学奠定了坚实的计量经济学基础,为解决经济学"最后的前沿问题"——将"空间"引入主流经济学和推动包括经济、社会和政治等因素在内的更加一般性的区位理论做出了贡献。

在本书所介绍的 GeoDa 软件家族中,GeoDa 和 GeoDaSpace 是基于图形用户界面的空间计量分析软件。其中,GeoDa 是最早的也是最知名的软件包,于 2002 年发布第一版,2003 年发布了一个改进版,即版本 0.9.5-i。2009 年,第一个开源测试版 GeoDa 发布,现在也被称为遗留版 GeoDa,是用 C++ 编程语言,基于美国环境系统研究所(ESRI)的 MapObjects 图形库编写而成的,是只能在 Windows XP 操作系统上运行的桌面软件系统。2011 年,安索林院士团队发布了官方版本基于图形用户界面的 GeoDa 1.0。该版本采用开源的 GPL3.0 许可,支持 Windows、Mac OS X 和 Lunix 三种操作系统,而且在每一个操作系统的系统外观和用户体验上都有所不同。GeoDa 具有强大的地理可视化(包括异常值图、速率平滑、统计图和地图动画等),探索性数据分析(包括统计图表、平行坐标图、条件图),特别是探索性空间数据分析(ESDA),创建和操作空间权重(如邻近权重、距离权重、k 最近邻权重),建立和估计各种空间回归模型,以及构建空间数据集(如点坐标 shape 文件、泰森多边形、质心)等空间计量分析功能,其发布极大地降低了空间计量分析的学习成本,提升了用户体验,推动了空间计量分析的普及和使用。

GeoDaSpace 是一个包含在 PySAL spreg 模块中的有关空间回归代码的图形用户界面软件,其图形是基于 wxWidgets C++库的一个 Python 包——wxPython 模块而开发的,它适用于 Windows 和 Mac OS X 操作系统。GeoDaSpace 能够为用户提供先进的空间计量分析功能,包括创建和设置空间权重,以及主流空间计量模型的估计方法和统计检验。

PySAL 是一个空间计量分析的 Python 库,是用 Python 语言开发的用于进行空间计量分析的开源跨平台库。由于该库不是基于图形用户界面的,因此只能基于命令行对它进行操作,相应地,其用户也主要是那些习惯于使用命令行界面的使用者和程序员。该库包含了读入及导出数据、创建和操作空间权重矩阵、空间数据分析、空间回归分析和空间动力学分析等功能。要完成上述功能,我们主要需要用到 PySAL 的 weights 和 spreg 两个模块。

GeoDa 软件的安装包可以从美国芝加哥大学空间数据科学研究中心网站的软件下载页面下载,也可以从 github(开源和私有软件项目托管平台)网站下载。其网址分别是:

(1) https://spatial.uchicago.edu/software

(2) https://geodacenter.github.io/

2. 案例数据集说明

安索林院士团队提供了数十项可用于检验 GeoDa 软件家族可行性的案例数据集。这些数据集可以从美国芝加哥大学空间数据科学研究中心网站的数据下载页面下载,或者从 github 网站下载。其网址分别是:

(1) https://spatial.uchicago.edu/

(2) https://geodacenter.github.io/data-and-lab

本书用来进行操作示范的数据集主要有两个,即美国马里兰州巴尔的摩市的房价数据集和美国县级犯罪数据集。分别说明如下:

巴尔的摩市房价数据集：

巴尔的摩市房价数据集是一个记录了1978年美国马里兰州巴尔的摩市住房销售价格和房屋特征的数据库，存储于 baltim.dbf 文件之中，用于对影响住房价格的各种因素进行空间享乐分析。其原始数据来自美国俄亥俄州克利夫兰凯斯西部研究大学管理学院的罗宾·A.杜宾（Robin A. Dubin）教授。其主要特征如下：

(1) 文件类型：点形状文件；
(2) 投影：基于马里兰网格（Maryland grid）的投影坐标，具体投影类型未知；
(3) 观察值：211个；
(4) 变量数：17个；
(5) 年份：1978年。

主要变量描述如下：

表1 巴尔的摩市房价数据集变量说明

变量	说明
STATION	唯一标识码 ID variable
PRICE	房屋销售总价（单位为千美元） sales price of house in $1 000（MLS）
NROOM	所含房间数 number of rooms
DWELL	所含卧室数（1表示该房层有独立卧室） 1 if detached unit, 0 otherwise
NBATH	所含浴室数 number of bathrooms
PATIO	露台的指示变量（1表示该房屋有露台） 1 if patio, 0 otherwise
FIREPL	壁炉的指示变量（1表示该房屋有壁炉） 1 if fireplace, 0 otherwise
AC	空调的指示变量（1表示该房屋有空调） 1 if air conditioning, 0 otherwise
BMENT	地下室的指示变量（1表示该房屋有地下室） 1 if basement, 0 otherwise
NSTOR	房屋层数 number of storeys
GAR	车库的车位数（0表示没有车位） number of car spaces in garage（0 = no garage）

续表

变量	说明
AGE	房产的年龄 age of dwelling in years
CITCOU	地区变量（1 表示该房屋位于巴尔的摩县） 1 if dwelling is in Baltimore County, 0 otherwise
LOTSZ	建筑面积（单位为百平方英尺） lot size in hundreds of square feet
SQFT	室内面积（单位为百平方英尺） interior living space in hundreds of square feet
X	X 坐标 x coordinate on the Maryland grid
Y	Y 坐标 y coordinate on the Maryland grid

美国县级犯罪数据集：

美国县级犯罪数据集是一套记录了美国大陆县（不包括阿拉斯加州和夏威夷州）的犯罪数据,包括 1960 年、1970 年、1980 年和 1990 年四个人口普查年份的凶杀案以及有关的社会经济特征数据[①]。其基本特征如下：

(1) 文件类型：面形状文件；

(2) 观察值：3 085 个；

(3) 变量数：73 个；

(4) 投影：未知投影,经纬度格式。

该数据集以三个不同的文件进行存储,即 NAT.dbf,natregimes.dbf 和 south.dbf。其中,前两者所包含的是所有大陆县的犯罪数据,而后者只包含了美国南部地区的犯罪数据。我们用这套数据来研究美国各县的犯罪率与其潜在社会经济影响因素之间的相互关系。其主要变量描述如下：

表 2 美国县级犯罪数据集变量说明

变量	说明
NAME	县名 county name

---

① 详见：Messner, S., Anselin, L., Hawkins, D., Deane, G., Tolnay, S., & Baller R. (2000). An Atlas of the Spatial Patterning of County—Level Homicide, 1960—1990. Pittsburgh: National Consortium on Violence Research (NCOVR).

续表

变量	说明
STATE_NAME	州名 state name
STATE_FIPS[①]	州 FIPS 代码（字符型） statefips code (character)
CNTY_FIPS	县 FIPS 代码（字符型） countyfips code (character)
FIPS	州和县组合 FIPS 代码（字符型） combined state and countyfips code (character)
STFIPS	州 FIPS 代码（数字型） statefips code (numeric)
COFIPS	县 FIPS 代码（数字型） countyfips code (numeric)
FIPSNO	州和县组合 FIPS 代码（数字型） fips code as numeric variable
SOUTH	南方县哑元变量（南方县取值为1） dummy variable for Southern counties (South = 1)
HR**	每十万人犯罪率（四个年份） homicide rate per 100 000 (1960, 1970, 1980, 1990)
HC**	杀人案件数（以四个年份为基础取前后三年的平均值） homicide count, three year average centered on 1960, 1970, 1980, 1990
PO**	县域人口数量（四个年份） county population, 1960, 1970, 1980, 1990
RD**	资源匮乏（主成分，四个年份） resource deprivation, 1960, 1970, 1980, 1990 (principal component)
PS**	人口结构（主成分，四个年份） population structure, 1960, 1970, 1980, 1990 (principal component)
UE**	失业率（四个年份） unemployment rate, 1960, 1970, 1980, 1990
DV**	14 岁及以上男性离婚百分比（四个年份） divorce rate, 1960, 1970, 1980, 1990 (% males over 14 divorced)
MA**	年龄中位数（四个年份） median age, 1960, 1970, 1980, 1990
POL**	人口的对数值（四个年份） log of population, 1960, 1970, 1980, 1990
DNL**	人口密度的对数值（四个年份） log of population density, 1960, 1970, 1980, 1990

---

① FIPS，即美国联邦信息处理标准（the Federal Information Processing Standards）。

续表

变量	说明
MFIL**	平均家庭收入的对数值(四个年份) log of median family income, 1960, 1970, 1980, 1990
FP**	贫困家庭百分比(四个年份) % families below poverty, 1960, 1970, 1980, 1990 (see Codebook for details)
BLK**	黑人占比(四个年份) % black, 1960, 1970, 1980, 1990
GI**	家庭收入不平等的基尼系数(四个年份) Gini index of family income inequality, 1960, 1970, 1980, 1990
FH**	女性户主家庭的百分比(四个年份) % female headed households, 1960, 1970, 1980, 1990
WEST	西部地区虚拟变量 west region dummy
REGIONS	地区变量。南部地区的该变量值为0,北部和中部地区的该变量值为1,西部地区的该变量值为2. region dummy

注:**指有四个年份的数据。

上述变量说明中没有时间变量说明,事实上所有变量都和时间有关,在本书所有的案例演示中,我们把时间信息放在变量名中加以体现,如1960年的犯罪率变量名为HR60,1970年的犯罪率变量名为HR70,如此类推。部分案例出现的REGIONS为地区变量,即表示某个县所在的区域的虚拟变量,南部地区的该变量取值为0,北部和中部地区的该变量取值为1,而西部地区的该变量则取值为2。

本书所有案例中所涉及的上述两个案例数据集及其变量,都采取以上的描述,后文不再一一进行说明。

3. 有关术语说明

从简化书写以及方便阅读的目的出发,本书使用了很多计量经济学,特别是空间计量经济学的术语及其简称。为了便于读者将本书与沈体雁教授编著的《空间计量经济学》(第二版)[①]整合阅读,在此将本书中出现的各种术语简称以及空间计量经济学常用的术语简称及其中英文对照进行列举,后文不再一一说明。

CLR,经典线性模型(Classical Linear Regression Model)

---

① 详见:沈体雁,于瀚辰.空间计量经济学(第二版).北京:北京大学出版社,2019.

FAR,单变量一阶空间自回归模型(Simultaneous Univariate First-Order Spatial Autoregression Model)

SEM,空间误差模型(Spatial Error Model)

SLM/SAR,空间滞后模型(Spatial Lag Model/ Spatial Autoregressive Model)

SLX,自变量空间滞后模型(Spatial Lag of X Model)

SDM,空间杜宾模型(Spatial Durbin Model)

SDEM,空间杜宾误差模型(Spatial Durbin Error Model)

SAC,广义空间模型(General Spatial Autocorrelation Model)

GNS,广义嵌套空间模型(General Nesting Spatial Model)

SMA,空间移动平均模型(Spatial Moving Average Model)

SEC,空间误差分量模型(Spatial Error Components Model)

SSUR,空间似无关回归模型(Spatial Seemingly Unrelated Regression Model)

OLS,最小二乘估计(Ordinary Least Squares)

2SLS,两阶段最小二乘法(Two Stage Least Squares)

GLS,广义最小二乘(Generalized Least Squares)

WLS,加权最小二乘(Weighted Least Squares)

IV,工具变量法(Instrumental Variable Estimation)

MLE,最大似然估计(Maximum Likelihood Estimation)

GM,矩估计方法(Method of Moments)

GMM,广义矩估计方法(Generalized Method of Moments)

HAC,异方差和自相关一致估计方法(Heteroscedastic and Autocorrelation Consistent)

S2SLS,空间两阶段最小二乘法(Spatial Two Stage Least Squares)

FGS2SLS,可行广义空间两阶段最小二乘估计(Feasible Generalized Spatial Two-Stage Least Squares)

BLUE,最小方差的线性无偏估计量(Best Linear Unbiased Estimator)

LM,拉格朗日乘子检验(Lagrange Multiplier Test)

RLM,稳健的拉格朗日乘子检验(Robust Lagrange Multiplier Test)

LR,似然比检验(Likelihood Ratio Test)

MCMC,马尔可夫链蒙特卡洛方法(Markov Chain Monte Carlo Method)

ESF,特征向量空间滤波法(Eigenvector Spatial Filter)

EDM,特征函数分解法(Eigenfunction Decomposition Method)

GWR,地理加权回归(Geographically Weighted Regression)

SGWR,半参数地理加权回归(Semi-Parameter Geographically Weighted Regression/Mix Geographically Weighted Regression)

MGWR,多尺度地理加权回归(Muti-Scale Geographically Weighted Regression)

AIC,赤池信息量准则(Akaike Information Criterion)

AICc,修正的赤池信息量准则(Corrected Akaike Information Criterion)

GIS,地理信息系统(Geographic Information System)

R&D,研究与开发(Research and Development)

MAR,马歇尔-阿罗-罗默外部性(Marshal-Arrow-Romer Externalities)

LISA,局部空间关联指标(Local Indicators of Spatial Association)

NEG,新经济地理学(New Economic Geography)

EDA,探索性数据分析(Exploratory Data Analysis)

ESDA,探索性空间数据分析(Exploratory Spatial Data Analysis)

SP,空间过程(Spatial Processes/ Spatial Stochastic Processes)

MAUP,可变面元问题(Modifiable Areal Unit Problem)

GWPR,地理加权泊松回归(Geographical Weighted Poisson Regression)

GWLR,地理加权 Logistic 回归(Geographical Weighted Logistic Regression)

AGWR,地理加权空间自回归(Autoregressive Geographical Weighted Regression)

PGW,地理加权 Probit 回归(Probit Model with Geographical Weighted)

GWRR,地理加权岭回归(Geographical Weighted Ridge Regression)

GWL,地理加权套索回归(Geographical Weighted Lasso)

SWIM,空间加权相互作用模型(Spatially Weighted Interaction Models)

GTWR,时空地理加权回归(Geographical and Temporal Weighted Regression)

GAM,广义加性模型(Generalized Additive Model)

ENP,有效参数数量(Effective Number of Parameters)

ICT,信息、通信和技术(Information, Communication and Technology)

BIC,贝叶斯信息准则(Bayesian Information Criterion)

HQC,汉南-奎因准则(Hannan-Quinn Criterion)

空间计量经济学(Spatial Econometrics)

空间效应(Spatial Effect)

空间溢出效应(Spatial Spillover Effects)

计量经济学(Econometrics)

经典计量经济学(Classical Econometrics)

高斯-马尔科夫假定(Gauss-Markov Assumptions)

非经典计量经济学(Non-Classical Econometrics)

现代时间序列计量经济学(Time Series Econometrics)

微观计量经济学(Micro-Econometrics)

非参数计量经济学(Nonparametric Econometrics)

面板数据计量经济学(Panel Data Econometrics)

国际区域科学协会(Regional Science Association International)

《区域科学杂志》(*Journal of Regional Science*)

空间统计学(Spatial Statistics)

计算科学(Computational Science)

联立方程(Simultaneous Equation)

离散选择(Discrete Choice)

截面数据(Cross-Sectional Data)

时间序列数据(Time-Series Data)

面板数据(Panel Data)

截断数据(Truncation Data)

归并数据(Censored Data)

持续时间数据(Duration Data)

离散选择数据(Discrete Choice Data)

计数数据(Count Data)

空间数据(Spatial Data)

空间计量经济学会(Spatial Econometrics Association)

美国国家地理信息与分析中心(National Center for Geographic Information and Analysis)

区域创新集群(Regional Innovation Cluster)

局域知识溢出(Local Knowledge Spillovers)

干中学(Learning by Doing)

隐性知识(Tacit Knowledge)

局域地理溢出(Local Geographical Spillover)

全域地理溢出(Global Geographical Spillover)

横截面相关(Cross-Sectional Dependence)

空间参照数据(Spatial Referenced Data)

地理参照数据(Georeferenced Data)

时空数据立方(Space-Time Data Cube)

空间数据矩阵(Spatial Data Matrix)

多元时间序列(Multivariate Time Series)

高斯过程(Gaussian Processes)

严格平稳性(Strictly Stationary)

遍历性(Strictly Ergodic)

各向同性(Isotropic)

各向异性(Anisotropic)

一致非退化(Uniform Non-Degeneracy)

李雅普诺夫有界(Lyapunov Boundedness)

空间抽样(Spatial Sampling)

随机抽样(Random Sampling)

系统抽样(Systematic Sampling)

分层抽样(Stratified Sampling)

空间机制(Spatial Regimes)

伪回归(Spurious Regression)

条件似然(Conditional Likelihood)

附带参数问题(Incidental Parameter Problem)

部分似然(Partial Likelihood)

重力模型(Gravity Model)

网络自相关效应(Network Autocorrelation Effect)

过度离散(Over-Dispersion)

离散平衡(Equi-Dispersion)

泊松-伽马分布(Poisson-Gamma Distribution)

正交性(Orthogonality)

伪T检验(Pseudo T-Test)

后退拟合算法(Back-Fitting Algorithm)

平滑项变化比例(Change in the Smoother)

残差平方和变化比例(Proportional Change in the Residual Sum of Squares)

特征价格模型(Hedonic Price Model)

目 录

上篇 基于图形用户界面的空间计量分析软件：GeoDa 和 GeoDaSpace

第 1 章 GeoDa 和 GeoDaSpace 简介 …………………………………… (3)
    1.1　GeoDa ………………………………………………………………… (3)
    1.2　GeoDaSpace …………………………………………………………… (5)

第 2 章 软件使用预备知识 ……………………………………………… (7)
    2.1　GeoDa 界面 …………………………………………………………… (7)
    2.2　GeoDaSpace 界面 …………………………………………………… (14)

第 3 章 GUI 中的邻接权重矩阵 ………………………………………… (23)
    3.1　GeoDa 中的邻接权重矩阵 ………………………………………… (23)
    3.2　GeoDaSpace 中的邻接权重矩阵 …………………………………… (31)

第 4 章 GUI 中的距离权重矩阵 ………………………………………… (40)
    4.1　GeoDa 中的距离权重矩阵 ………………………………………… (40)
    4.2　GeoDaSpace 中的距离权重矩阵 …………………………………… (45)

第 5 章 GUI 中的最小二乘估计 ………………………………………… (53)
    5.1　模型创建 …………………………………………………………… (53)
    5.2　基本的 OLS 回归结果 ……………………………………………… (55)

    5.3　非空间回归分析 ………………………………………………………… (59)
    5.4　空间效应分析 …………………………………………………………… (61)
    5.5　预测值和残差 …………………………………………………………… (67)
    5.6　鲁棒系数标准误估计 …………………………………………………… (70)

第6章　GUI中的两阶段最小二乘估计 …………………………………………… (76)
    6.1　模型创建 ………………………………………………………………… (76)
    6.2　基本估计结果 …………………………………………………………… (78)
    6.3　空间效应分析 …………………………………………………………… (79)
    6.4　鲁棒系数标准误估计 …………………………………………………… (80)

第7章　GUI中的空间滞后模型的空间两阶段最小二乘估计 …………………… (83)
    7.1　模型创建 ………………………………………………………………… (83)
    7.2　基本估计结果 …………………………………………………………… (85)
    7.3　S2SLS的空间效应分析 ………………………………………………… (91)
    7.4　鲁棒系数标准误估计 …………………………………………………… (91)
    7.5　包含内生变量的S2SLS ………………………………………………… (94)

第8章　GUI中的空间滞后模型的最大似然估计 ………………………………… (100)
    8.1　模型创建 ………………………………………………………………… (100)
    8.2　ML的基本估计结果 …………………………………………………… (102)
    8.3　ML面板高级设置 ……………………………………………………… (105)

第9章　GUI中的空间误差模型的广义矩估计 …………………………………… (108)
    9.1　模型创建 ………………………………………………………………… (108)
    9.2　GM估计 ………………………………………………………………… (111)
    9.3　包含异方差性的GMM估计 …………………………………………… (114)
    9.4　包含同方差性的GMM估计 …………………………………………… (120)
    9.5　估计值的比较 …………………………………………………………… (122)

第10章　GUI中的空间误差模型的最大似然估计 ……………………………… (124)
    10.1　模型创建 ……………………………………………………………… (124)
    10.2　基本估计结果 ………………………………………………………… (126)
    10.3　ML-预测值和残差 …………………………………………………… (127)

第 11 章　GUI 中的复合模型	(130)
11.1　模型创建	(130)
11.2　复合模型的 GM 估计	(134)
11.3　复合模型的 GMM 估计	(137)

下篇　基于 Python 的空间计量分析库：PySAL

第 12 章　PySAL 软件简介与安装	(145)
第 13 章　PySAL 和 spreg 计算包的基本原理	(148)
13.1　PySAL spreg 的逻辑原理	(148)
13.2　样本数据录入	(149)
第 14 章　PySAL 中的邻接权重矩阵	(153)
14.1　空间权重对象	(153)
14.2　从 shape 文件生成空间邻接权重对象	(163)
14.3　从矩形方格生成空间邻接权重对象	(165)
14.4　分块权重	(167)
14.5　高阶权重	(168)
14.6　空间滞后变量的生成	(169)
第 15 章　PySAL 中的距离权重矩阵	(171)
15.1　从 shape 文件生成空间距离权重对象	(171)
15.2　核权重对象的生成	(177)
第 16 章　PySAL spreg 中的普通最小二乘估计	(181)
16.1　回归运算的准备工作	(181)
16.2　普通最小二乘命令	(182)
16.3　普通最小二乘对象	(184)
16.4　OLS 与怀特检验	(188)
16.5　OLS 与空间相关性检验	(189)
16.6　OLS 与怀特标准误	(190)
16.7　OLS 与 HAC 标准误	(193)

  16.8 单独获取底层函数 ……………………………………………………………… (194)

第 17 章 PySAL spreg 中的两阶段最小二乘估计 ……………………………… (195)

  17.1 回归运算的准备工作 …………………………………………………………… (195)
  17.2 两阶段最小二乘命令 …………………………………………………………… (196)
  17.3 两阶段最小二乘对象 …………………………………………………………… (198)
  17.4 两阶段最小二乘的两个阶段 …………………………………………………… (200)
  17.5 2SLS 与空间相关性检验 ……………………………………………………… (202)
  17.6 2SLS 与怀特标准误 …………………………………………………………… (202)
  17.7 2SLS 与 HAC 标准误 ………………………………………………………… (204)

第 18 章 PySAL spreg 中的空间滞后模型的空间两阶段最小二乘估计 ……… (205)

  18.1 回归运算的准备工作 …………………………………………………………… (205)
  18.2 GM_Lag 命令 …………………………………………………………………… (206)
  18.3 GM_Lag 对象 …………………………………………………………………… (207)
  18.4 GM_Lag 与空间相关性检验 …………………………………………………… (213)
  18.5 GM_Lag 与怀特标准误 ………………………………………………………… (214)
  18.6 GM_Lag 与 HAC 标准误 ……………………………………………………… (215)
  18.7 含有内生解释变量的 GM_Lag 运算 ………………………………………… (216)

第 19 章 PySAL spreg 中的空间滞后模型的最大似然估计 ……………………… (218)

  19.1 回归运算的准备 ………………………………………………………………… (218)
  19.2 ML_Lag 命令 …………………………………………………………………… (218)
  19.3 ML_Lag 对象 …………………………………………………………………… (219)
  19.4 ML_Lag 估计中的选项 ………………………………………………………… (221)

第 20 章 PySAL spreg 中的空间误差模型的广义矩估计 ………………………… (223)

  20.1 回归运算的准备 ………………………………………………………………… (223)
  20.2 GM_Error 命令 ………………………………………………………………… (225)
  20.3 GM_Endog_Error 命令 ………………………………………………………… (227)
  20.4 GM_Error_Het 命令 …………………………………………………………… (230)
  20.5 GM_Endog_Error_Het 命令 …………………………………………………… (234)
  20.6 GM_Error_Hom 命令 ………………………………………………………… (235)

  20.7 GM_Endog_Error_Hom 命令 ……………………………………………（238）

第 21 章 PySAL spreg 中的空间误差模型的最大似然估计 ……………（242）
  21.1 回归运算的准备 …………………………………………………（242）
  21.2 ML_Error 命令 ……………………………………………………（242）
  21.3 ML_Error 对象 ……………………………………………………（243）
  21.4 ML_Error 估计中的选项 …………………………………………（245）

第 22 章 PySAL spreg 中的滞后与误差共存的广义空间两阶段最小二乘估计 ………（247）
  22.1 回归运算的准备 …………………………………………………（247）
  22.2 GM_Combo 命令 …………………………………………………（249）
  22.3 GM_Combo_Hom 命令 ……………………………………………（253）
  22.4 GM_Combo_Het 命令 ……………………………………………（256）

参考文献 ……………………………………………………………………………（260）

上篇 基于图形用户界面的空间计量分析软件:GeoDa 和 GeoDaSpace

第 1 章 GeoDa 和 GeoDaSpace 简介

1.1 GeoDa

目前,国内主流的空间计量分析软件中,GeoDa 是最古老的,也是最知名的。它最先由美国国家科学基金会资助的空间综合社会科学中心在 2002 年发布,2003 年发布了一个改进版,即 GeoDa 0.9.5-i。这个版本一直保留,直到 2009 年被 GeoDa 的第一个开源测试版本所取代。旧版遗留版 GeoDa 的软件是用 C++写的,只能在 Windows XP 操作系统上运行,且其大部分地图功能依赖于美国环境系统研究所(ESRI)的 MapObjects 库。它是最早的完全对其所有的开放窗口(地图、表格和统计图表)实施动态链接和刷新的桌面程序之一,并且迅速地取得了广泛的用户基础。

遗留版 GeoDa 强调地理可视化(如异常值图、速率平滑、统计图、地图动画)、探索性数据分析(如统计图表、平行坐标图、条件图),尤其是探索性空间数据分析(ESDA)对全局和局部的空间自相关统计的计算和可视化。它也提供了大量的函数,用以构建空间数据集(如点坐标的 shape 文件、泰森多边形、质心),创建和操作空间权重(如邻近权重、距离权重、k 邻近权重)。

GeoDa 从一开始就包含了一个带有空间回归功能的集合。普通最小二乘回归被用来分析空间自相关,包括 Moran's I 指数和拉格朗日统计数据。另外,最大似然估计支持空间滞后模型和空间误差模型,它以对大数据集进行估算的特殊算法为基础。然而,最大似然估计的局限性在于,它只适用于那些权重矩阵对称的模型,而不适用于权重。

卢克·安索林在2005年提供了一组比较全面的案例和插图后，在2006年又对遗留版GeoDa的功能进行了扩展描述。

在2005年，GeoDa从根本上改变了软件结构，并把它变为开源、跨平台的系统。这就要求完全重新编写代码（仍然用C++编写），引用了标准的开源库，如C++标准模板库（STL），提供了跨平台图形用户界面的wxWidgets，具有图形功能的Boost C++库，以及用于访问多源数据库的OGR简单要素库（1.6版）。所得产品的测试版本首次在2009年发布。2011年10月发布了官方版本1.0，它采用开源的GPL3.0许可。该版本支持三种操作系统，能分别在Windows、Mac OS X和Lunix操作系统中运行，但在每一个操作系统中的外观和用户体验有所不同。

开源版GeoDa包含遗留版GeoDa的所有功能，但是界面更为优化，底层数据结构更为稳健。就本书提到的空间计量方法而言，与遗留版并无太大的差别。除此之外，用户界面稍做了一些修改，但是产品的外观和体验是和以前完全相同的。本书采用的版本是2014年春季发布的1.6版本。

如下载GeoDa软件，可以在GeoDa Center网站上下载二进制文件，网址为https://spatial.uchicago.edu/software。网站的页面结构如图1.1所示。点击最右侧一栏的"Free Download"，我们可以获取软件的二进制文件，并可用于Windows（7及以上版本）、Mac OS X（10.6及以上版本）和两种Lunix系统（Ubuntu 12.x和Fedora Core 6）。在下载之前，用户需要创建账号，若已有账号则需要登录。

软件的安装很简单：将下载的文件复制到指定目录，双击可执行文件或者GeoDa图标［如图1.2(a)所示］来启动程序。Mac OS X操作系统的用户需要先右击GeoDa图标并确认想运行所下载的软件。这一步仅需操作一次，之后正常的双击便可以启动程序。

网址https://geodacenter.github.io/中介绍了其他特定数据库连接的安装，并介绍了所支持的不同格式。GeoDa的源代码保存为一个Google代码项目，可以从网址http://code.google.com/p/geoda上浏览和下载。它采用开源的 GPL3.0 许可。

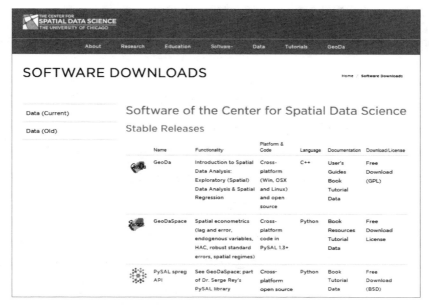

图 1.1　https://spatial.uchicago.edu/software 页面

（a）GeoDa　　　　　（b）GeoDaSpace

图 1.2　软件图标

1.2　GeoDaSpace

　　GeoDaSpace 是包含在 PySAL spreg 模块中的基于图形用户界面的空间回归软件。其图形是基于 wxPython 模块而开发的，wxPython 是 wxWidgets C++库的一个 Python 包。值得说明的是，GeoDa 的图形也是同一个库。因此，GeoDaSpace 和 GeoDa 的回归界面以及输出方式都非常相似。

　　GeoDaSpace 能为用户提供先进的且可以用在空间计量经济学领域的功

能,这些功能包含在 spreg 模块中。它隐藏了很多操作和技术上的细节,把重点放在最普通的操作和选项上面,这包括了所有的估计方法和统计检验。然而,在 spreg 模块中也有一些功能被 GeoDaSpace 排除在外,这些功能只能通过命令行来执行。

GeoDaSpace 的 1.0 版本是在 2014 年夏季发布的,它与 PySAL 1.8 版本相一致。软件的 Alpha 和 Beta 版本从 PySAL 1.3 版本(2010 年 1 月)起就开始流通。作为对空间回归功能的补充,GeoDaSpace 中也增加了创建和设置空间权重的功能,这个功能是基于底层的 PySAL 中的权重模块。

软件适用于 Windows 和 Mac OS X 操作系统,安装包可以从 GeoDa Center 网站上下载,网址是 https://spatial.uchicago.edu/software。所下载的文件是可执行文件,可以复制到任意目录。它包含 Python 本身以及所有与之相关的文件,包括 numpy 和 scipy 模块。因此它是完全自我封装的,把技术上的细节隐藏起来。

程序的运行非常简单,如双击 GeoDaSpace 图标[如图 1.2(b)所示],或者调用可执行文件。

第 2 章 软件使用预备知识

2.1 GeoDa 界面

GeoDa 可以以最普通的方式运行,如双击桌面上的 GeoDa 图标[如图 1.2(a)所示],或者调用可执行文件,便可以打开数据源浮动工具条和主菜单,如图 2.1 所示。

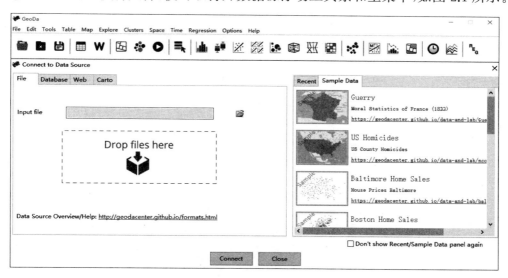

图 2.1　GeoDa 浮动工具条和主菜单

GeoDa 的功能远比我们在这里展示得多,在此我们主要关注空间回归功能。启动 GeoDa 1.12 版本,会自动连接数据源。在早期的版本中,打开的数据源只支持 shape 文件和 dBase 数据库文件。而在 1.12 版本中扩展了很多文件格式,还有关系数据库的连接和网络功能服务。

要进行回归运算,必须打开一个项目,可以选择创建新项目或者打开一个项目文件。项目文件是 XML 格式的文本文件,包含一个项目的元数据,如数据文件的路径(如果是文件)、变量名称和时空特性,这种文件的扩展名为.gda。开启 GeoDa 1.12 会自动打开一个新项目。打开项目后,程序就会连接数据源,并确保能够对变量进行分析。工具条最左边的三个图标分别代表了对项目进行新建和打开、关闭及保存。左边第一个图标用于新建和打开项目,如图2.2所示。这些功能也包含在菜单栏中,在 File＞ New 目录下,如图2.3所示。

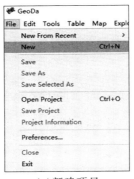 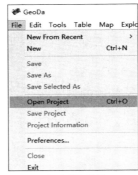

(a)新建项目　　　　　　　(b)打开项目

图 2.2　在 GeoDa 中新建或打开一个项目

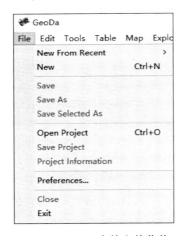

图 2.3　GeoDa 中的文件菜单

当打开一个现有的项目时,会连接到数据源,变量被读入内存中且屏幕上会显示一幅基础底图。此时,便可以开始进行回归分析。

在新建项目之前,需要先完成几步操作。首先,会弹出一个对话框选择连接文件、数据库或者 Web 服务作为数据源,如图 2.4 所示。当点击对话框中的打开文件图标时,会弹出一列文件格式,如图 2.5 所示。这些所支持的文件格式范围来自 OGR 简单要素库。目前,GeoDa 支持以下十种文件格式:

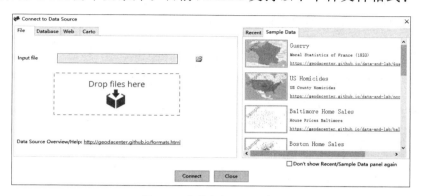

图 2.4 连接数据源对话框

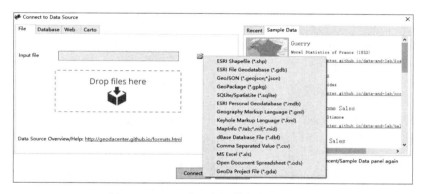

图 2.5 GeoDa 中可打开的数据文件格式

- ESRI shape 文件(﹡.shp);
- Excel 所生成的逗号分隔文本文件(﹡.csv);
- dBase 数据库文件(﹡.dbf);
- ESRI 地理数据库文件(﹡.gdb);
- GeoJSON 文件(﹡.geojson,﹡.json);
- 地理标记语言(GML)文本文件(﹡.gml);
- Google KML(前 Keyhole Markup Language)文本文件(﹡.kml);
- Mapinfo 文件(﹡.tab,﹡.mif,﹡.mid);
- 微软 Excel 电子表格文件(﹡.xls);

- SQLite/SpatiaLite 数据库文件（*.sqlite）。

选择其中一种数据格式，将会打开一个常见的文件对话框（不同的操作系统有不同的特点），对话框里的内容与刚刚选择的文件类型相对应。

举例来说，如果选择 dbf 格式，我们在对话框中可以使用 NAT.dbf 示例数据集，如图 2.6 所示。点击打开，就连接到文件，系统把数据读入内存，并显示出数据表。此时，便可以进行回归分析。

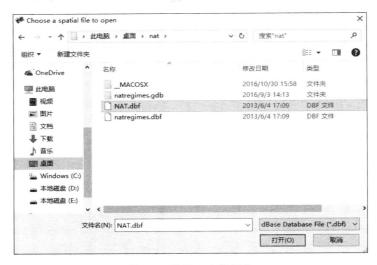

图 2.6 选择一个数据集

Connect To Data Source 对话框有两个选项卡来获取进行分析的数据，每个选项卡有不同的界面设置。Database 选项卡中能连接到三种数据库格式，如图 2.7（a）所示。目前，GeoDa 支持 Oracle Spatial、PostgreSQL/PostGIS 和 MySQL Spatial 三种数据库格式。Web 可以连接并访问统一资源定位符 URL，包括 GeoJson URL 和 WFS URL，如图 2.7（b）所示。单击 Connect 按钮将弹出一个对话框，指定连接的类型，以输入建立连接的必要参数（如数据库主机，端口和名称，用户名称，密码，表名称）。一旦建立连接，数据就会被载入，GeoDa 也就做好了回归分析的准备。

建立回归分析有两种方法，一是从主菜单栏点击 Regression，如图 2.8（a）所示；二是单击工具栏最右边的图标，如图 2.8（b）所示。在一个项目打开以后，所有的变量就会加载到回归分析界面,并且可以指定一个模型,下文我们会详细介绍该内容。

(a)连接数据库

(b)连接网上的数据集

图 2.7　连接数据库和网上数据集

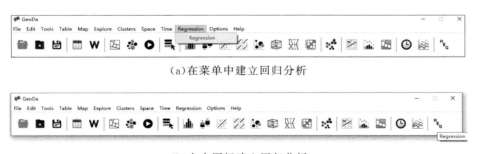

(a)在菜单中建立回归分析

(b)点击图标建立回归分析

图 2.8　GeoDa 中建立回归分析

最后,我们来介绍一下另外两个图标,分别是 Save 和 Close,如图 2.9 所示,这两个图标在 File 菜单里面也有对应项(见图 2.3)。它们的意义很容易理解,此处不再解释。

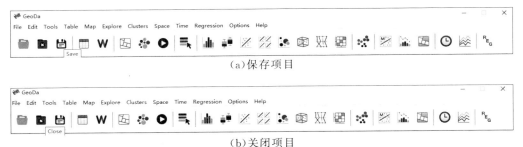

(a)保存项目

(b)关闭项目

图 2.9　GeoDa 中保存和关闭项目

GeoDa 和 GeoDaSpace 这两个基于 GUI(图形用户界面)的软件程序在使用上颇为相似。当数据源指定后，其中的数据便可用于回归模型。GeoDa 的初始界面如图 2.10 所示，左上角有一个框叫作 Variables，里面列举了所有变量。

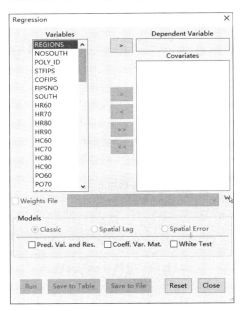

图 2.10　GeoDa 中建立回归分析的主界面

界面主要分为三个部分，如图 2.10 所示的三个框。第一部分与实际模型规范有关。因变量(Dependent Variable)和解释变量(Covariates)可以通过两种方式加载，一是通过双击列表中的变量名称，二是先选中变量，通过中间的箭头来将变量移到相应的框中。图 2.11 展示了一个完成设置后的回归分析主界面。在这个例子中,我们用到了 NAT.dbf 示例数据集,选取 HR90 作为因变量,RD90 和 UE90 作为解释变量。

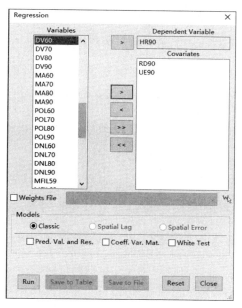

图 2.11 GeoDa 中完成设置后的回归分析主界面

位于中间的第二个框用于选择空间权重文件。选择一个文件后最小二乘回归结果也会分析空间效应。另外,空间权重文件也用于执行空间滞后回归和空间误差回归。GeoDa 还有一个功能是创建和操作空间权重的,后面的章节将会对其进行详细介绍。

选定了变量和权重文件后,我们就可以选择回归模型了。Models 框中有三种回归模型可供选择,分别是标准非空间回归模型(Classic Model)、空间滞后模型(Spatial Lag Model)以及空间误差模型(Spatial Error Model)。标准非空间回归模型采用普通最小二乘回归,并当指定空间权重文件时分析空间效应,这部分内容将在第 5 章进行深入讨论。GeoDa 中空间滞后模型和空间误差模型采用最大似然法进行估计,这将在第 8 章和第 10 章进行详细说明。

"模型选择"部分下方的复选框提供了三个扩展输出的选项。第一个复选框与预测值和残差的估计相关。鉴于预测值和残差总是通过计算得到的,它们不在标准输出内容之内。尤其是对大容量的观测数据集进行处理的过程中,这很快就会变得难以处理。只有少数情况是理想的,所以该选项默认是关闭的。当然我们可以将预测值和残差加载到当前数据表中,而不是将它们列为标准回归输出的一部分,这样更方便我们进行进一步的分析和可视化。完成这一步需要单击进度条下面的 Save to Table 按钮(这个按钮只有在回归完成以后才能点击,这将在第 5 章讨论最小二乘回归时进行详细的说明)。

第二个复选框与参数方差或协方差的估计相关。同样,它也是通过计算得到的,不在标准输出内容之内。勾选 Coefficient Variance Matrix 即可启用此选项,并且将方差或协方差矩阵附加到输出结果中。

第三个复选框与异方差的怀特检验相关。这个检验统计量要求计算所有解释变量之间的叉乘,所以在计算解释变量较多的大数据集时将会花费一些额外的时间。该复选框默认是关闭的。如果选中了 White Test,其结果会出现在非空间回归分析中。

最后,在界面的最底部有四个工具按钮。点击 Run 按钮便开始执行估计。此时,复选框下面的进度条能够显示估计的执行进程。对于最小二乘估计来说,这个过程一般很短暂,但是对于有着大量观测数据的空间模型来说,这个过程需要几秒钟的时间。

点击 Save to File 按钮会弹出一个打开文件对话框,选择一个文件夹来保存输出文件。若不指定此项,输出文件将只出现在屏幕上,但是不能作为之后的参考。Reset 按钮将界面中的内容清除,以便选择新的模型。而如上所述,Save to File 按钮能够将预测值和残差加载到当前数据表中。

2.2　GeoDaSpace 界面

与 GeoDa 相同,GeoDaSpace 也可以以最普通的方式运行,如双击桌面上的 GeoDaSpace 图标[如图 1.2(b)所示],或者正确地调用目录下的可执行文件,便可以弹出主界面,如图 2.12 所示。

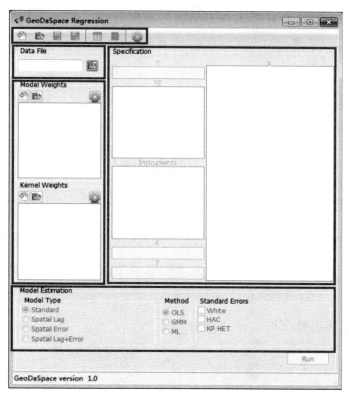

图 2.12　GeoDaSpace 中建立回归分析的主界面

主界面分为五个部分，即图中五个不同的方框。第一部分是顶部的七个图标，代表了一些快捷功能，如打开新模型或设置高级偏好。我们会在后续章节中进行详细的介绍。

第二部分是上述七个图标下面的 Data File 部分，用于指定数据集。其右边是 Specification 部分，这一部分是建模时所用到的各种变量，如变量 Y、外生解释变量 X、内生解释变量 YE、工具变量 Instruments 以及机制变量 R。T 框当前是不可用的，在时空分析中才会用到。

第三部分用于设置空间权重。其中，一部分是用于选择模型权重（Model Weights），用来分析空间自相关关系以及识别使用的是空间滞后模型还是空间误差模型；另一部分用于选择 HAC 估计中需要用到的核权重（Kernel Weights）。

第四部分是主界面底部的许多单选框和复选框。其中,前两部分用于选择模型类型和估计方法,后一部分是计算估计值的标准误时需要用到的选项。GeoDaSpace 扩展了 GeoDa 的功能,增加了 2SLS 估计、空间滞后模型的 IV/GMM 估计(除最大似然之外)、空间误差模型的 GM/GMM 估计(除最大似然之外),以及同时包含空间滞后和空间误差的估计。

第五部分是主界面最底部的版本信息(有些操作系统中会列出发布时间)。

2.2.1 GeoDaSpace 中的回归模型

在 GeoDaSpace 中,所有分析的第一步都是选择数据集。有两种方式可以选择数据集,第一种是点击 GUI 中左上角第一个图标创建新模型[如图2.13(a)所示],第二种是点击 Data File 面板中的打开文件图标[如图 2.13(b)所示],这两种方式都会弹出标准的文件选择对话框。

(a)选择数据集方式 1

(b)选择数据集方式 2

图 2.13　GeoDaSpace 中选择数据集文件

GeoDaSpace 支持包含在 PySAL 的 FileIO 模块中的数据格式。目前,它支持的格式包括 dBase 数据库文件(文件扩展名为 dbf)、以逗号分隔值文本文件,如 Excel 所生成的电子表格(文件扩展名为 csv)等。选择数据文件后,其内容就可被程序使用了。数据文件面板中会把文件名显示出来,并在一个新的 Variable 窗口中列出数据集的文件名,包含所有能用于分析的变量,如图 2.14 所示。与之前一样,我们使用 NAT.dbf 示例数据集,现在它已经被列入 GUI 的 Data File 面板中。

我们以一个简单的回归分析来说明,把 HR90 作为因变量,RD90 和 UE90 作为解释变量,如图 2.15 所示。

如要建立一个模型,请点击变量名称并将其从列表中拖拽到面板上的合适位置。任何模型都至少需要两个变量,即因变量 Y 和外生解释变量 X。其他的是有选择性的,取决于特定的案例。例如,当用内生解释变量 YE 评估一个模型时,要用到工具变量 Instruments。类似地,对于空间滞后模型和空间误差模型,就要选择空间权重文件。如果这些必备的变量和文件不包含在 GUI 中,将会弹出警告或错误信息。

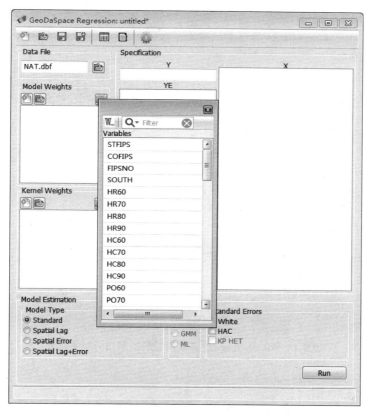

图 2.14　GeoDaSpace 中创建模型时可用的变量

如图 2.15 所示,通过将变量 HR90 拖到 Y 窗口,将变量 RD90 和 UE90 拖到 X 窗口,可以建立模型;通过点击关闭按钮可以从界面中移除变量列表窗口。通过 GUI 顶部的 Open the Variable List 图标(右起第三个图标),可以随时将关闭的窗口恢复,如图 2.16(a)所示。

在底部面板中选择某种类型的模型,并点击执行,弹出结果窗口。在进行分析时的任何一个时间点,这个窗口可以通过 GUI 顶部右起第二个图标打开,如图 2.16(b)所示。有关回归模型输出的更多细节将在后文相应的章节中做进一步的讨论。

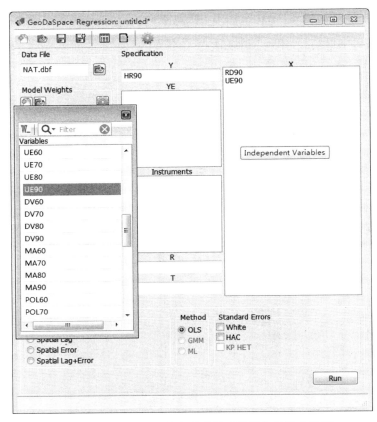

图 2.15　GeoDaSpace 中完成设置后的回归分析主界面

(a)打开变量列表　　　　　　　　　(b)显示结果窗口

图 2.16　打开变量列表和结果显示窗口

2.2.2　GeoDaSpace 中的偏好设置

GeoDaSpace GUI 中顶部最右边的图标用以调用高级设置,如图 2.17(a)所示。点击图标会弹出设置面板,可以指定模型和方法等选项,如图 2.17(b)所示。

Std Dev,GMM,ML,Instruments 和 Regimes 的设置将会在相应估计方法的章节中进行介绍。Output 和 Other 中的一些设置是通用的,能用到所有的模型中。

(a)高级设置

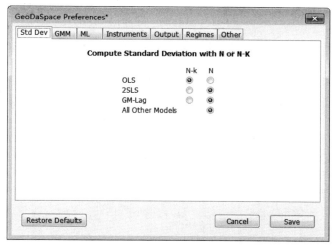

(b)高级设置界面

图 2.17 高级设置的调用与显示

当 Preference 面板中的设置更改后,需要点击面板右下角的 Save 按钮进行保存以使新的设置生效。在 GeoDaSpace 中,这个更改后的设置将一直用于后续的分析中,直到用户再次调整设置并保存,或者点击 Restore Defaults 按钮。这种偏好设置的机制可能会引起一些混乱,所以最好在进行一个新的分析前检查偏好设置。

与 GeoDa 中的例子一样,GeoDaSpace 中标准的回归输出既不包含估计系数的协方差矩阵,也不包含残差和预测值。为了列出这些结果,必须选中面板中相应的选项,如图 2.18(a)所示。与 GeoDa 不同,残差和预测值不能加载到当前数据集中。

最后,Preferences 面板中 Other 选项卡下的两个通用项是多重处理选项,也能处理缺失值。对于 spreg 模块乃至 GeoDaSpace 来说,可以在计算时使用多核(Multi-Core)计算。但是因为这不是在所有操作系统上都能实现的,所以默认的设置是不勾选 Multi-Core 选项。而要使用多核计算时,就需要勾选这个选项。在这种情况下,会在操作系统支持下在计算中使用所有可用的内核。

一般来说,在存在空间相关性的模型中应该避免缺失值。为了避免它们出现在数据集中,最好的方法是给它们赋予一个特定值,这样它们就能和其他观测值区分开来。Preferences 面板中 Other 选项卡下的 Data 选项就提供了一个这样的机会,用一个给定的值来取代缺失值,如面板中指定的那样[如图 2.18(b)所示]。这个选项只有当必要时才能使用,因为用特定的数值替代缺失的观测值可能会产生误导性的结果。

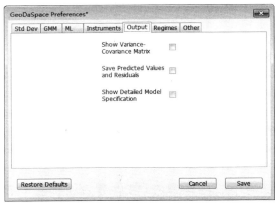

(a)Output 高级设置界面

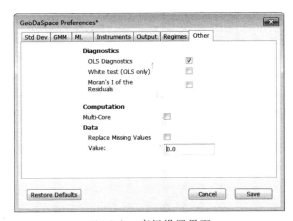

(b)Other 高级设置界面

图 2.18　GeoDaSpace 中常用的高级设置界面

2.2.3　模型的保存与打开

在 GeoDaSpace 中，模型不需要每次都从头开始输入。我们可以先保存模型，以后使用时再重新将其加载进来。保存模型需要点击左起第四个菜单图标 Save Model As…，如图 2.19(a)所示。点击它将会弹出常见的文件保存界面，并需要指定文件名，该文件的扩展名以 mdl 为结尾。这种模型文件是一个简单的文本文件，它以 Python 字典的形式包含了有关模型的所有信息。而且，如果确定对当前的模型完成了修正或编辑，可以用 Save Model…图标保存当前的模型文件，如图 2.19(b)所示。

(a) Save Model As…

(b) Save Model…

图 2.19　保存当前模型

在保存以后，该模型文件可以通过点击左起第二个菜单图标 Open Existing Model:Choose.mdl File 来重新打开，如图 2.20 所示。这样就不用重新打开所有的变量和重新更改选项。例如，在打开文件对话框中选择 NAT1.mdl 文件，则会弹出一个填充好的界面，如图 2.21 所示。模型文件的名称就列在界面的顶部的标题框内。

图 2.20　打开之前保存的模型

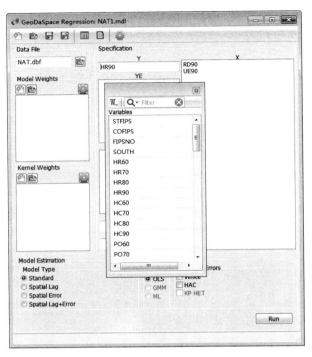

图 2.21 打开之前已创建的模型文件后的界面

第 3 章　GUI 中的邻接权重矩阵

3.1　GeoDa 中的邻接权重矩阵

在 GeoDa 中,空间权重矩阵可以由任意文件、数据库等方式生成。一旦打开一个项目,这个空间权重矩阵就将在之后的回归模型中使用,不需要明确指定(与 1.6 版本之前的 GeoDa 相反)。有两种方法可以创建权重,一种是从菜单中创建,依次点击 Tools＞Weights Manager＞Create[如图 3.1(a)所示],另一种是通过工具条的权重矩阵图标创建[如图 3.1(b)所示],从而进入权重管理窗口[如图 3.1(c)所示]。另外,也可以选择菜单中的 Tools＞Weights Manager＞Load 将已有的文件读入。

在 GeoDa 的空间回归中,矩阵总是以行标准化的形式使用空间权重。

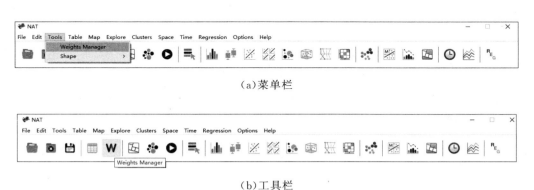

(a)菜单栏

(b)工具栏

图 3.1　GeoDa 中的权重矩阵创建

(c)权重管理窗口

图 3.1　GeoDa 中的权重矩阵创建(续)

3.1.1　权重矩阵设置界面

GeoDa 中创建权重矩阵文件的对话框如图 3.2(a)所示。它主要包含两个部分,在图中由两个框表示。最上面的框用于选择 ID 变量。这个变量的每个观测值包含了一个独立的整数值,以便空间权重矩阵能与数据集中的观测值精确匹配。例如,在图 3.2(b)中 ID 变量设为 FIPSNO。

当数据集中没有可选择的 ID 变量时,点击 Add ID Variable 按钮可以加载一个变量。在实践中经常遇到一个问题,一个看似取整数值的变量不能被识别出来作为 ID 变量,Add ID Variable 这个功能可以确保整数序列号能够插入数据集中。这个变量会自动获取默认标签 POLY_ID,用户也可以在对话框中改为任意一个唯一的变量名称。

第二个框用于设置权重矩阵,这部分内容将在下两节做进一步讨论。

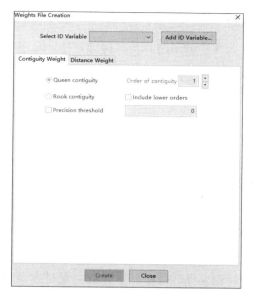
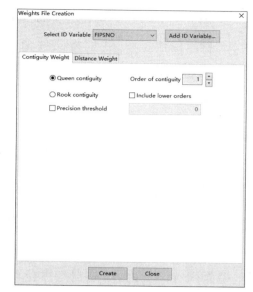

（a）创建权重矩阵文件的界面　　　　（b）ID 变量的选择

图 3.2　GeoDa 中邻接权重矩阵的创建

3.1.2　创建邻接权重矩阵

1. 一阶邻接

创建邻接权重矩阵有 Queen 准则和 Rook 准则两种方法，可以通过在对话框中勾选相应的单选按钮来实现，如图 3.3 所示。其中，默认的是一阶邻接矩阵，相应的在 Order of contiguity 文本框中的值为 1。

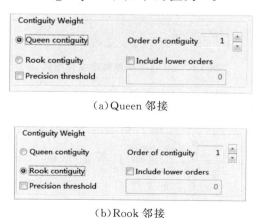

（a）Queen 邻接

（b）Rook 邻接

图 3.3　GeoDa 中设置邻接方式

此时，单击 Create 按钮会弹出文件保存对话框，并命名新的权重文件。在图 3.4 所示的例子中，我们将文件命名为 NAT_test.gal。实际上，Queen 权重与示例数据文件中的 nat_queen.gal 是一样的，但我们用了不同的名字以免覆盖示例文件。

图 3.4　为新的邻接权重矩阵文件命名

gal 格式文件中前三个观测值包含的内容如图 3.5 所示。第一行是标题行，里面列有四项内容，分别是占位符 0、观测数量 3085、原 shape 文件的名称 NAT 以及 ID 变量 FIPSNO。接下来是三个观测量，每个占两行。第一个观测量的第一行是 ID 27077 和相邻的数量 3；第二行是与其相邻的三个观测量的 ID：27007、27135、27071。其他观测量也按照同样的次序排列。gal 格式文件是一个简单的文本文件，所以对它编辑起来很容易。然而，当你试图编辑时一定要非常小心，必须保持数据的对称性。

图 3.5　gal 邻接权重矩阵文件格式

另外，Contiguity Weight 对话框也包含一个 Precision threshold 的选项。在多数情况下，不应该勾选这个选项。只有在地理信息系统（GIS）中存在一些小误差，且用户对这些误差的数量级有着清晰的认识时才能用到。如果 Precision threshold 不为 0 的话，那么我们可以进行模糊对比，来判定两个多边形是否有公共的顶点。当然，系统默认的是精确对比，它假定多边形的拓扑结构是正确的。Precision threshold 选项提供了一种处理小误差的方法，以避免返回 GIS 去修改拓扑结构,不过它不能完全取代 GIS 的功能。

2.高阶邻接

高阶邻接的权重可以通过改变 Order of contiguity 选项的值来获取,默认值是 1,可以改为任意值。例如,图 3.6(a)展示了二阶邻接。在空间权重中高阶邻接矩阵有一个选项是结果中包括低阶邻接矩阵。默认的是不包括[如图 3.6(a)所示],这样可以减少邻接权重矩阵中多余的元素。然而,在某些情况下需要包括低阶邻接权重矩阵,在这些情况下,Include lower orders 选项需要勾选,如图 3.6(b)所示。

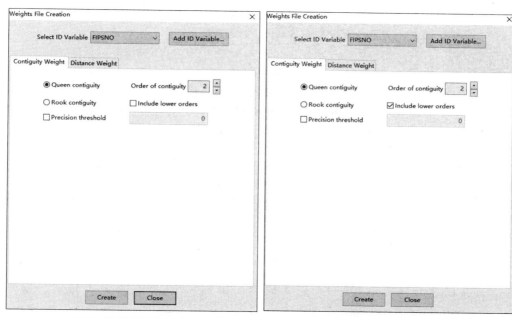

(a)二阶邻接权重矩阵　　　　　　(b)包括低阶邻接权重矩阵

图 3.6　GeoDa 中设置高阶邻接权重矩阵

3.1.3　邻接权重矩阵属性

在 GeoDa 中,权重矩阵属性可由连通直方图得出,分别可以通过点击 Tools＞Weights Manager＞Histogram[如图 3.1(a)所示]和点击权重工具条最右侧的图标[如图 3.1(b)所示]两种方法来调用。其结果是一个特殊的 GeoDa 直方图,其中横轴表示相邻空间单元的个数,如图 3.7 所示。

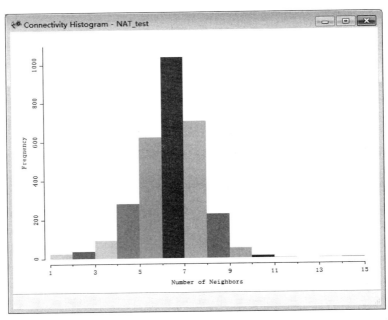

图 3.7 GeoDa 邻接权重矩阵直方图

相邻空间单元个数分布的可视化表示可以通过直方图的 Display Statistics 选项进一步量化显示。这能通过右击显示的窗口并选择"View>Display Statistics"来实现。所得结果是直方图下面列出的一组描述性统计量,如图 3.8 所示。最底部一行是我们特别感兴趣的,它列出了邻接数的最小值、最大值、中值和平均值。在我们的案例中,四个相应的值分别是 1、14、6 和 5.889 14。

为了防止有离散值,我们不仅要将最小值设为 0(直方图中将会有一个柱对应于这个值),而且要就这种情况产生一个警告信息。

3.1.4 构建空间滞后变量

在 GeoDa 中,空间滞后变量的计算是 Variable Calculation 功能的一部分,位于 Table 菜单栏中。如图 3.9(a)所示,它可以从主菜单栏选择 Table > Calculator 来调用;或者还可以通过右击数据框来启用,点击后会弹出 Calculator 对话框,如图 3.9(b)所示。Spatial Lag 计算可以通过点击对话框顶部的第四个选项卡来选择。当一个权重文件生成后,它就会列在对话框中,就如我们的案例中,NAT_test.gal 文件显示在 Weight 框下,如图 3.9(b)所示。如果没有显示,则需要点击图标来创建权重矩阵。下一个步骤是命名这个新的空间滞后变量[如图 3.10(a)中的 W_HR60],并从下拉列表中选择一个需要计算的空间滞后变量[如图 3.10(b)中的 HR60]。点击 Apply 将会计算这个新的变量并将其插入数据表中,如图 3.11 所示。此时,这个变量就能用于 GeoDa 中的所有分析。

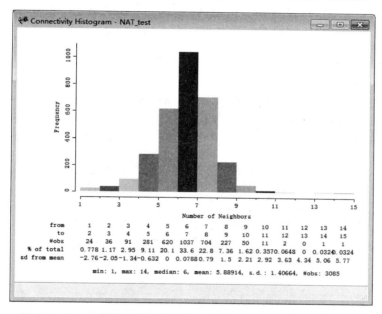

图 3.8 GeoDa 邻接权重矩阵直方图中显示相邻空间单元个数分布

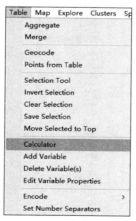

(a)变量计算

图 3.9 GeoDa 中空间滞后计算

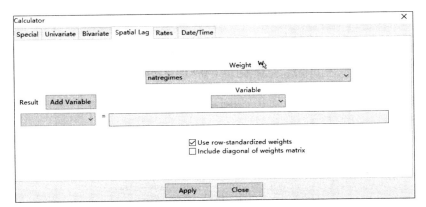

(b)空间滞后设置

图 3.9　GeoDa 中空间滞后计算(续)

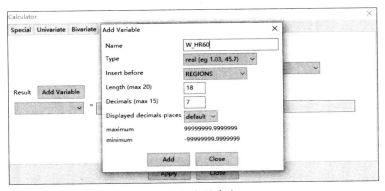

(a)为新变量命名

(b)选择变量

图 3.10　GeoDa 中空间滞后变量的选择

图 3.11 将新变量插入数据表中

3.2 GeoDaSpace 中的邻接权重矩阵

3.2.1 权重矩阵设置界面

GeoDaSpace 中,创建和读取空间权重矩阵的功能包含在回归界面的模型权重(Model Weights)和核权重(Kernel Weights)两部分中(如图 2.12 所示)。邻接权重矩阵通过 Model Weights 部分来进行操作,如图 3.12 所示。Kernel Weights 是一种基于距离的权重矩阵,将在第 4 章做进一步讨论。

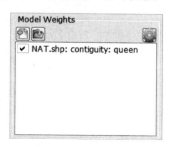

(a)初始界面　　　　　　　(b)邻接权重文件创建完成

图 3.12 GeoDaSpace 中权重矩阵界面

关于对邻接权重矩阵的操作可通过顶部的三个图标来调用。最左边的图标 Create Weights 是创建权重矩阵,第二个图标 Open Weights 是打开已有的权重文件,最右边齿轮状的图标 Properties 用来查看权重矩阵的属性。接下来我们依次介绍。

3.2.2 创建权重矩阵

点击 Model Weights 面板中的 Create Weights 图标,弹出对话框,与 GeoDa 中的界面极其相似。对话框中也列出了当前的 shape 文件作为 Input File,有两个选项卡可以选择:Contiguity 权重或者 Distance 权重。我们首先选择左边 Contiguity 权重选项。

Contiguity 权重对话框里的单选框可以选择 Queen 准则或者 Rook 准则两种方法,分别如图 3.13(a)和图 3.13(b)所示。与 GeoDa 中相同,ID 变量必须唯一确定。在我们的案例中,我们仍然选择 FIPSNO。如果在数据集中没有合适的 ID 变量,点击"+"符号,增加一个序列号来作为 ID(默认的变量名称是 POLY_ID)。

默认的邻接权重矩阵是一阶邻接。高阶邻接权重可以通过 Order of contiguity 选项的值来改变。与 GeoDa 中相同,通过勾选相应的选项可以将低阶邻接权重矩阵包括进来。

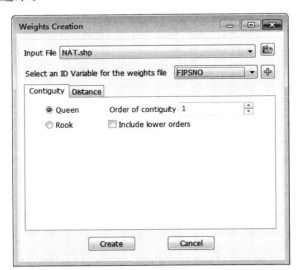

(a)Queen 邻接

图 3.13　GeoDaSpace 中邻接方式的选择

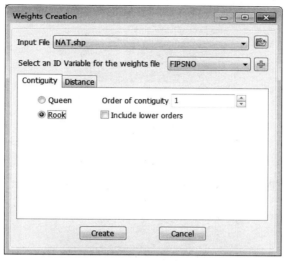

(b)Rook 邻接

图 3.13　GeoDaSpace 中邻接方式的选择(续)

点击 Create 按钮后,弹出文件保存对话框,需要对新生成的空间权重文件命名。该文件会以 gal 为扩展名来保存。另外,Model Weights 窗口中会提示一个邻接权重文件已经被创建,如图 3.12(b)所示。需要注意的是,这里不是文件名称(如 GeoDa 中我们使用 NAT_test.shp),而是赋予了它原 shape 文件的名称(NAT.shp)。这样就能将新创建的权重文件和读入的文件区分开来。

3.2.3　读取邻接权重矩阵

GeoDaSpace 支持 PySAL 权重模块的所有权重矩阵文件格式,不仅包括标准的 gal 和 gwt 格式,还包括 ArcGIS,MatLab,Stata 等软件的权重矩阵文件格式。点击 Model Weights 面板中的 Open Weights 菜单按钮,就可以从文件对话框的列表中看到所有系统支持的权重矩阵文件格式,如图 3.14 所示。

在文件打开对话框中选择所要读取的权重文件,完成后,文件名称将会列入 Model Weights 面板中。在本案例中,我们使用示例数据 queen 邻接权重矩阵 nat_queen.gal。如图 3.15 所示,所得结果的文件名已被列入面板中。与前一部分相反,此处所列的是实际名称。

图 3.14　GeoDaSpace 支持的所有权重矩阵文件格式

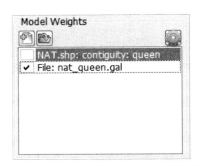

图 3.15　nat_queen.gal 文件中的 queen 邻接权重矩阵

3.2.4　邻接权重矩阵属性

邻接权重矩阵的属性可以通过点击 Model Weights 面板中的齿轮状图标来获取。点击后将会打开 Weights Properties Editor 面板，面板中列举了一些非常有用的空间权重矩阵的属性，如图 3.16 所示。

顶部是一个选择栏，列出了现有的权重矩阵文件。在我们的案例中，此处选择nat_queen.gal。如果在当前会话中创建了权重矩阵，在此下拉菜单中也可以选择。权重文件的名称会在 Name 文本框中重复一遍(File：nat_queen.gal)，与进入 Model Weights 面板时相对应。

跳到 Properties 项下的第四个标签 Neighbors of，我们可以看到相邻接的观测值的列表，显示 ID 值 27077(也就是 FIPSNO = 27077)及列出的相应的权重值。与之相邻的是 FIPSNO 为 27007、27071 和 27135 的县，它们的权重值为 0.333。此处的邻接信息与图 3.5 中 gal 文件中相应的信息是一样的。对于其他观测值也可以获取相应的信息,只需滚动 Neighbors of 标签下面的下拉列表,选择指定的 ID 值即可。

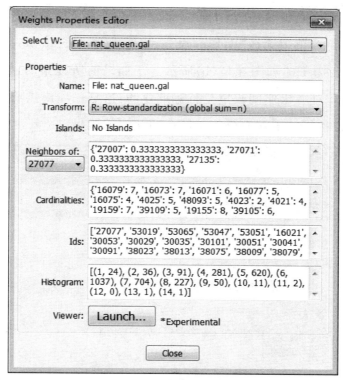

图 3.16　空间权重矩阵的属性

最后,Ids 标签下给出了 ID 变量值的完整列表。检查这个列表以确保权重文件和数据集之间没有错配。

1.空间权重矩阵形式

Weights Properties Editor 面板中的第二个图框(Transform)给出了当前权重矩阵的形式。GeoDaSpace 中默认的是对所有的 Model Weights 文件执行 row-standardization 方法。在文本框中显示的是"R：Row-standardization (global sum = n)"。然而,这个选项不仅列出了当前权重矩阵的形式,还允许用户去改变。系统设置了五种可选的形式,如图 3.17(a)所示,分别是:

- B：Binary；
- R：Row-standardization；

- D:Double-standardization;
- V:Variance stabilizing;
- O:Restore original transformation。

我们在下拉菜单中选择"B:Binary"。结果显示,Neighbors of 图框中的权重值由 0.333 变为 1.0,如图 3.17(b)所示。正如之前所提到的,GeoDaSpace 中所有的估计过程都要求空间权重是行标准化的,这是一项提供给高级用户的功能,高级用户往往能够更加充分地了解这项功能的后果。

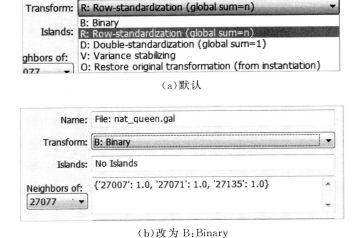

(a)默认

(b)改为 B:Binary

图 3.17 GeoDaSpace 中权重矩阵形式的选择

2.权重属性可视化

Weights Properties Editor 面板中还有三个图框,它们包含了一些有用的空间权重矩阵信息。其中,第三个图框 Islands,表明了该权重是否与其他观测值相接。在本书的案例中,并没有岛的出现,因此文本框中是 No Islands。如果有孤立的观测值,则该面板中会显示它们的 ID 变量。

第五个图框 Cardinalities,给出了每个观测量邻居的数目,并按照 ID 排列。它也成为面板最下方的 Histogram 的基础。它是与图 3.7 中 Connectivity Histogram 相对应的列表。每一对数据分别代表了邻居的数量以及拥有相同邻居数量的观测量的数量。在本书的案例中,最小和最大的邻居数量为 1 和 14,分别有 24 和 1 个观测量与之相对应。

Weights Properties Editor 面板中的最后一个特性 Viewer。点击 Launch 按钮,弹出一个交互视窗,它基于特定的空间权重矩阵将选中的单元的邻居可视化表达出来。选择文件对话框中相应的 shape 文件名称,系统将生成一张地图。在 Weights Inspector 窗口中,用户可以用鼠标在地图上浏览,选中的单元其相应的邻居也会在地图上高亮显示出来。窗口底部列出了所选单元的 ID、其邻居的 ID 以及相应的权重。它会随着所选单元的变化而不断改变。

3.2.5 创建空间滞后变量

在 GeoDaSpace 图形用户界面中,要从变量列表中创建空间滞后变量。如图 3.18 所示,可以通过点击变量列表窗口左上角的 W 图标来调用。

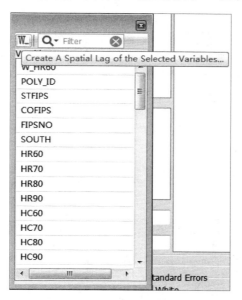

图 3.18 从变量列表中创建空间滞后变量

点击图标后弹出一个选择变量和权重的对话框,如图 3.19 所示。需要选择已有的权重文件,如本案例中的 nat_queen.gal,变量是从下拉菜单中进行选择的,如图 3.19(a)。每当选中一个变量,会生成一个 W_ 前缀的新变量名并在窗口中列出,如图 3.19(b)所示。点击 OK 按钮,弹出保存文件对话框,用户需要指定一个新的数据名称(文件扩展名为 dbf)。换句话说,这个新的空间滞后变量不会添加到当前数据集中,而是包含在一个新的 dbf 文件中(如本案例中的 natlag.dbf,如图 3.20 所示)。

在完成文件保存的过程中,新的数据文件会作为数据集保存在 GUI 中,随之空间滞后变量也被添加到变量列表之中,如图 3.21 所示。此时我们就可以将这些空间滞后变量运用到任何空间回归模型中了。

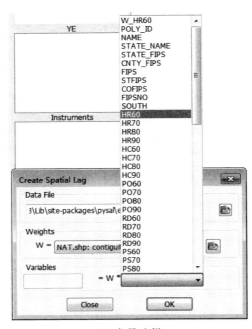

(a)变量选择

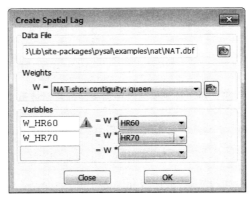

(b)变量命名

图 3.19　GeoDaSpace 中空间滞后变量界面

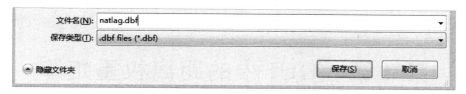

图 3.20　保存带有空间滞后变量的文件

图 3.21　将空间滞后变量添加到变量列表中

第 4 章　GUI 中的距离权重矩阵

4.1　GeoDa 中的距离权重矩阵

在 GeoDa 中创建基于距离的权重矩阵在很大程度上与创建邻接权重矩阵是非常相近的，一些操作甚至相同，比如权重矩阵的可视化和空间滞后变量的计算，这些方面的讨论我们可以参照第 3 章。本章我们专注于基于距离的空间权重矩阵和 k 最近邻权重矩阵的创建工作。

4.1.1　距离

在 GeoDa 中，创建距离权重矩阵的界面与邻接权重矩阵相同，点击 Distance Weight 选项卡（如图 4.1 所示）。在本案例中，我们使用数据集 batlim.shp，并选择 STATION 作为 ID 变量（位于对话框顶部）。

通过滑动 Specify bandwidth 下方标签来调用 max-min 距离的计算，其结果将显示在后面的面板中（21.319 006）。案例中，美国巴尔的摩市（Baltimore）的房价数据是经过精心准备的，我们可以使用欧几里得距离（Euclidean Distance）来计算距离权重。当然，如果没有一些必要的信息，我们就无法推断度量距离的最小单元。这里可以通过移动对话框中的滑块或者输入一个特定值来改变距离。

点击 Create 按钮，弹出保存文件对话框，为文件指定一个名称，将该文件保存为 gwt 格式，文件内容如图 4.2 所示。在标题行之后（与 gal 格式相同），每一行包含三部分，分别是观测量的 ID 和它的邻居，以及它们之间的距离。这个距离值在后面将会被忽略,只记录邻居。如前所述,在 GeoDa 中权重矩阵总是用行标准化的形式。

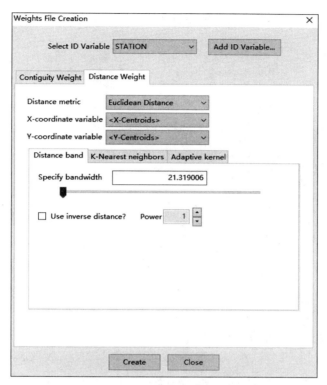

图 4.1 GeoDa 中距离权重矩阵界面

图 4.2 GeoDa 中 gwt 格式的权重矩阵文件

在图 4.1 所示界面中,默认坐标显示为 X-coordinate variable 和 Y-coordinate variable。如果不是点而是图形,那么我们就默认存储的是图形中心点的 (x,y) 坐标。

我们可以将这些 (x,y) 坐标作为计算距离的基础。例如,在图 4.3 中,我们选择 baltim.dbf 数据集中的 X 和 Y 变量,它们刚好与点的坐标相同,所以这里的选择是没有必要的。然而,此处可选的变量不仅限于点坐标。实际上任意两个变量都可以用来计算其距离值。程序会计算最大、最小距离,以确保每个观测量都至少有一个邻居,即使这个距离不一定是基于地理上的概念。

图 4.3　选择 baltim.dbf 数据集中的 X 和 Y 变量计算距离

下面我们具体介绍一下弧距。从 Distance metric 下拉菜单中选择 Arc Distance 选项以计算弧距。在本书的案例中,我们选择美国的县的 shape 数据 (NAT.shp),将 FIPSNO 作为 ID 变量。在图 4.4 中,默认的列表已经给出,Specify bandwidth 的值为 1.465 776。这是利用县所在的经纬度并以欧几里得距离为度量方式计算出来的,是不正确的。选择 Arc Distance(mi)后,结果变为了 90.865 247,如图 4.5 所示。此处用英里来度量两个县的中心之间的距离,就确保了每个县至少有一个邻居。最后,对于 Arc Distance(km),相应的值变为了 146.233 441,度量单位为千米(如图 4.6 所示)。在其他方面,用弧距创建权重矩阵的操作与用欧几里得距离创建权重矩阵的操作相同。

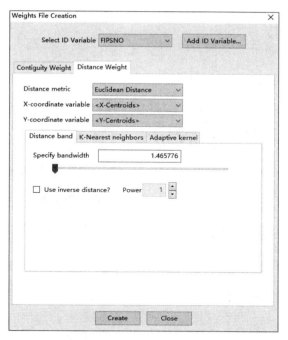

图 4.4 利用经纬度计算欧式距离

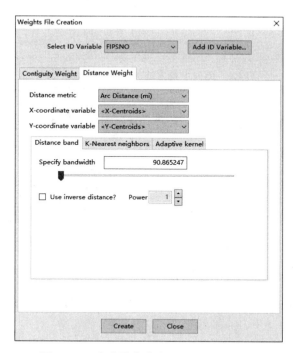

图 4.5 距离度量方式为 Arc Distance(mi)

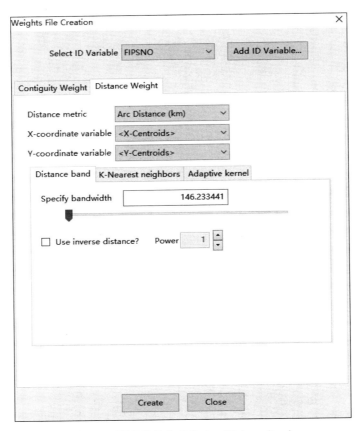

图 4.6　距离度量方式为 Arc Distance(km)

4.1.2　k 最近邻算法

在 GeoDa 中,运用 k 最近邻算法计算空间权重矩阵需要从权重创建对话框中选择相应的 Distance Weight 选项卡下的 K-nearest neighbors 选项卡,如图 4.7 所示。k 的默认值是 4,但是用户可以将 Number of neighbors 改为任意值。

所创建的权重矩阵保存为 gwt 格式的文件。同样地,两个观测量之间的距离也被存储在文件的第三列,但是程序不会调用这一列数据。在其他方面,用 k 最近邻算法创建权重矩阵的操作与用欧几里得距离创建权重矩阵的操作相同。

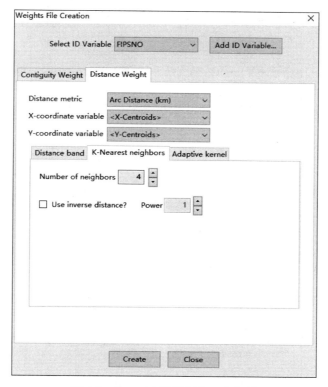

图 4.7 GeoDa 中最近邻的 k 个邻居

4.2 GeoDaSpace 中的距离权重矩阵

在 GeoDaSpace 中，要创建基于距离或者 k 最近邻算法计算的距离权重矩阵，都要通过与创建邻接权重矩阵相同的 Model Weights 界面（如图 3.13 所示）。唯一不同的是，这次需要选择右边的选项卡，如图 4.8(a) 所示。

核权重矩阵的创建是点击 Adaptive Kernel 选项卡，将会弹出核权重对话框，如图 4.8(b) 所示。

两个例子都用了 NAT.shp 数据集，选取 FIPSNO 作为 ID 变量。我们将在之后讨论核权重矩阵。在那之前，我们先来回顾一下距离度量的选择，包括 k 最近邻距离、二进制距离以及倒数距离的计算。

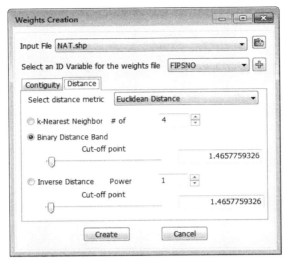

(a)创建距离权重矩阵界面

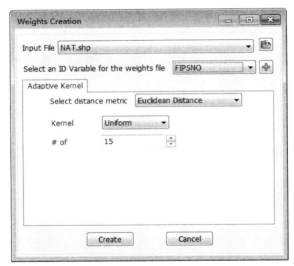

(b)创建核权重矩阵界面

图 4.8　GeoDaSpace 中距离权重矩阵界面

4.2.1　距离度量的选择

图 4.8(a)中将 Euclidean Distance 作为默认的距离度量。二进制距离(Binary Distance Band)与倒数距离(Inverse Distance)界面中都有最小距离,其值是 1.465 775 932 6,与 GeoDa 中给出的值相同(除了由于四舍五入带来的误

差),如图 4.4 所示。正如之前所指出的,这是不正确的,因为美国的县的中心点是十进制的经纬度坐标,这些坐标是未经投影的。

在 GeoDaSpace 中,距离度量的下拉菜单中还包含两个选项,这两个选项用来计算弧距,如图 4.9 所示。当选择英里作为单位时,距离阈值是 90.865 247 381 5,而除去一些四舍五入带来的误差,这也与图 4.5 中由 GeoDa 得出的值相同。当选择千米作为单位时,该阈值是 146.233 440 682(额外的小数由 Python 的默认输出所决定,但是它在度量距离时并没有很大的意义,保留四位小数就足以满足精度要求)。

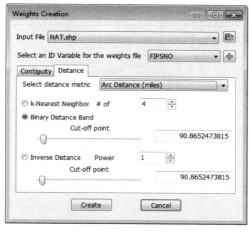

(a)以英里为单位

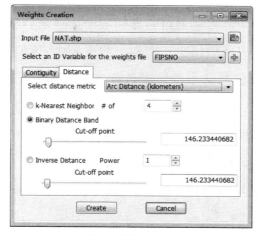

(b)以千米为单位

图 4.9 弧距的单位选择

4.2.2 k 邻近算法

可以通过勾选相应的单选按钮来创建 k 邻近权重矩阵。对于未投影的数据,我们需要选择计算弧距的选项,选择英里或者千米作为单位都可以。与在 GeoDa 中一样,默认的邻居数是 4,但是可以改为任意值。点击 Create 按钮同样会弹出文件保存对话框。

该权重文件保存为 gwt 格式。与 GeoDa 中创建的文件不同(如图 4.2 所示),GeoDaSpace 生成的文件中第三列没有记录观测值之间的距离,而是值为 1,如图 4.10 所示。该权重矩阵也是行标准化的。

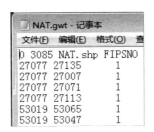

图 4.10 GeoDaSpace 中 gwt 格式的权重矩阵文件

4.2.3 二进制距离权重矩阵

二进制距离权重矩阵可以通过勾选相应的选项来创建,如图 4.11(a)所示。默认的距离阈值已在界面中给出。在本书的案例中,该值对应于以千米为单位的弧距。我们可以通过移动小滑块来改变它,但总的来说我们并不推荐这样做。另外,我们还可以直接在面板中输入一个值来改变它。当给定一个具有很强的理论基础的距离阈值时,它才可能是有用的。然而在实际中,我们必须确保这样做不会产生新的孤立点。

与 k 邻近权重矩阵的例子相同,二进制距离权重矩阵也保存为 gwt 格式的文件(图 4.10 中的格式)。

4.2.4 倒数距离权重矩阵

倒数距离权重矩阵也可以通过勾选相应的单选按钮来创建,如图 4.11(b) 所示。默认的是一次幂,但可以改为任意值。此时默认使用同样的距离阈值,当然这也可以改变。例如,有的人可能需要获取不带阈值的倒数距离来计算距离的衰减,并最终在某个点之后接近零值。

(a)二进制距离

(b)倒数距离

图 4.11　GeoDaSpace 中二进制距离权重矩阵和倒数距离权重矩阵的创建

与其他基于距离的权重矩阵相反，倒数距离权重矩阵的值存储在 gwt 文件的第三列，如图 4.12 所示。然而，GeoDaSpace 中权重矩阵是行标准化的。例如，图 4.13(a)中，在 Properties 界面中的观测量 27077，其邻居 27089 的权重值为 0.099…，与 gwt 文件中的值不同(图 4.12 中该值为 0.008…)。这是预想中的结果，因为权重已经行标准化了。比如说，如果我们要创建一个变量(倒数距离平方加权之和)，使用倒数距离或倒数距离平方的实际值，则 Transform 选项需要设为 O：Restore original transformation，如图 4.13(b)所示。那样得到的 27089 的权重值则为0.008…，与 gwt 文件中的值相同。

NAT.gwt - 记事本
文件(F) 编辑(E) 格式(O) 查看

```
0 3085 NAT FIPSNO
27077 27069 0.00726107
27077 27071 0.00989003
27077 27135 0.0149938
27077 27089 0.00856348
27077 27007 0.0112879
```

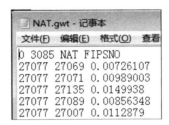

图 4.12　GeoDaSpace 中 gwt 格式的倒数距离权重矩阵文件

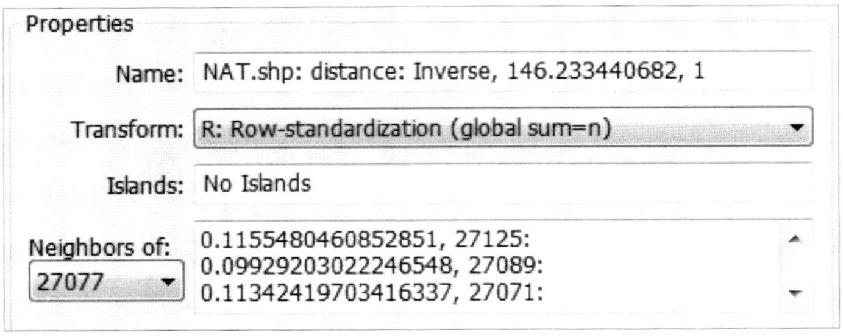

(a)二进制距离

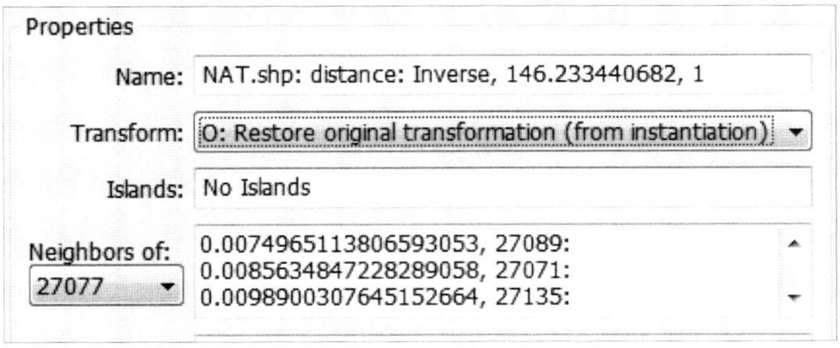

(b)倒数矩阵

图 4.13　GeoDaSpace 中二进制距离权重矩阵和倒数距离权重矩阵的属性

4.2.5 核权重矩阵

核权重矩阵(Kernel Weights)从相应的对话框中创建,如图 4.8(b)所示。本书的案例中,我们仍旧使用 NAT.shp 文件作为 Input File,FIPSNO 作为 ID 变量。为了使核权重的计算更加准确,我们需要将默认的 Euclidean Distanc 改为两个弧距选项中的一个。

核权重矩阵是一种自适应权重矩阵,它不是基于一个固定的带宽,而是基于一个固定的最近邻居数目。这个邻居的数目需要足够大,以便于 HAC 估计量的渐进特性能够表现出来。在 GeoDaSpace 中,默认的最小值(经四舍五入后)是观测量数目的方根。如图 4.8(b)所示,对于 NAT.shp 数据集来说,这个值为 15。最近邻居数目中较大的值可以在对话框中修改,但较小的值不可以。

核权重矩阵在根本上是不同于模型权重矩阵的,因为它的对角线是非零值。为了使核的平滑估计更加准确,我们需要将对角线上的值设为 1。

点击 Create 按钮后,仍然是弹出我们所熟悉的文件保存对话框。核权重矩阵文件保存为扩展名为 kwt 的文件。图 4.14(a)的例子中选择的是 Triangular 方法,并使用了英里单位的弧距来表达。如图 4.14(b)所示,文件中的第三项是核权重的值。其中,每个观测量也是其本身的邻居,权重值为 1。

核权重矩阵能够正确地运用到 HAC 估计中,但是它不能被当作模型权重矩阵去使用。

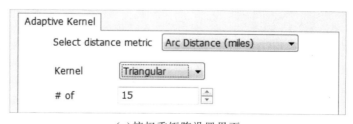

(a)核权重矩阵设置界面

图 4.14 GeoDaSpace 中的核权重矩阵设置

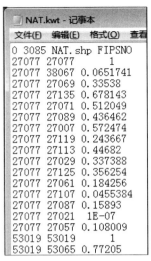

(b) kwt 格式的核权重矩阵文件

图 4.14　GeoDaSpace 中的核权重矩阵设置(续)

第 5 章 GUI 中的最小二乘估计

5.1 模型创建

在 GeoDa 和 GeoDaSpace 的 GUI 中组建回归模型的基本原则已在第 2 章做了概述,有关细节请参阅相关章节。

为了清晰起见,我们简要地重复一下这个过程中的主要步骤,这在两个软件中都是很有必要的:

- 选择一个数据集;
- 在变量列表中选择独立变量,并将其移到 GUI 的相应图框中;
- 在变量列表中选择解释变量,并将它们移到 GUI 的相应图框中;
- (可选)选择用于空间分析的空间权重矩阵文件;
- (在 GeoDaSpace 中可选)选择用于 HAC 误差计算的核权重矩阵文件;
- 调整参数或选项;
- 运行模型;
- 保存结果。

如第 2 章所述,两个界面略微有所差别,但基本的操作都是相同的。

我们使用 Baltimore 房价数据的案例来说明最小二乘(OLS)估计,由 baltim.dbf 文件访问数据。该模型中将房屋成交价格(PRICE)作为独立变量,而解释变量对应于房屋的几个特征,如房间的数量(NROOM)、浴室的数量(NBATH)。

模型操作如图 5.1 和图 5.2 所示,分别对应于 GeoDa 和 GeoDaSpace 两个软件的操作。在此我们只考虑了标准 OLS 的结果,因而不用指定空间权重矩阵,也不用在 GeoDaSpace 中勾选任何标准误差(Standard Errors)的选项。在 GeoDa 中,OLS 被称为经典模型,需要选择相应的单选按钮,如图 5.1 所示;而在 GeoDaSpace 中,则要勾选 Standard 和 OLS 两个按钮,如图 5.2 所示。

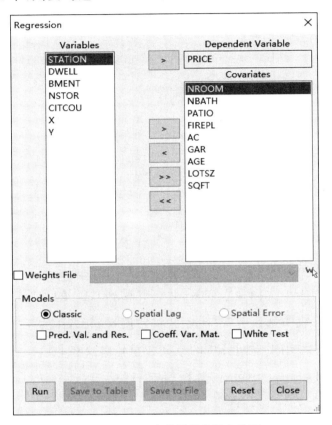

图 5.1　GeoDa 中的回归分析主界面

如第 2 章所述,在 GeoDaSpace 中,我们可以将模型保存为模型文件,以便后续使用。

此时,点击 Run 按钮启动运行过程,回归结果会显示在一个新的窗口中。在 GeoDa 和 GeoDaSpace 中,该结果可以保存为文本文件。

我们接下来讨论基本的 OLS 回归结果。

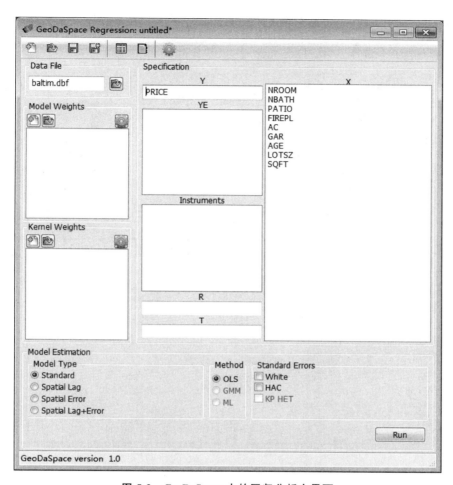

图 5.2　GeoDaSpace 中的回归分析主界面

5.2　基本的 OLS 回归结果

OLS 估计的输出结果在两个软件中的格式相同,分别如图 5.3 和图 5.4 所示。输出结果主要分为四个部分(如图 5.3 中画出的四个框),在 GeoDa 和 GeoDaSpace 中布局相同。

第一个方框中提供了一些基本的描述信息,包括数据集的文件名(baltim)、因变量(PRICE)及其平均值(44.307 2)、标准偏差(23.550 1)以及观测量总数(211)、变量个数(10)和自由度(201)。变量个数中包括常数项,它也是模型规范的一部分。GeoDaSpace 中也包含同样的信息。

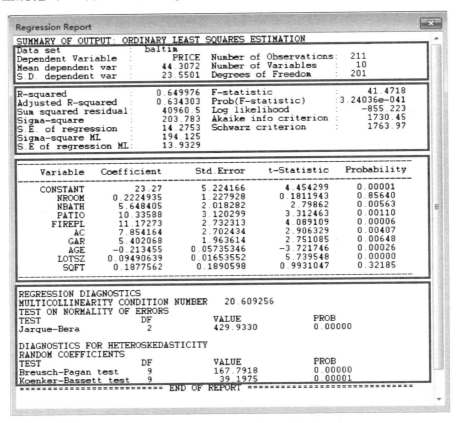

图 5.3 GeoDa 中 OLS 估计的结果

第二个方框中包含了模型若干经典的拟合优度,以及一些非经典的拟合优度。后者是为了便于与利用最大似然法估计的空间回归模型进行比较。

在我们的案例中,R^2 等于 0.649 976。在标准的假设下,这说明我们的模型解释了总方差的 2/3。我们也可以通过这个方框中的其他信息来手动地计算出 R^2。根据公式 $R^2 = 1 - \dfrac{\text{RSS}}{\text{SST}}$,我们首先获取平方的总数(SST)。这要通过两个步骤来完成。首先,我们对因变量的标准偏差进行无偏估计,对所得结果取平方(GeoDaSpace 输出结果中的 S.D. dependent var),得到的值是 $23.6061^2 = 557.247\,957$。这个结果乘以 $(n-1)=210$[因为方差是总偏差的平方和的均值,除以$(n-1)$],得到的 SST 为 117 022.071。R^2 的值就是 1.0 减去 RSS 与 SST 的比值,即

$$R^2 = 1.0 - \frac{40\,960.463}{117\,022.071} = 0.650\,0$$

如果规定保留四位小数,则这与 OLS 输出的结果相同。

```
REGRESSION
----------
SUMMARY OF OUTPUT: ORDINARY LEAST SQUARES
-----------------------------------------
Data set              :  baltim.dbf
Dependent Variable    :      PRICE      Number of Observations:      211
Mean dependent var    :     44.3072     Number of Variables   :       10
S.D. dependent var    :     23.6061     Degrees of Freedom    :      201
R-squared             :      0.6500
Adjusted R-squared    :      0.6343
Sum squared residual:     40960.463     F-statistic           :      41.4718
Sigma-square          :     203.783     Prob(F-statistic)     :     3.24e-41
S.E. of regression    :      14.275     Log likelihood        :     -855.223
Sigma-square ML       :     194.125     Akaike info criterion :     1730.446
S.E of regression ML:      13.9329      Schwarz criterion     :     1763.965

-----------------------------------------------------------------------------
       Variable     Coefficient      Std.Error     t-Statistic    Probability
-----------------------------------------------------------------------------
       CONSTANT      23.2699963      5.2241658      4.4542989      0.0000140
             AC       7.8541637      2.7024343      2.9063292      0.0040671
            AGE      -0.2134550      0.0573535     -3.7217456      0.0002568
          FIREPL     11.1727277      2.7323132      4.0891094      0.0000626
            GAR       5.4020685      1.9636140      2.7510848      0.0064824
          LOTSZ       0.0949064      0.0165355      5.7395480      0.0000000
          NBATH       5.6484051      2.0182820      2.7986204      0.0056318
          NROOM       0.2224935      1.2279277      0.1811943      0.8563976
          PATIO      10.3358755      3.1202987      3.3124635      0.0010966
           SQFT       0.1877562      0.1890598      0.9931047      0.3218530
-----------------------------------------------------------------------------

REGRESSION DIAGNOSTICS
MULTICOLLINEARITY CONDITION NUMBER           20.609

TEST ON NORMALITY OF ERRORS
TEST                         DF      VALUE           PROB
Jarque-Bera                   2      429.933         0.0000

DIAGNOSTICS FOR HETEROSKEDASTICITY
RANDOM COEFFICIENTS
TEST                         DF      VALUE           PROB
Breusch-Pagan test            9      167.792         0.0000
Koenker-Bassett test          9       39.197         0.0000
=============================== END OF REPORT ===============================
```

图 5.4　GeoDaSpace 中 OLS 估计的结果

在 GeoDa 中,Adjusted R-square 给出的值是 0.634 303,而在 GeoDaSpace 中,这

个值舍为 0.634 3。同样地,我们可以根据公式 $R_a^2 = R^2 - \frac{(1-R^2)(k-1)}{n-k}$ 来手动计算。$R^2 = 1.0 - 0.649\ 98 = 0.350\ 02$,调整比率为 $(10-1)/201 = 0.044\ 776$。所以,原本的 0.649 98 应该与 $0.350\ 02 \times 0.044\ 776 = 0.015\ 672$ 相减,即 $0.649\ 98 - 0.015\ 672 = 0.634\ 3$,与图 5.3 和图 5.4 中得出的值一样。

第二个方框中左边一栏剩下的值来源于残差平方和。针对误差方差和相应的标准误有两种不同的估计方法。第一种方法是 Sigma-square,它是对方差(203.783)和标准误(14.275 3)的无偏估计,通过用残差平方和除以自由度得到。举例来说,对于方差,它的值为 $40\ 960.463/201 = 203.783$(标准误是这个值的平方根)。与此相反,第二种方法是 Sigma-square ML,它是对误差方差的一致估计,通过用残差平方和除以观测值的数量获取(即 $40\ 960.463/211 = 194.125$),其平方根为相应的标准误(13.932 9)。

第二个方框中右边一栏中,排列在最前面的是 F 统计量的值(41.471 8),它是由公式 $F = \frac{RSS_c - RSS_u}{k-1} / \frac{RSS_u}{n-k}$ 计算得到的,其次是与之相关的 p 值(3.240 5e-41)。我们可以想到,这个值是非常重要的。

其余的几个结果都是基于一种标准回归模型的似然方法。对于正态分布的误差项,OLS 估计与最大似然估计是等价的。因此它们也能够用来计算相应的最大似然函数,参见公式 $L = -\frac{n}{2}\ln 2\pi - \frac{n}{2}\ln \sigma_{ML}^2 - \frac{1}{2}e'e/\sigma_{ML}^2$。在我们的例子中,最大似然函数的值为 -855.223。我们通过比较不同的模型,最好的似然函数是与最佳模型相关联的。

有两个量可以用解释变量的函数来代替似然函数,一是公式 $AIC = -2L + 2k$ 中的 Akaike info criterion(1 730.45),二是公式 $SC = -2L + k\ln(n)$ 中的 Schwarz criterion(1 763.965)。例如,AIC 是 $-2 \times (-855.223) + 2 \times 10$,或者 $1\ 710.446 + 20 = 1\ 730.45$。这个量与似然函数相反,它的最小值对应最佳模型。

第三个方框中是输出结果的主要内容,包括估计值以及与之相对应的标准误、t 统计量和 p 值。我们注意到除两个系数外,其他系数的 $p = 0.01$,都很显著(这两个系数分别是 NROOM 和 SQFT,不显著)。所有的系数都与预测的相符,除 AGE 之外的其他系数都是正值,而 AGE 是负值,我们很容易对此进行解释,年代久远的房屋价格更低,其他系数与之相反。

第四个方框中包含的是标准非空间模型分析的结果,我们将在下一节进行分析。

5.3 非空间回归分析

图 5.3 和图 5.4 最下方的方框中包含一组常见的非空间回归分析结果。特别地,里面还包含多重共线性的指标、Jarque-Bera 正态性检验统计量和一些异方差性检验统计量。

多重共线性的指标是 20.609 256,这并没有显示出什么潜在问题(依据经验该值要大于 30)。Jarque-Bera 正态性检验统计量的值是 429.933 0,χ^2 变量的显著性很高,自由度为 2,表明它有很高的非正态性。

这两个软件中都记录了异方差性检验。Breusch-Pagan 检验 [BP = $(1/2)[f'Z(Z'Z)^{-1}Z'f] \sim \chi^2(P+1)$)]的值是 167.791 8,Koenker-Bassett 检验 [KB = $(1/\text{Var}[u_i^2])[f'Z(Z'Z)^{-1}Z'f] \sim \chi^2(P+1)$)]的值是 39.197 5。两个值的 χ^2 变量的显著性很高,自由度为 9,表明它有很强的异方差性。这两个检验统计量值的差异也证实了潜在误差的非正态性,因为如果是正态的话这两个值应该大致相同。

下面我们来看一下怀特检验统计。异方差性的第三个检验统计量是怀特检验,它在输出结果中的显示与其他值不同。在 GeoDa 中,需要勾选 White Test 选项,如图 5.5(a)所示。在 GeoDaSpace 中,则需要在 Preferences 的设置中勾选 Other 选项卡下的该选项,如图 5.5(b)所示。

两个软件中的结果略有不同。当解释变量的平方和叉积趋于极端多重共线性时,在 GeoDa 中便不会再计算统计量的值。在我们的案例中它的值记为

N/A,自由度为 54,如图 5.6 所示。

在 GeoDaSpace 中,输出的结果如图 5.7 所示。我们注意到它的自由度 (51)与 GeoDa 中的自由度(54)不同。这是因为在计算时舍去了一些叉积或平方项,以避免极端多重共线性。怀特检验统计量值为 164.335,又进一步证实了观测量的异方差性。

(a)GeoDa

(b) GeoDaSpace

图 5.5　怀特检验的设置

图 5.6　GeoDa 中怀特检验的结果

```
DIAGNOSTICS FOR HETEROSKEDASTICITY
RANDOM COEFFICIENTS
TEST                          DF        VALUE         PROB
Breusch-Pagan test            9         167.792       0.0000
Koenker-Bassett test          9         39.197        0.0000

SPECIFICATION ROBUST TEST
TEST                          DF        VALUE         PROB
White                         51        164.335       0.0000
```

图 5.7 GeoDaSpace 中怀特检验的结果

5.4 空间效应分析

到目前为止，我们尚未考虑空间效应分析。如果进行回归时没有空间权重矩阵，那么默认不考虑空间效应分析。选择权重矩阵文件后，两个软件中都会默认计算空间滞后、空间误差和空间自回归移动平均的拉格朗日乘子统计量。在 GeoDa 中还会计算 Moran's I 指数，但在 GeoDaSpace 中则不会，因为该选项需要在 Preferences 对话框中设定。

5.4.1 选择权重矩阵文件

在两个软件中选择空间权重矩阵文件略有不同。我们使用 Baltimore 房价数据点的 k 最近邻权重矩阵来展示这种不同，k 值设为 4。baltim_k4.gwt 文件已经被纳入示例数据集中。

在 GeoDa 中，空间权重矩阵可以通过勾选回归对话框中 Weights File 旁边的单选框来进行初始化，如图 5.1 所示。选择一个权重矩阵文件后，当前默认的文件会列在中间的框中。如果没有显示，则点击右边的 W 图标就会弹出选择权重矩阵文件对话框。在这个对话框中，我们可以选择创建一个新的权重矩阵文件（通过点击 Create 图标），或者通过 Load 图标载入一个已有的权重矩阵文件，如图5.8(a)所示。当我们创建或者载入一个权重矩阵文件后，它将会显示在中间的框中，如图5.8(b)所示。点击 OK 按钮，回到 Regression 对话框，此时空间权重矩阵文件的名称已经显示在 Weights File 旁边的框中，如图 5.9 所示。

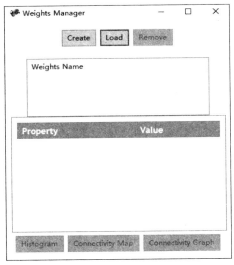
（a）选择文件之前

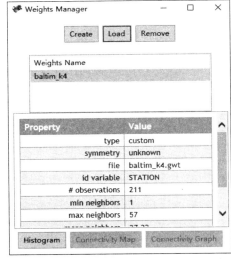
（b）选择文件之后

图 5.8　GeoDa 中权重矩阵文件选择界面

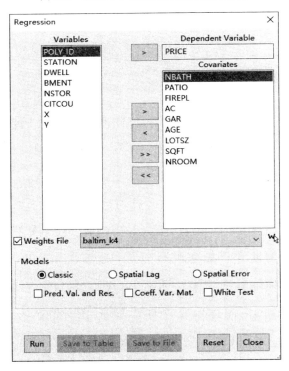

图 5.9　确定权重矩阵后的 GeoDa 回归分析主界面

在 GeoDaSpace 中，权重矩阵文件在回归对话框中的 Model Weights 界面中进行选择。在界面中我们可以通过选择相应的图标来创建新的权重矩阵文件或者载入已有的文件，如图 5.10 所示。当确定权重矩阵文件后，其文件名会显示在 Model Weights 面板中，如图 5.11 所示。

（a）创建新的权重矩阵文件　　　（b）打开已有的权重矩阵文件

图 5.10　GeoDaSpace 中权重矩阵文件选择界面

图 5.11　确定权重矩阵后的 GeoDaSpace 回归分析主界面

5.4.2 拉格朗日乘子统计量

在两个软件中选好空间权重矩阵文件后,用 OLS 计算拉格朗日乘子统计量的空间依赖。它们的输出结果在显示上有所不同。在 GeoDa 中,空间权重矩阵文件是添加到分析结果中的,如图 5.15 所示;而在 GeoDaSpace 中,它则列在输出结果顶部第二行,如图 5.12 所示。

```
SUMMARY OF OUTPUT: ORDINARY LEAST SQUARES
------------------------------------------
Data set            : baltim.dbf
Weights matrix      :File: baltim_k4.gwt
Dependent Variable  :      PRICE
```

图 5.12　GeoDaSpace 回归结果中的权重矩阵文件

检验统计量的值排列在非空间回归分析的下面。图 5.13 给出了我们案例中的相应值。GeoDaSpace 中的格式与 GeoDa 不同,正如我们在之前所提到的,Moran's I 指数在 GeoDa 中是默认计算的(如图 5.15 所示)。

```
DIAGNOSTICS FOR SPATIAL DEPENDENCE
TEST                          MI/DF    VALUE       PROB
Lagrange Multiplier (lag)       1      30.912      0.0000
Robust LM (lag)                 1      28.466      0.0000
Lagrange Multiplier (error)     1       5.442      0.0197
Robust LM (error)               1       2.996      0.0835
Lagrange Multiplier (SARMA)     2      33.908      0.0000
```

图 5.13　GeoDaSpace 中空间依赖性分析结果

记录中的第一个统计量是关于空间滞后自相关的测试。因为检验统计量的顺序并没有什么影响,而我们将它放在第一位,是考虑到忽略一个空间滞后项造成的后果远比忽略空间误差自相关的后果要严重得多。LM_ρ 统计量 $[LM_\rho = \dfrac{d_\rho^2}{D} \sim \chi^2(1)]$ 表示为 Lagrange Multiplier(lag),其值为 30.912。χ^2 变量的显著性很高,自由度为 1,表明它有很强的空间自相关。

第二个统计量是关于空间滞后的鲁棒性检验,LM_ρ^* 统计量 $[LM_\rho^* =$

$\frac{(d_\rho - d_\lambda)^2}{(D-T)} \sim \chi^2(1)$]表示为 Robust LM(lag),其值为 28.466。χ^2 变量的显著性很高,自由度为 2。相对于值为 30.912 的 LM 统计量,它的值几乎没有影响,这表明空间滞后模型很可能是正确的替代性选择。

接下来是两个针对空间误差自相关的检验统计量。LM_λ 统计量[$LM_\lambda = \frac{d_\lambda^2}{T} \sim \chi^2(1)$]排列在 Lagrange Multiplier(error)下面,值为 5.442。χ^2 变量略微有些显著性,自由度为 1,$p = 0.02$。与之相反,LM_λ^* 统计量[$LM_\lambda^* = \frac{(d_\lambda - TD^{-1}d_\rho)^2}{[T(1-TD)]} \sim \chi^2(1)$]表示为 Robust LM(error),值为 2.996,它已经不再显著($p = 0.08$)。所以在此情况下,统计量由微弱的显著性($p = 0.02$)变为不显著。这表明空间自相关取决于空间滞后的选择,而不是空间误差自相关。

空间依赖性分析的最后一行是 $LM_{\rho\lambda}$ 统计量[$LM_{\rho\lambda} = \frac{d_\lambda^2}{T} + \frac{(d_\lambda - d_\rho)^2}{(D-T)} \sim \chi^2(2)$]的结果。它排列在 Lagrange Multiplier(SARMA)下面,值为 33.908,自由度为 2。这个值具有很高的显著性。这个结果表明高阶模型能正确地替代回归模型,但必须对其进行谨慎的解释。事实上,因为这个检验自由度为 2,边缘检测(本案例中的空间滞后检验)中一个很高的值会导致拒绝联合原假设,即使这个正确的替代模型只包含一个空间参数。

5.4.3 Moran's I 指数

在 GeoDa 中,Moran's I 指数($I = \frac{e'We/S_0}{e'e/n}$)与空间分析放在一起;而在 GeoDaSpace 中,只有在 Preferences 面板中明确地选择相应的选项后才会计算。该选项在 Other 选项卡下,如图 5.14 所示。勾选该选项,点击 Save 按钮,使 Moran's I 指数能用于后续所有的分析中,直到恢复默认。

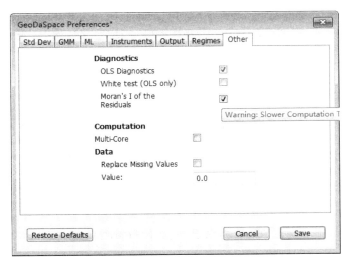

图 5.14 GeoDaSpace 中 Moran's I 指数的设置界面

两个软件中的列表是相同的,我们在图 5.15 中给出了 GeoDa 的结果。其中,位于第一项的统计量是 Moran's I(error),它列出了 Moran's I 指数的值及相应的标准化的 z 值和 p 值的大小。在我们的案例中,Moran's I 指数的值为 0.107 3,z 值为 2.649 0,$p=0.008$,它具有显著性。也就是说,在没有空间自相关时,Moran's I 指数拒绝原假设。然而,这并不能让我们了解空间误差模型或者空间滞后模型能否合理地进行空间回归。因此,我们更倾向于根据拉格朗日乘子统计量的结果来寻找一些新的策略。

```
DIAGNOSTICS FOR SPATIAL DEPENDENCE
FOR WEIGHT MATRIX : baltim_k4.gwt
   (row-standardized weights)
TEST                              MI/DF      VALUE         PROB
Moran's I (error)                 0.1073     2.6490        0.00807
Lagrange Multiplier (lag)         1          30.9119       0.00000
Robust LM (lag)                   1          28.4663       0.00000
Lagrange Multiplier (error)       1          5.4417        0.01966
Robust LM (error)                 1          2.9961        0.08347
Lagrange Multiplier (SARMA)       2          33.9080       0.00000
```

图 5.15 GeoDa 中空间依赖分析的结果

5.4.4 空间模型的选择

现在我们来讨论空间规范搜寻的应用,这里,我们使用的是 LM 统计的结果(如图 5.13 所示)。

如果我们设 p 值为 0.01,并在我们的分析中将其作为推算的基础,则 LM_ρ 值将会变得显著($p=0.0000$),但是 LM_λ 值不显著(因为 $p=0.0197$ 不符合 $p=0.01$ 的标准)。因此,此时我们应该进行的是空间滞后模型的估计。

或者,如果我们将 p 值设为更常规的 0.05,则两个统计量都将变得显著,之后我们一直执行直到通过鲁棒性检验。需要记住,鲁棒拉格朗日乘子只有在 LM_ρ 和 LM_λ 都拒绝原假设时才予以考虑,当其中一个统计量(或两个)没有拒绝时就不能考虑。在我们的案例中,鲁棒性检验统计量的滞后选择显著性很强,$p=0.0000$;相反,误差选择就不显著,$p=0.08$。因此,我们将继续评估空间滞后模型。

5.5 预测值和残差

GeoDa 和 GeoDaSpace 两个软件对预测值和残差的处理有所不同。在 GeoDa 中,有两个选项能分别将残差和预测值输出在回归结果中,还有可能将它们作为新变量添加到数据表中。在 GeoDaSpace 中,对预测值和残差的处理可以在 Preferences 面板中进行设置。

5.5.1 GeoDa

在 GeoDa 中,要将预测值和残差作为新变量添加到数据表中,就要在执行完回归后点击 Save to Table 按钮,如图 5.16 所示。点击后会弹出一系列对话框,选择添加预测值还是残差(或两者都添加),并定义一个变量名称(如果作为新变量的话)和数据格式,如图 5.17 所示。通常情况下,保持默认设置就可以了。

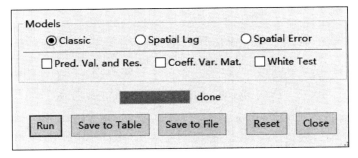

图 5.16 GeoDa 中把结果保存进数据表

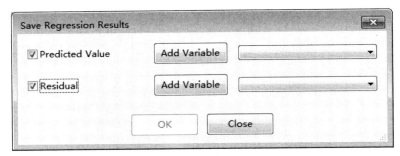

(a)添加变量

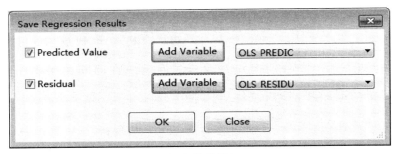

(b)变量已添加

图 5.17 添加预测值和残差

这个步骤完成后,新的变量就被添加到数据表中了,如图 5.18 所示。这些新变量可以应用到 GeoDa 的所有分析中,如创建一个预测值和残差的示意图,或者执行一个标准的图形化回归分析。例如,预测值和残差的图形化显示可以用于异方差性可视化分析。

	CITCOU	LOTSZ	SQFT	X	Y	OLS_PREDIC	OLS_RESIDU
1	0.000000	5.700000	11.250000	907.000000	534.000000	0.8702636	46.1297364
2	1.000000	279.510000	28.920000	922.000000	574.000000	109.1514684	3.8485316
3	1.000000	70.640000	30.620000	920.000000	581.000000	78.8050222	86.1949778
4	1.000000	174.630000	26.120000	923.000000	578.000000	99.5257883	4.7742117
5	1.000000	107.800000	22.040000	918.000000	574.000000	65.1220733	-2.6220733
6	1.000000	139.640000	39.420000	900.000000	577.000000	82.0216209	-12.0216209
7	1.000000	250.000000	21.880000	918.000000	576.000000	102.4584788	25.0415212
8	1.000000	100.000000	36.720000	907.000000	576.000000	55.5474655	-2.5474655
9	1.000000	115.900000	25.600000	918.000000	562.000000	70.7263300	-6.2263300
10	1.000000	365.070000	44.120000	897.000000	576.000000	121.1928286	23.8071714
11	1.000000	81.100000	19.880000	916.000000	569.000000	53.5945329	9.9054671
12	1.000000	91.000000	12.080000	908.000000	573.000000	61.3416429	-2.4416429
13	1.000000	74.350000	10.990000	913.000000	566.000000	38.1728625	26.8271375
14	1.000000	46.170000	13.600000	910.000000	574.000000	50.8871214	1.1128786
15	1.000000	23.100000	12.800000	922.000000	569.000000	33.6084992	14.3915008
16	0.000000	14.400000	29.790000	913.000000	536.000000	33.1684399	-29.6684399
17	0.000000	8.970000	14.300000	919.000000	533.500000	31.0956704	-18.2956704
18	0.000000	10.220000	13.720000	917.500000	535.000000	19.7022544	-2.2022544

图 5.18 GeoDa 中包含预测值和残差的数据表

5.5.2 GeoDaSpace

在 GeoDaSpace 中,对预测值和残差的处理取决于 Preferences Output 选项卡中的设置,如第 2 章的图 2.18(a)所示。勾选了该选项后,执行回归时会触发一个请求,来为预测值和残差指定文件名。例如,在图 5.19 中,我们选择使用默认名称 baltim_predY_resid.csv。这一步将会创建一个逗号分隔格式的 csv 文件,它包含观测量的 ID、独立变量的值、预测值和残差,图 5.20 中显示的是 Baltimore 回归中的前 10 个观测量。

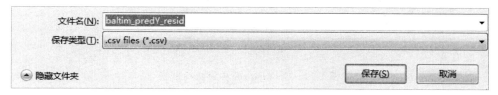

图 5.19 GeoDaSpace 中预测值和残差文件的保存

IDs	PRICE	standard	standard_resid
1	47	0.8703	46.1297
2	113	109.1515	3.8485
3	165	78.805	86.195
4	104.3	99.5258	4.7742
5	62.5	65.1221	-2.6221
6	70	82.0216	-12.0216
7	127.5	102.4585	25.0415
8	53	55.5475	-2.5475
9	64.5	70.7263	-6.2263
10	145	121.1928	23.8072

图 5.20　GeoDaSpace 中预测值和残差文件的部分内容

5.6　鲁棒系数标准误估计

在 GeoDaSpace 中，可以通过一些操作来估计鲁棒系数标准误。目前在 GeoDa 中还没有这个选项。

5.6.1　怀特标准误

异方差一致性判断是基于对系数的怀特检验，如公式 $Var[\hat{\beta}] = n \times [X'X]^{-1}\hat{V} \times [X'X]^{-1}$。在 GUI 中要通过勾选 Model Estimation 面板中的 White 选项来调用该功能，如图 5.21 所示。其他参数都不需要再调整，因为数据和模型的相关选项都与前面的例子相同。

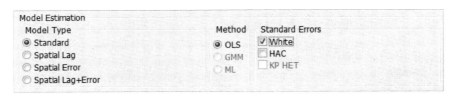

图 5.21　GeoDaSpace 中怀特标准误

选中 White 选项后，在回归结果中就多了一张表，包括估计值、标准误、t 统计量和 p 值，如图 5.22 所示。

我们注意到，回归估计值与标准 OLS 估计的结果相同（如图 5.4 所示）。两个输出表的不同之处在于怀特异方差鲁棒标准误差估计,这将会引起 t 统计量和对应的 p 统计量的变化。

```
White Standard Errors
-----------------------------------------------------------------
     Variable     Coefficient    Std.Error    t-Statistic    Probability
-----------------------------------------------------------------
     CONSTANT     23.2699963     6.5488415     3.5532997      0.0004741
           AC      7.8541637     3.1147472     2.5216055      0.0124581
          AGE     -0.2134550     0.1082717    -1.9714745      0.0500417
        FIREPL    11.1727277     3.0235003     3.6952957      0.0002831
          GAR      5.4020685     3.2537312     1.6602688      0.0984196
         LOTSZ     0.0949064     0.0260489     3.6433902      0.0003425
         NBATH     5.6484051     2.4995696     2.2597511      0.0249092
         NROOM     0.2224935     1.3934904     0.1596663      0.8733042
         PATIO    10.3358755     4.1978783     2.4621665      0.0146520
          SQFT     0.1877562     0.2099744     0.8941860      0.3722918
-----------------------------------------------------------------
```

图 5.22 包含怀特标准误估计的 OLS 结果

OLS 的默认设置按照公式 $Var[\hat{\beta}] = \dfrac{n}{n-k}[X'X]^{-1}[X'SX][X'X]^{-1}$,实现最初怀特结果的一个经过调整后的小样本。这取决于 Preferences 面板中 Std Dev 选项卡下的 OLS 选项。默认的是执行此功能,如图 5.23(a)中 N-K 列的单选按钮已选中。要使用原怀特变量,如公式 $Var[\hat{\beta}] = [X'X]^{-1}[X'SX][X'X]^{-1}$,则需要选中 N 列的单选按钮,如图 5.23(b)所示。

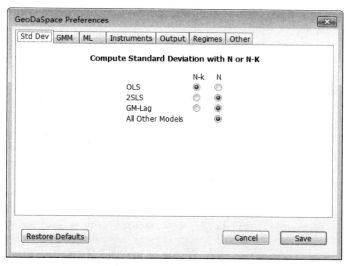

(a)默认设置 Std Dev = N-K

图 5.23 标准误计算设置界面

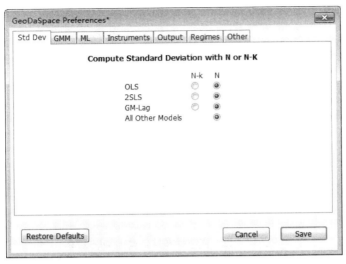

(b) Std Dev = N

图 5.23 标准误计算设置界面(续)

未经调整的怀特标准误的结果如图 5.24 所示。正如预期的那样,标准误小于经过调整后的版本,导致其 t 值较高而 p 值较小。我们可以很容易地计算出比例因子达到 $n/(n-k)$ 或 $211/201=1.04975$。例如,如果我们将标准误设为 CONSTANT,则进位后的值为 6.548 841 5(如图 5.22 所示),调整前的值为 6.391 772 1(如图 5.24 所示)。这两个数的比值等于 1.024 573 7,其平方是 1.049 75,与理论上的比例因子相同。

```
White Standard Errors
-----------------------------------------------------------------------
     Variable     Coefficient      Std.Error      t-Statistic    Probability
-----------------------------------------------------------------------
     CONSTANT     23.2699963       6.3917721      3.6406174      0.0003459
           AC      7.8541637       3.0400421      2.5835707      0.0104876
          AGE     -0.2134550       0.1056749     -2.0199209      0.0447190
       FIREPL     11.1727277       2.9509837      3.7861028      0.0002020
          GAR      5.4020685       3.1756927      1.7010678      0.0904767
        LOTSZ      0.0949064       0.0254242      3.7329217      0.0002464
        NBATH      5.6484051       2.4396191      2.3152815      0.0216067
        NROOM      0.2224935       1.3600685      0.1635899      0.8702183
        PATIO     10.3358755       4.0971951      2.5226710      0.0124216
         SQFT      0.1877562       0.2049383      0.9161595      0.3606811
-----------------------------------------------------------------------
```

图 5.24 Std Dev 设置为 N 时的怀特标准误结果

在较大的数据集中,比例因子的影响就变得微不足道了,但在小至中等的数据集中,它还是能产生一定的影响的。例如,在我们的结果中,AGE 这个系

数的 p 值为 0.045，这是未经过调整得到的怀特标准误（如图 5.24 所示），但是比例因子将其 p 值变为 0.050（如图 5.22 所示）。也就是说，我们的推断会由显著性变为非显著性。它相当于使用标准误的经典 OLS 估计，p 值为 0.000 3（如图 5.4 所示）。

5.6.2 异方差和自相关一致性标准误（HAC）

在 GUI 中，HAC 鲁棒系数标准误的估计要通过勾选 Standard Errors 项下相应的选项，如图 5.25 所示。GeoDa 中没有这个选项。

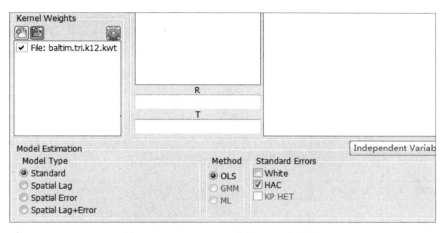

图 5.25　GeoDaSpace 中的 HAC 标准误

除勾选相应的选项外，HAC 估计还需要一个核权重矩阵文件。在 GeoDaSpace 中，还是采用常用的那两种方式：创建新的权重矩阵文件或者打开已有的文件，与 Model Weights 的图标相同（如图 5.10 所示），只不过该图标位于 Kernel Weights 面板中。在我们的案例中，我们用的是基于 $k=12$ 的最近邻居的三角核，并选取点数据 baltim.shp 作为示例数据集。将其载入后，核权重矩阵文件的名称就列于面板中，如图 5.25 中的 baltim.tri.k12.kwt 文件。

与之前怀特标准误的例子相似，它与标准 OLS 估计输出结果的唯一不同之处就是它产生了一组新的标准误，以及相应的 t 统计量和 p 值，如图 5.26 所示。除了数值结果，输出表的顶部还列出了引用的核权重矩阵文件，即 baltim.tri.k12.kwt。

```
HAC Standard Errors; Kernel Weights: File: baltim.tri.k12.kwt
-----------------------------------------------------------------
      Variable     Coefficient     Std.Error     t-Statistic     Probability
-----------------------------------------------------------------
      CONSTANT     23.2699963      6.7557588     3.4444682       0.0006964
      AC            7.8541637      3.2786033     2.3955822       0.0175113
      AGE          -0.2134550      0.1067463    -1.9996471       0.0468849
      FIREPL       11.1727277      2.9682469     3.7640829       0.0002194
      GAR           5.4020685      3.5732510     1.5118077       0.1321534
      LOTSZ         0.0949064      0.0251785     3.7693418       0.0002151
      NBATH         5.6484051      2.4853389     2.2726901       0.0241027
      NROOM         0.2224935      1.3841623     0.1607424       0.8724578
      PATIO        10.3358755      4.4904056     2.3017688       0.0223729
      SQFT          0.1877562      0.1867879     1.0051842       0.3160167
-----------------------------------------------------------------
```

图 5.26 包含 HAC 标准误的 OLS 估计

5.6.3 标准误比较

我们来总结一下 OLS 回归,在表 5.1 中我们将标准情况下的标准误估计、怀特标准误估计[调整后标记为(1),未调整的标记为(2)]和 HAC 标准误估计放在了一起。为了保持它的完整性,系数估计也列入其中。

表 5.1 OLS 的标准误比较

Variable	Estimate	OLS	White(1)	White(2)	HAC
CONSTANT	23.270	5.224	6.549	6.392	6.756
AC	7.854	2.702	3.115	3.040	3.279
AGE	−0.213	0.057	0.108	0.106	0.107
FIREPL	11.173	2.732	3.024	2.951	2.968
GAR	5.402	1.964	3.254	3.176	3.573
LOTSZ	0.095	0.017	0.026	0.025	0.025
NBATH	5.648	2.018	2.500	2.440	2.485
NROOM	0.222	1.228	1.393	1.360	1.384
PATIO	10.336	3.120	4.198	4.097	4.490
SQFT	0.188	0.189	0.210	0.205	0.187

结果表明了一种常见的模式,在多数情况下,用怀特和 HAC 方法比常规 OLS 估计得到的标准误要大。

在我们的案例中,异方差性的影响很明显。怀特的所有系数和标准误比 OLS 要大,有时甚至是后者的两倍。例如,对 GAR 变量 OLS 的标准误是 1.964,而怀特的标准误是 3.254。这也导致了 p 值的差异,由 OLS 的 $p=0.006$

变为怀特的 $p=0.098$。也就是说,有些参数在常规 OLS 的标准误下被认为是显著的,而在异方差鲁棒标准误估计时则不显著。AGE 变量的模式与之相似,虽然两个值的差距没那么明显,标准误由 0.057 变为 0.108(相应的 p 值由 OLS 的 $p=0.0003$ 变为怀特的 $p=0.050$)。NBATH 变量的标准误由 2.018 变为 2.500(相应的 p 值由 OLS 的 $p=0.006$ 变为怀特的 $p=0.025$)。

相对于常规 OLS 估计,使用 HAC 估计的影响与怀特相似。在所有情况下(除去 SQFT,它在任何情况下都不显著),HAC 的标准误比 OLS 的标准误要大。另外,HAC 的标准误也几乎总是大于未经调整的怀特的标准误,而对于调整后的怀特的标准误则不然。相对于 OLS 和怀特的差异来说,怀特和 HAC 的差异就没有那么显著。这表明在这个案例中,错误设定的主要影响可能与异方差性有关,而不是空间自相关。这与空间效应的分析结果相一致,表明这是空间滞后模型,而不是空间误差模型。

第6章　GUI 中的两阶段最小二乘估计

6.1　模型创建

在 GeoDaSpace 中建立一个回归模型的基本方法已经在之前做了介绍,此处不再赘述。两阶段最小二乘(2SLS)的步骤与 OLS 相似,但是它有两个额外要求:至少要选择一个内生变量,以及指定至少与内生变量个数相同的工具。

总而言之,创建 2SLS 回归模型的步骤变为:
- 选择数据集(dbf 文件);
- 从变量列表中选择一个独立变量,并将其拖到 Y 文本框中;
- 从变量列表中选择一个解释变量,并将其拖到 X 文本框中;
- 从变量列表中选择至少一个内生变量,并将其拖到 YE 文本框中;
- 从变量列表中选择工具,其数目至少与内生变量相同,并将其拖到 Instruments 文本框中。

默认选择的模型是 Standard,在本书的案例中,Standard 模型包含内生变量,但没有空间效应(如没有空间滞后独立变量或空间自回归误差)。

为了更好地阐述 2SLS 模型,我们选用关于美国县级犯罪的 NAT.shp 示例数据集。如图 6.1 所示,独立变量是 1990 年的县级犯罪率(HR90);解释变量是资源剥夺指数(RD90)、人口结构指标(PS90)、平均年龄(MA90)以及失业率(UE90),所有的解释变量都是 1990 年的数据。

我们将失业率作为内生变量,并添加了三个工具变量去控制它:1989 年低于贫困线的家庭比例(FP89)、1989 年县的基尼系数(GI89)以及 1990 年女性做主的家庭比例(FH90)。

由于我们只考虑了标准情况,在图 6.1 中没有指定空间权重,因此我们没有勾选 Standard Errors 面板中的选项。就像 GeoDaSpace 中的所有模型一样,我们可以将这个规范保存为模型文件供以后使用。

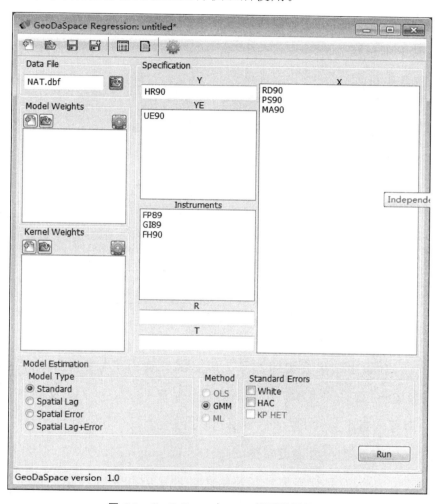

图 6.1　GeoDaSpace 中 2SLS 模型设置界面

点击 Run 按钮开始执行。此时,回归结果会显示在一个新的窗口中。点击 Save Results File As... 图标可以将结果保存为文件。文本的大小可以通过"+"和"-"图标来调整。

接下来我们讨论 2SLS 的基本估计结果。

6.2 基本估计结果

所有的估计方法都以相同的组织方式输出结果。图 6.2 所示是 2SLS 的输出结果,其中不包括分析。

```
REGRESSION
----------
SUMMARY OF OUTPUT: TWO STAGE LEAST SQUARES
------------------------------------------
Data set            :    NAT.dbf
Dependent Variable  :       HR90        Number of Observations:       3085
Mean dependent var  :     6.1829        Number of Variables   :          5
S.D. dependent var  :     6.6414        Degrees of Freedom    :       3080
Pseudo R-squared    :     0.3570

------------------------------------------------------------------------------
        Variable      Coefficient       Std.Error     z-Statistic    Probability
------------------------------------------------------------------------------
        CONSTANT       15.6455516       1.3545018      11.5507796      0.0000000
            MA90       -0.0983758       0.0299492      -3.2847583      0.0010207
            PS90        1.8770506       0.1070934      17.5272273      0.0000000
            RD90        5.7292488       0.2129126      26.9089171      0.0000000
            UE90       -0.9144554       0.0986831      -9.2665854      0.0000000
------------------------------------------------------------------------------
Instrumented: UE90
Instruments: FH90, FP89, GI89
============================ END OF REPORT =================================
```

图 6.2 2SLS 的主要结果

如前所述,输出结果分为四部分。第一部分列出了数据集(NAT.dbf)、独立变量(HR90)及其平均值(6.182 9)、标准误(6.641 4)以及观测量个数(3 085)、解释变量个数(5,包括常数项)和自由度。

第二部分是作为拟合度度量的 Pseu1do R-squared(0.357 0)。注意这里不是我们常见的 R^2,而是观测值和预测值之间的平方相关性。在此设定下,计算预测值时要包含实际观测量的内生变量。通常对 R^2 的解释是将方差分解成一个解释分量和一个残余分量,在这里也已经不再适用。在模型的选择上它可以作为一个粗略的指导方针,但不能指示解释标准误(std.Error)的比例。

第三部分包含估计值、标准误、渐近 t 检验(z 统计量)以及相应的 p 值。在本书的案例中,所有的变量都具有很高的显著性,平均年龄和失业率是负值

（变量的值越高,犯罪率越低),人口结构和资源剥夺是正值。

第四部分是内生变量(记为 Instrumented)以及在估计中用到的工具变量(Instruments)。

最后,当选中 Preferences 面板中的 Output 选项卡时,如第 2 章中的图 2.18(a)所示,运行回归会发起一个请求来为预测值和残差指定一个文件名。输出的文件与 OLS 格式相同,如图 6.3 所示。

IDs	HR90	standard	standard_resid
1	0	1.1852	-1.1852
2	15.8856	-6.2857	22.1713
3	6.4625	0.3504	6.1121
4	6.9965	4.109	2.8875
5	7.478	-2.8202	10.2982
6	4.0006	-3.0012	7.0018
7	5.7205	-5.3591	11.0796
8	2.8145	3.2525	-0.4381
9	5.5001	3.9545	1.5456
10	6.6059	4.0001	2.6058

图 6.3 2SLS 的预测值和残差文件

6.3 空间效应分析

GeoDaSpace 中,当用户界面的 Model Weights 部分存在空间权重矩阵项时我们就可以进行空间效应分析。权重矩阵文件可以新建,也可以从已有的权重矩阵文件中读取。两种情况下都会在 Model Weights 面板中列出文件名。指定空间权重矩阵文件后,就会执行 Anselin-Kelejian(AK)权重,并添加到估计结果中。

在图 6.4 中,我们使用 NAT.dbf 示例数据集的例子来阐述,一阶 queen 邻接文件作为模型权重矩阵(包含在 nat_queen.gal)。图中还包含一个核权重矩阵,现在暂时不考虑,我们将会在计算 HAC 标准误时用到它。

选择模型权重矩阵后,2SLS 估计的输出结果与标准情况下的结果相同,除去包括权重矩阵文件的名称(nat_queen.gal)以及残差空间自相关的 AK 检验

(Anselin-Kelejian Test)，如图 6.5 所示。在本书的案例中，统计量的值为 124.415，显著性极高（$p=0.0000$）。这表明这个模型中存在残差空间自相关。然而，这个检验结果并不能表明替代模型是滞后模型还是误差模型。

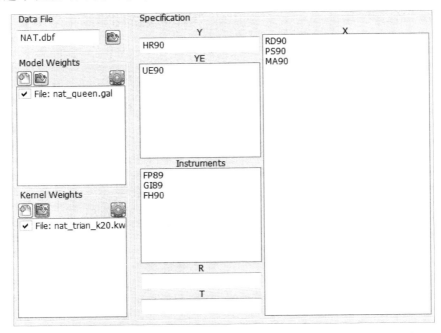

图 6.4　带有空间权重矩阵的 2SLS 模型

图 6.5　2SLS 中空间自相关的 AK 检验

6.4　鲁棒系数标准误估计

与 OLS 的例子相同，鲁棒系数标准误估计也能用于 2SLS，其基本原则和正式的结果也与 OLS 相同，不同之处在于，用于怀特标准误或者 HAC 标准误计算的残差来自 2SLS。

在 GeoDaSpace 中,要通过勾选 GUI 中的相应选项来执行怀特或 HAC 标准误的计算。如图 6.6 所示,两个选项都被选中。用 HAC 方法计算时,需要指定 Kernel Weights。如图 6.4 所示,我们选择了三角核权重矩阵功能,将其设定为基于 20 个最近邻居的自适应带宽(nat_trian_k20.kw)。

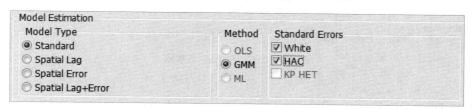

图 6.6　计算 2SLS 的鲁棒系数标准误

6.4.1　怀特标准误估计

怀特标准误(White Standard Error)的结果如图 6.7 所示,与 OLS 的格式相同。估计值与标准 2SLS 估计的值相同,如图 6.2 所示,但是标准误、z 统计量和相应的 p 值则不同。

```
White Standard Errors
------------------------------------------------------------------------------
         Variable     Coefficient     Std.Error     z-Statistic     Probability
------------------------------------------------------------------------------
         CONSTANT     15.6455516      1.5393092     10.1640082      0.0000000
             MA90    -0.0983758      0.0316213     -3.1110577      0.0018642
             PS90     1.8770506      0.1688432     11.1171261      0.0000000
             RD90     5.7292488      0.3053397     18.7635242      0.0000000
             UE90    -0.9144554      0.1384631     -6.6043272      0.0000000
------------------------------------------------------------------------------
Instrumented: UE90
Instruments: FH90, FP89, GI89
```

图 6.7　2SLS 的怀特标准误

6.4.2　HAC 标准误估计

HAC 标准误的结果如图 6.8 所示,与 OLS 的格式相同。同样地,估计值与标准 2SLS 估计的值相同,但是标准误、z 统计量和相应的 p 值则不同。另外,核权重矩阵的名字也列在表格顶部。

```
HAC Standard Errors; Kernel Weights: File: nat_trian_k20.kwt
------------------------------------------------------------------
     Variable       Coefficient      Std.Error     z-Statistic    Probability
------------------------------------------------------------------
     CONSTANT      15.6455516       1.6404233      9.5375088      0.0000000
         MA90      -0.0983758       0.0340391     -2.8900797      0.0038514
         PS90       1.8770506       0.1981754      9.4716612      0.0000000
         RD90       5.7292488       0.3292923     17.3986729      0.0000000
         UE90      -0.9144554       0.1429948     -6.3950252      0.0000000
------------------------------------------------------------------
Instrumented: UE90
Instruments: FH90, FP89, GI89
```

图 6.8　2SLS 的 HAC 标准误

6.4.3　标准误比较

在表 6.1 中我们将三个标准误估计值放在一起进行比较。标准误以通常的模式显示,其值由标准 2SLS 到怀特和 HAC 依次增加。尽管我们建议在分析标准 2SLS 结果时应该谨慎,但在本书的案例中结果并没有受到影响。所有系数都具有很高的显著性,即使是在 HAC 标准误中也不例外,换句话来说,在这个模型中空间误差自相关和异方差性的效应是最小的。

表 6.1　2SLS 的三个标准误之比较

Variable	Estimate	SE-standard	SE-White	SE-HAC
CONSTANT	15.646	1.355	1.539	1.641
MA90	−0.098	0.030	0.032	0.034
PS90	1.877	0.107	0.169	0.198
RD90	5.729	0.213	0.305	0.330
UE90	−0.914	0.099	0.138	0.143

这个案例清楚地表明,标准 2SLS 的系数标准误结果可能会出现某种错误的精度。在一些应用中精度起着十分重要的作用,比如在计算某个项目的成本和效益时,我们就必须考虑到精度问题。

第 7 章　GUI 中的空间滞后模型的空间两阶段最小二乘估计

7.1　模型创建

在 GeoDaSpace 中,空间滞后估计的设置与 OLS 基本模型估计的设置基本上是一致的。唯一的不同在于它需要在 Model Weights 面板中指定一个空间权重矩阵文件,并且必须将 Model Type 设为 Spatial Lag。估计方法默认设为 GMM。我们在此处不再重复基本的设置过程。

首先我们讨论只包含一个外生解释变量的模型的创建。我们会在下文讨论拥有内生变量的模型。我们注意到,在 Instruments 面板中,不必明确地指定一个空间滞后解释变量,唯一需要指定的是内生变量。

我们仍然使用 Baltimore 房价数据的例子,其数据包含在 baltim.dbf 示例数据集中。完整的模型创建的设置如图 7.1 所示。独立变量是房屋价格(PRICE);解释变量有九个,分别是房间个数(NROOM)、浴室个数(NBATH)、是否有阳台(PATIO)、是否有壁炉(FIREPL)、是否有空调(AC)、是否有车库(GAR)、房产的年龄(AGE)、建筑面积(LOTSZ)和使用面积(SQFT)。关于空间权重矩阵的计算我们选择 k 最近邻算法,设 $k=4$,从文件 baltim_k4.gwt(包含在示例数据集中)可以得到。回顾之前给出的方法,图 5.13 中空间依赖性分析结果表明,选择空间滞后模型能正确地替代非空间模型。我们继续介绍空间滞后模型的空间两阶段最小二乘(S2SLS)估计。

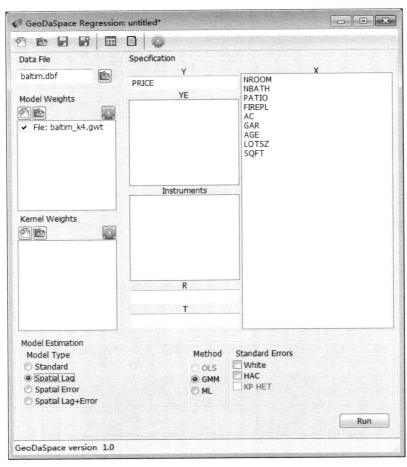

图 7.1　S2SLS 空间滞后模型设置界面

我们在之前讨论方法时曾指出，校正空间滞后项内生性最好的工具变量是空间滞后解释变量。空间滞后的阶数可以在 Instruments 选项卡中设置。默认的是用一阶邻接，如图 7.2(a)所示。高阶邻接可以通过点击旁边的箭头来设置。例如，图 7.2(b)选择了二阶邻接。

必须点击 Save 才能保存更改。已保存的更改会作为 GeoDaSpace 设置的一部分，并用于后续分析（甚至重新打开项目后仍然可以使用）。因此在执行一个估计之前，最好先检查一下设置面板。若要恢复到默认设置，可以点击 Restore Defaults 按钮，然后点击 Save 保存。

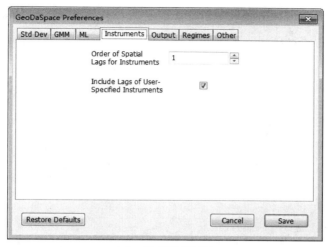

(a)一阶邻接(默认)

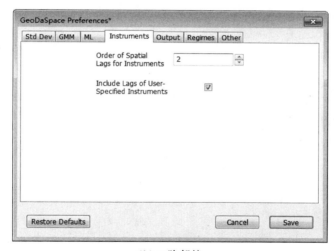

(b)二阶邻接

图 7.2　**Instruments** 设置界面

7.2　基本估计结果

空间滞后模型的 S2SLS 估计结果如图 7.3 所示。输出结果与前文相似,分为五部分。第一部分是顶部的标题和各种描述性统计量,其中在 Weights matrix 后面列出了空间权重矩阵的名称,在本书的案例中,该文件是 baltim_k4.gwt。当然,我们也可以新建该文件。此外是两个拟合优度,我们将在之后进行讨论。

```
REGRESSION
----------
SUMMARY OF OUTPUT: SPATIAL TWO STAGE LEAST SQUARES
--------------------------------------------------
Data set            : baltim.dbf
Weights matrix      :File: baltim_k4.gwt
Dependent Variable  :      PRICE      Number of Observations:    211
Mean dependent var  :    44.3072      Number of Variables   :     11
S.D. dependent var  :    23.6061      Degrees of Freedom    :    200
Pseudo R-squared    :    0.7064
Spatial Pseudo R-squared:  0.6856

----------------------------------------------------------------------
       Variable      Coefficient    Std.Error     z-Statistic   Probability
----------------------------------------------------------------------
       CONSTANT       1.3276578    5.7718694      0.2300222     0.8180746
             AC       6.4790945    2.4253311      2.6714268     0.0075530
            AGE      -0.0942686    0.0544832     -1.7302327     0.0835887
         FIREPL       7.1552855    2.5203968      2.8389519     0.0045262
            GAR       3.6751527    1.7756639      2.0697344     0.0384772
          LOTSZ       0.0674761    0.0153788      4.3875982     0.0000115
          NBATH       5.6036165    1.8043761      3.1055700     0.0018991
          NROOM       0.8894675    1.1026083      0.8066940     0.4198428
          PATIO       7.0709845    2.8348494      2.4943069     0.0126203
           SQFT       0.0750551    0.1699164      0.4417178     0.6586934
        W_PRICE       0.4780523    0.0738868      6.4700639     0.0000000
----------------------------------------------------------------------
Instrumented: W_PRICE
Instruments: W_AC, W_AGE, W_FIREPL, W_GAR, W_LOTSZ, W_NBATH, W_NROOM,
             W_PATIO, W_SQFT

DIAGNOSTICS FOR SPATIAL DEPENDENCE
TEST                       MI/DF       VALUE        PROB
Anselin-Kelejian Test        1         3.390       0.0656
============================== END OF REPORT =========================
```

图 7.3　S2SLS 结果:一阶邻接空间滞后

第二部分是一个表格,记录了变量、估计值、标准误、z 统计量以及相应的 p 值,与之前的其他估计方法格式相同。我们注意到,空间自回归系数(系数 W_PRICE,值为 0.478 052 3)具有较高的显著性,这证明了我们在 OLS 估计时空间诊断的结果。

有些系数的估计值与 OLS 的结果有很大的不同,无论是从量级还是显著性上。在空间滞后模型中,显著性系数估计值的绝对值都比非空间模型的值要小,说明后者吸收了一些空间自相关的回归系数的估计。变化最大的是 CONSTANT 项,由 OLS 中的 23.270 变为了 1.328,并且不再显著。还有一些系数的估计值受到了影响,包括 FIREPL(由 11.173 变为了 7.155)、PATIO(由

10.336 变为了 7.071)和 AC(由 7.854 变为了 6.479)。NROOM 和 SQFT 仍然是非显著的,但也有其他系数在空间滞后模型中不再显著。以 p 值为 0.01 为标准,CONSTANT、AGE、GAR 和 PATIO 都变为非显著(在 p 值为 0.05 时,GAR 和 PATIO 都是显著的)。

第三部分,即在输出结果的下方,是一个内生变量的列表,记为 Instrumented 变量(即空间滞后独立变量 W_PRICE),以及使用的工具变量(Instruments)。这些工具变量包含空间滞后的解释变量,它们的名称都以 W_ 为开头。

第四部分,即输出结果的底部是空间独立性检验,我们将在之后进行讨论。

第五部分是结果保存。当 Preferences 面板中 Output 选项卡上的 Save Predicted Values and Residuals 选项被选中后,我们需要为输出的预测值和残差制定一个文件名。如图 7.4 所示,输出的文件现在已包含两组预测值和残差。第一组中,predy 和 resid 对应于其定义(公式 $E[y \mid X] = \hat{y} = \hat{\rho}Wy + X\hat{\beta}$),空间滞后独立变量的值($Wy$)在公式的右边。第二组中,predy_e 和 e_pred 见公式 $\hat{y}_R = (I - \rho W)^{-1} X\hat{\beta}$。在两个预测值中,predy_e 更为可信,因为它在公式的右边只用了外生变量。需要指出的是,相应的预测误差(e_pred)会保持空间自相关。这是因为它是关于 $(I - \rho W)^{-1} u$ 的估计,而于 $(I - \rho W)^{-1} u$ 是空间自回归的。与之相反,残差 resid 则不存在空间自相关,因为空间滞后效应已经转移。

```
IDs,PRICE, predy, resid, predy_e, e_pred
1, 47.0000, 9.0245, 37.9755, 12.1494, 34.8506,
2, 113.0000, 113.1604, -0.1604, 117.0124, -4.0124,
3, 165.0000, 96.7137, 68.2863, 99.5586, 65.4414,
4, 104.3000, 118.8232, -14.5232, 112.8278, -8.5278,
5, 62.5000, 86.1198, -23.6198, 86.2352, -23.7352,
6, 70.0000, 90.2309, -20.2309, 87.3913, -17.3913,
7, 127.5000, 118.5144, 8.9856, 115.0287, 12.4713,
8, 53.0000, 63.4268, -10.4268, 65.6548, -12.6548,
9, 64.5000, 56.9669, 7.5331, 57.6531, 6.8469,
10, 145.0000, 114.5343, 30.4657, 116.0161, 28.9839,
```

图 7.4 S2SLS 预测值和残差

7.2.1 拟合优度

有两种不同的方法来计算空间滞后模型的预测值,对应 Pseudo

R-squared。在 2SLS 估计的情况下，这些度量的计算与观测值和独立变量预测值之差的平方有关。

Pseudo R-squared(0.7064)的度量是基于粗略的预测值，如公式 $E[y \mid X] = \hat{y} = \hat{\rho}Wy + X\hat{\beta}$。除此之外，被称为 Spatial Pseudo R-squared(0.6856)的度量是基于减小形式下的预测值，如公式 $\hat{y}_R = (I - \hat{\rho}W)^{-1}X\hat{\beta}$。我们在前面指出过，粗略的预测值往往具有更好的拟合度，与结果相一致。

要记住，所有这些度量都不是真正的 R^2，在这个意义上，它们不对应于模型所解释的标准误。当没有其他替代时，空间 Pseudo R-squared 是以特定方式评估模型相对拟合度的首选指标。

7.2.2 使用高阶邻接

图 7.5 和图 7.6 中展示了选择不同阶邻接时解释变量的空间滞后效应。

```
REGRESSION
----------
SUMMARY OF OUTPUT: SPATIAL TWO STAGE LEAST SQUARES
--------------------------------------------------
Data set            :  baltim.dbf
Weights matrix      :File: baltim_k4.gwt
Dependent Variable  :      PRICE         Number of Observations:         211
Mean dependent var  :    44.3072         Number of Variables   :          11
S.D. dependent var  :    23.6061         Degrees of Freedom    :         200
Pseudo R-squared    :     0.7061
Spatial Pseudo R-squared:  0.6845

------------------------------------------------------------------------------------
        Variable     Coefficient       Std.Error     z-Statistic     Probability
------------------------------------------------------------------------------------
        CONSTANT       0.8965615       5.7234031       0.1566483       0.8755220
              AC       6.4520788       2.4264263       2.6590871       0.0078353
             AGE      -0.0919270       0.0543559      -1.6912033       0.0907980
           FIREPL      7.0763557       2.5180454       2.8102574       0.0049502
             GAR       3.6412243       1.7757744       2.0504994       0.0403157
           LOTSZ       0.0669372       0.0153583       4.3583650       0.0000131
           NBATH       5.6027365       1.8055518       3.1030605       0.0019153
           NROOM       0.9025714       1.1030756       0.8182316       0.4132249
           PATIO       7.0068398       2.8343528       2.4721128       0.0134317
            SQFT       0.0728409       0.1699806       0.4285248       0.6682691
         W_PRICE       0.4874444       0.0719813       6.7718234       0.0000000
------------------------------------------------------------------------------------
Instrumented: W_PRICE
Instruments: W2_AC, W2_AGE, W2_FIREPL, W2_GAR, W2_LOTSZ, W2_NBATH, W2_NROOM,
             W2_PATIO, W2_SQFT, W_AC, W_AGE, W_FIREPL, W_GAR, W_LOTSZ,
             W_NBATH, W_NROOM, W_PATIO, W_SQFT
DIAGNOSTICS FOR SPATIAL DEPENDENCE
TEST                            MI/DF      VALUE         PROB
Anselin-Kelejian Test              1       3.622        0.0570
================================ END OF REPORT ================================
```

图 7.5　S2SLS 结果：二阶邻接空间滞后

```
REGRESSION
----------
SUMMARY OF OUTPUT: SPATIAL TWO STAGE LEAST SQUARES
--------------------------------------------------
Data set            :   baltim.dbf
Weights matrix      :File: baltim_k4.gwt
Dependent Variable  :       PRICE        Number of Observations:       211
Mean dependent var  :      44.3072       Number of Variables   :        11
S.D. dependent var  :      23.6061       Degrees of Freedom    :       200
Pseudo R-squared    :       0.7063
Spatial Pseudo R-squared:   0.6852

------------------------------------------------------------------------------
    Variable      Coefficient       Std.Error       z-Statistic     Probability
------------------------------------------------------------------------------
    CONSTANT       1.1925852        5.6945102        0.2094272       0.8341148
          AC       6.4706298        2.4250725        2.6682212       0.0076254
         AGE      -0.0935349        0.0542496       -1.7241593       0.0846791
       FIREPL      7.1305549        2.5148945        2.8353296       0.0045778
         GAR       3.6645221        1.7744380        2.0651734       0.0389066
        LOTSZ      0.0673072        0.0153360        4.3888340       0.0000114
        NBATH      5.6033408        1.8047248        3.1048173       0.0019040
        NROOM      0.8935732        1.1024449        0.8105378       0.4176312
        PATIO      7.0508864        2.8318830        2.4898226       0.0127807
         SQFT      0.0743614        0.1698795        0.4377300       0.6615820
      W_PRICE      0.4809951        0.0709521        6.7791488       0.0000000
------------------------------------------------------------------------------
Instrumented: W_PRICE
Instruments:  W2_AC, W2_AGE, W2_FIREPL, W2_GAR, W2_LOTSZ, W2_NBATH, W2_NROOM,
              W2_PATIO, W2_SQFT, W3_AC, W3_AGE, W3_FIREPL, W3_GAR, W3_LOTSZ,
              W3_NBATH, W3_NROOM, W3_PATIO, W3_SQFT, W_AC, W_AGE, W_FIREPL,
              W_GAR, W_LOTSZ, W_NBATH, W_NROOM, W_PATIO, W_SQFT

DIAGNOSTICS FOR SPATIAL DEPENDENCE
TEST                       MI/DF      VALUE         PROB
Anselin-Kelejian Test        1        3.494         0.0616
================================ END OF REPORT ================================
```

图 7.6 S2SLS 结果:三阶邻接空间滞后

在图 7.3 和图 7.5 中,我们使用的是一阶和二阶邻接,而在图 7.6 中则是三阶邻接。它显示在输出结果底部的 Instruments 列表中。对于二阶邻接,这些变量名都以 W2_为开头;而对于三阶邻接,这些变量名都以 W3_为开头。

7.2.3 估计值对比

表 7.1 中列出了各项系数的估计值,包含非空间模型的估计值(OLS)以及三组 S2SLS 估计值(Lag1、Lag2、Lag3),这三组数据分别是阶数由一至三的空间滞后模型。另外,表中还包含最大似然估计值(ML),由第 8 章的图 8.9 所得。

表 7.1　估计值对比

Variable	OLS	Lag1	Lag2	Lag3	ML
CONSTANT	23.270	1.328	0.897	1.193	7.444
AC	7.854	6.479	6.452	6.471	6.862
AGE	−0.213	−0.094	−0.092	−0.094	−0.127
FIREPL	11.173	7.155	7.076	7.131	8.275
GAR	5.402	3.675	3.641	3.665	4.157
LOTSZ	0.095	0.067	0.067	0.067	0.075
NBATH	5.648	5.604	5.603	5.603	5.616
NROOM	0.222	0.889	0.903	0.894	0.704
PATIO	10.336	7.071	7.007	7.051	7.981
SQFT	0.188	0.075	0.073	0.074	0.106
W_PRICE		0.478	0.487	0.481	0.345

表 7.1 展示了 S2SLS 估计值间有轻微的差异,空间自回归参数值 $\hat{\rho}$ 分别为 0.478、0.487 和 0.481。回归系数也略有不同,但是这三个空间滞后阶数下的显著性相一致。相反,ML 估计值更小,值为 0.345。它产生了介于 OLS 和 S2SLS 之间的其他系数的估计值。也就是说,由于滞后的系数更小,空间乘子的影响就更小,所以可能会低估该值。

考虑到解释变量 LOTSZ 的估计,它在非空间模型(OLS)的估计值为 0.095,在空间滞后模型的三个阶数的估计值都为 0.067(ML 估计值为 0.075),0.067 的值反映了所谓的直接影响。如前所述,连续的解释变量,其变化的总效应可以由 $\hat{\beta}/(1-\hat{\rho})$ 来计算。使用 $\hat{\rho}$ 值的一阶空间滞后工具,所得 LOTSZ 值 0.067/0.522=0.130,几乎是初始估计值的两倍。对于总效应 0.130 而言,其中间接效应为 0.130−0.067=0.063,它归因于空间乘子。总效应估计值 0.130 也高于在非空间模型(OLS)的估计值 0.095。这说明在房价模型中空间乘子能改变边缘效应的程度。

7.3　S2SLS 的空间效应分析

空间滞后模型必须包含空间权重矩阵,该权重矩阵是在 Model Weights 面板中指定的,因此必须进行空间自相关检验。检验结果在输出结果的最底部,Instruments 的下面。

在本书的案例中,空间滞后的阶数为一阶时(如图 7.3 所示),统计量的值为 3.390,p 值为 0.065 6。这说明所包含的空间滞后项已经校正了大部分的空间自相关性,尽管不是所有的都能校正。如果我们保守地设置 p 值为 0.10,那么我们会发现它依然保持空间自相关。这表明我们需要使用 HAC 标准误估计来进一步推断。

选择其他阶数所得的结果也非常相似,二阶滞后的值为 3.622(p 值为 0.057 0),如图 7.5 所示,三阶滞后的值为 3.494(p 值为 0.061 6),如图 7.6 所示。

7.4　鲁棒系数标准误估计

与 OLS 和 2SLS 相似,S2SLS 中也有一个鲁棒估计的选项,用来计算方差-协方差矩阵的系数估计值。具体步骤与第 6 章中相同,此处不再赘述。唯一的差异是工具变量 Q 的矩阵包含空间滞后解释变量,但是所有的表达式都同样地应用于空间滞后模型中。

在 GUI 中要通过勾选 White 或 HAC 复选框来选择该选项,如图 7.7 所示。要计算 HAC 标准误,必须在 Kernel Weights 面板中生成一个核权重矩阵文件。在本书的案例中,我们对 Baltimore 房价数据点位置使用了三角核,基于 $k=12$ 最近邻居的自适应带宽(baltim.tri.k12.kwt)。

怀特标准误的计算结果如图 7.8 所示,HAC 标准误的计算结果如图 7.9 所示。此处列出的是解释变量的一阶滞后估计。估计值与图7.3中的值相同,而标准误、z统计量和p值则不同。

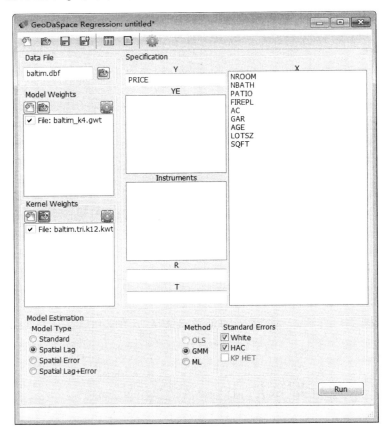

图7.7 含鲁棒系数标准误的S2SLS

```
White Standard Errors
------------------------------------------------------------------------------
      Variable     Coefficient      Std.Error      z-Statistic     Probability
------------------------------------------------------------------------------
      CONSTANT       1.3276578       7.0498787       0.1883235       0.8506231
            AC       6.4790945       2.6957981       2.4034050       0.0162432
           AGE      -0.0942686       0.0985737      -0.9563261       0.3389075
        FIREPL       7.1552855       2.4338903       2.9398554       0.0032837
           GAR       3.6751527       2.3904033       1.5374614       0.1241804
         LOTSZ       0.0674761       0.0251552       2.6823926       0.0073098
         NBATH       5.6036165       2.1970447       2.5505246       0.0107561
         NROOM       0.8894675       1.3949334       0.6376415       0.5237071
         PATIO       7.0709845       3.1925381       2.2148473       0.0267705
          SQFT       0.0750551       0.2227874       0.3368913       0.7361989
       W_PRICE       0.4780523       0.1265144       3.7786378       0.0001577
------------------------------------------------------------------------------
```

图7.8 S2SLS结果:怀特标准误

```
HAC Standard Errors; Kernel Weights: File: baltim.tri.k12.kwt
------------------------------------------------------------
     Variable    Coefficient    Std.Error    z-Statistic    Probability
------------------------------------------------------------
     CONSTANT     1.3276578    7.3836489     0.1798105      0.8573013
           AC     6.4790945    2.9269976     2.2135633      0.0268588
          AGE    -0.0942686    0.0965855    -0.9760116      0.3290587
        FIREPL    7.1552855    2.3991792     2.9823889      0.0028601
          GAR     3.6751527    2.4484638     1.5010035      0.1333547
        LOTSZ     0.0674761    0.0229780     2.9365494      0.0033189
        NBATH     5.6036165    2.1947209     2.5532251      0.0106730
        NROOM     0.8894675    1.4151498     0.6285324      0.5296552
        PATIO     7.0709845    3.1710955     2.2298238      0.0257591
         SQFT     0.0750551    0.1979195     0.3792205      0.7045241
      W_PRICE     0.4780523    0.1140102     4.1930674      0.0000275
------------------------------------------------------------
```

图 7.9 S2SLS 结果：HAC 标准误

为了比较三种方法的结果，我们在表 7.2 中分别列出了默认方法、怀特标准误和 HAC 标准误的结果。如前所述，估计值是基于解释变量的一阶滞后估计。

表 7.2 标准误之比较

Variable	Estimate	Standard	White	HAC
CONSTANT	1.328	5.772	7.050	7.384
AC	6.479	2.425	2.696	2.927
AGE	−0.094	0.054	0.099	0.097
FIREPL	7.155	2.520	2.434	2.399
GAR	3.675	1.776	2.390	2.448
LOTSE	0.067	0.015	0.025	0.023
NBATH	5.604	1.804	2.197	2.195
NROOM	0.889	1.103	1.395	1.415
PATIO	7.071	2.835	3.193	3.171
SQFT	0.075	0.170	0.223	0.198
W_PRICE	0.478	0.074	0.127	0.114

从表 7.2 中可以看出，除 FIREPL 外的所有系数，其怀特和 HAC 的标准误都比默认方法得到的值要大。在很多实例中，甚至显著性的评估也会改变。例如，对于 GAR 变量，其标准误在默认方法中为 1.776，而在怀特方法中为 2.390、HAC 方法中为 2.448。相应地，p 值分别为 0.04、0.12 和 0.13。然而，空间自回归项的显著性几乎不受影响。

有趣的是，HAC 方法的标准误并不总是最大的。对于 AGE、FIREPL、

LOTSZ、NBATH、PATIO、SQFT 和 W_PRICE 这几个变量,标准误最大的是怀特方法。这说明相对于剩余的空间误差自相关,异方差性的影响更强。这也与我们之前的发现相一致(见 7.2.3 节),即 AK 检验只表现出微弱的剩余的空间误差自相关($p<0.10$)。

7.5 包含内生变量的 S2SLS

到目前为止,我们只考虑到了模型中所有的解释变量都是外生性的情况(空间滞后项除外)。现在我们引入更多的复杂性,允许一部分解释变量是内生性的。这就需要引入一个新的工具来控制内生性,如第 6 章所述。

在此我们使用的数据集是美国县级犯罪率(NAT.dbf)数据,并选择 HR90 作为独立变量。外生解释变量是 RD90、PS90、MA90。变量 UE90 处理为内生性的,其工具变量有 FP89、GI89 和 FH90。基本的设置如图 7.10 所示。

当读入一个预先设定的模型文件时,需要注意 GUI 中各项参数是如何设定的。文件名列在顶部:NAT。为方便起见,我们也选择了一个模型权重矩阵文件和一个核权重矩阵文件。如第 3 章,模型权重矩阵我们使用一阶 queen 邻接(nat_queen.gal),核权重矩阵我们使用三角核函数,基于 20 个最近邻居的自适应带宽(nat_train.k20.kwt)。此处也同时选择 White 和 HAC 选项。也就是说,除 Spatial Lag 按钮被选中以外,图 7.10 中的界面与图 6.6 相同。

点击 Run 按钮,生成一个输出面板,它包含估计值和三组标准误:默认结果(如图 7.11 所示)、怀特标准误(如图 7.12 所示)和 HAC 标准误(如图 7.13 所示)。首先来看图 7.11 中的结果,系数的符号与非空间的 2SLS 中系数的符号相同(如图 6.2 所示)。在非内生性的情况下,包含空间滞后项的主要作用就是降低系数估计值的绝对值。空间自回归的系数是 0.212,显著性较高。其他变量的显著性只受到了轻微的影响,只有变量 MA90 的显著性受到了较大的影响,其 p 值由显著的 0.001 变为了不显著的 0.080。由 Pseudo R-squared 度量的模型拟合度,略优于在非空间模型下的拟合度(分别为 0.391 4 和 0.357 006)。

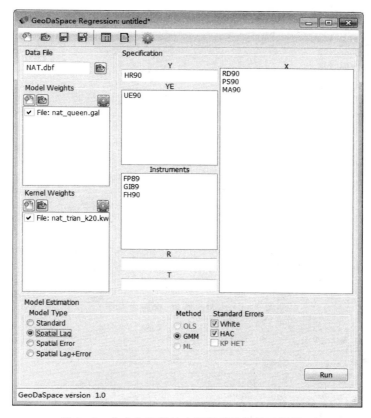

图 7.10　含内生变量的空间滞后模型的设置界面

在表格的底部,Instrumented(或者内生性的)变量为 UE90 和 W_HR90。同样地,工具变量中包含了变量的空间滞后,这些变量是在 Instruments 面板中指定的,也包含了空间滞后的解释变量。AK 检验的值似乎表明了空间滞后项的空间自相关已经校正了。对于非空间的 2SLS 结果,它的值为 124.4,具有很高的显著性,但是在这里它的值仅为 2.517,p 值为 0.112 7,本质上是非显著的。

正如我们之前所看到的,图 7.12 和图 7.13 中怀特标准误和 HAC 标准误比默认结果的值要大。然而,新的值也保持着同样的结论。例如,MA90 的 p 值在默认方法下为 0.080,怀特方法下为 0.086,HAC 方法下为 0.086。其他系数都保持很高的显著性。

```
REGRESSION
---------
SUMMARY OF OUTPUT: SPATIAL TWO STAGE LEAST SQUARES
-----------------------------------------------------
Data set            :   NAT.dbf
Weights matrix      :File: nat_queen.gal
Dependent Variable  :      HR90                Number of Observations:        3085
Mean dependent var  :    6.1829                Number of Variables   :           6
S.D. dependent var  :    6.6414                Degrees of Freedom    :        3079
Pseudo R-squared    :    0.4186
Spatial Pseudo R-squared:  0.3914

------------------------------------------------------------------------------
         Variable     Coefficient       Std.Error     z-Statistic     Probability
------------------------------------------------------------------------------
         CONSTANT      10.0338240       1.3616383       7.3689349       0.0000000
             MA90      -0.0500990       0.0286025      -1.7515613       0.0798493
             PS90       1.5813070       0.1084249      14.5843567       0.0000000
             RD90       4.4092974       0.2400482      18.3683863       0.0000000
             UE90      -0.5182722       0.0882736      -5.8712062       0.0000000
           W_HR90       0.2123364       0.0371805       5.7109639       0.0000000
------------------------------------------------------------------------------
Instrumented: UE90, W_HR90
Instruments: FH90, FP89, GI89, W_FH90, W_FP89, W_GI89, W_MA90, W_PS90,
             W_RD90

DIAGNOSTICS FOR SPATIAL DEPENDENCE
TEST                     MI/DF       VALUE          PROB
Anselin-Kelejian Test      1         2.517         0.1127
================================ END OF REPORT ================================
```

图 7.11 S2SLS 结果(含内生变量)

```
White Standard Errors
------------------------------------------------------------------------------
         Variable     Coefficient       Std.Error     z-Statistic     Probability
------------------------------------------------------------------------------
         CONSTANT      10.0338240       1.4996751       6.6906654       0.0000000
             MA90      -0.0500990       0.0291963      -1.7159378       0.0861734
             PS90       1.5813070       0.1984032       7.9701686       0.0000000
             RD90       4.4092974       0.3694435      11.9349702       0.0000000
             UE90      -0.5182722       0.1140551      -4.5440529       0.0000055
           W_HR90       0.2123364       0.0559928       3.7922065       0.0001493
------------------------------------------------------------------------------
```

图 7.12 内生变量和怀特标准误

```
HAC Standard Errors; Kernel Weights: File: nat_trian_k20.kwt
------------------------------------------------------------------------------
         Variable     Coefficient       Std.Error     z-Statistic     Probability
------------------------------------------------------------------------------
         CONSTANT      10.0338240       1.5046697       6.6684564       0.0000000
             MA90      -0.0500990       0.0291633      -1.7178792       0.0858187
             PS90       1.5813070       0.2123670       7.4461048       0.0000000
             RD90       4.4092974       0.3833659      11.5015392       0.0000000
             UE90      -0.5182722       0.1129401      -4.5889110       0.0000045
           W_HR90       0.2123364       0.0589212       3.6037330       0.0003137
------------------------------------------------------------------------------
```

图 7.13 内生变量和 HAC 标准误

在包含内生变量的空间滞后模型中,默认地在整体工具矩阵 Q 中包含了两个额外的工具变量和它们的空间滞后。图 7.14(a)展示了 Preferences 面板中 Instruments 选项卡下的默认值。我们可以更改默认值,并取消勾选 Include Lags of User-Specified Instruments 选项,如图 7.14(b) 所示。注意,要点击 Save 按钮才能使更改生效。

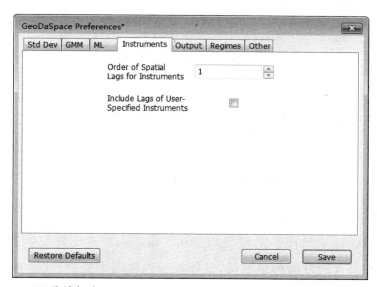

(a)默认设置

(b)取消勾选 Include Lags of User-Specified Instruments 选项

图 7.14 空间滞后 Instruments 设置

图 7.15 是使用新的工具变量后的估计结果。它对空间自回归系数估计的影响很小,其值由 0.212 变为 0.216。这会引起其他回归系数值的微小改变,但实质上主要是 MA90 显著性的改变。在图 7.11 中,变量 MA90 的 p 值是 0.080;而在图 7.15 中,其 p 值为 0.038。总的来说,当使用空间滞后的工具变量时,标准误更小一些,如果使用更多的工具变量,则可以更好地提高效率。与之相似,由 Spatial Pseudo R-squared 度量的拟合度,在包含滞后工具变量(0.3914)时略优于不包含(0.3802)时的拟合度。

```
REGRESSION
----------
SUMMARY OF OUTPUT: SPATIAL TWO STAGE LEAST SQUARES
--------------------------------------------------
Data set            :     NAT.dbf
Weights matrix      :File: nat_queen.gal
Dependent Variable  :        HR90      Number of Observations:        3085
Mean dependent var  :      6.1829      Number of Variables   :           6
S.D. dependent var  :      6.6414      Degrees of Freedom    :        3079
Pseudo R-squared    :      0.4076
Spatial Pseudo R-squared:   0.3802

----------------------------------------------------------------------------
        Variable     Coefficient       Std.Error     z-Statistic     Probability
----------------------------------------------------------------------------
        CONSTANT      11.2850228       1.4177538       7.9597903       0.0000000
            MA90      -0.0601274       0.0290474      -2.0722259       0.0382444
            PS90       1.6149324       0.1105060      14.6139849       0.0000000
            RD90       4.6642007       0.2537771      18.3791221       0.0000000
            UE90      -0.6580528       0.0951942      -6.9127375       0.0000000
          W_HR90       0.2163835       0.0389967       5.5487653       0.0000000
----------------------------------------------------------------------------
Instrumented: UE90, W_HR90
Instruments: FH90, FP89, GI89, W_MA90, W_PS90, W_RD90

DIAGNOSTICS FOR SPATIAL DEPENDENCE
TEST                       MI/DF        VALUE            PROB
Anselin-Kelejian Test          1        2.442            0.1182
============================ END OF REPORT ================================
```

图 7.15 S2SLS 结果:无空间滞后的工具变量

我们再回顾一下上述五种不同的方法,并将它们的估计值和标准误放到一起来进行比较,包括两种非空间模型(OLS 和 2SLS)和三种空间滞后模型(其中,有一种不包含额外的内生变量,另外两种包含内生变量,这两种方法的不同之处在于空间滞后工具变量的使用)。总结如表 7.3 所示。

表7.3 五种方法估计值和标准误比较

Variable	OLS	2SLS	Lag	LagEnd1[2]	LagEnd2[3]
CONSTANT	9.901 (1.033)	15.646 (1.355)	7.386 (1.105)	10.034 (1.362)	11.285 (1.418)
MA90	−0.052 (0.028)	−0.098 (0.030)	−0.029 (0.028)	−0.050 (0.029)	−0.060 (0.029)
PS90	1.711 (0.101)	1.877 (0.107)	1.510 (0.104)	1.581 (0.108)	1.615 (0.111)
RD90	4.545 (0.123)	5.729 (0.213)	3.869 (0.172)	4.409 (0.240)	4.664 (0.254)
UE90	−0.291 (0.040)	−0.914 (0.099)	−0.223 (0.041)	−0.518 (0.088)	−0.658 (0.095)
W_HR90			0.205 (0.038)	0.212 (0.037)	0.216 (0.039)
R^2	0.395	0.357	0.399	0.391	0.380

粗略地看一下拟合度的度量(除 OLS 估计以外皆为 R^2),大致可以表明不含内生性的空间滞后模型是最好的。大多数情况下,估计值之间的差异很小,但是有时也会很显著,例如变量 UE90。并且,标准误中最小的值都是由 OLS 产生的,这可能会产生一些误导,因为 OLS 忽略了异方差性和空间自相关。除变量 MA90 外,显著性实质上在所有的模型和方法中都是一致的。

第 8 章 GUI 中的空间滞后模型的最大似然估计

8.1 模型创建

为了更好地阐述 GeoDa 和 GeoDaSpace 中的空间滞后模型的最大似然（ML）估计，我们在此仍使用第 7 章中的案例。同样地，我们还是使用 Baltimore 房价数据，并选择相同的变量。然而，与 S2SLS 不同的是，我们不能使用 k 最近邻空间权重矩阵。这种矩阵实质上是不对称的，它违反了在 GeoDa 中执行的特征值估计的一个假设。虽然这种约束条件在 GeoDaSpace 中不存在，我们还是首先使用一个对称的权重矩阵，这个矩阵是对房屋点数据构建泰森多边形，并对其进行 Queen 邻接得到的，它包含在示例文件 baltim_q.gal 中。

在 GeoDa 中，其回归界面的布局与 OLS 的布局相同，只有两点不同之处。如图 8.1 所示，除变量列表中的独立变量和解释变量外，Spatial Lag 单选按钮也被选中了，并且空间权重矩阵文件也已指定好。

如图 8.2 所示，GeoDaSpace 的布局与图 7.1 中 S2SLS 的布局相同，除了 Model Weights 面板中的权重矩阵文件不同，以及在 Method 中选择了 ML 单选框。

同之前一样，点击 Run 按钮，弹出估计结果窗口。

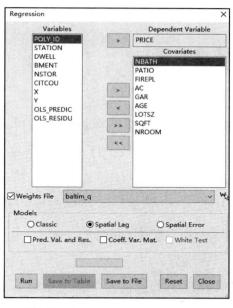

图 8.1　最大似然估计:GeoDa 中空间滞后模型的设置

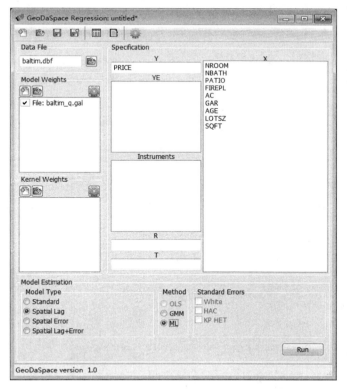

图 8.2　最大似然估计:GeoDaSpace 中空间滞后模型的设置

8.2 ML 的基本估计结果

图 8.3 是 GeoDa 中 ML 估计的空间滞后模型结果,图 8.4 是 GeoDaSpace 中的结果,这两者只有轻微的差异。其中最显著的差异是,空间滞后系数的估计值在 GeoDa 中排列在第一个,而在 GeoDaSpace 中排列在最后,与 S2SLS 的格式相同。并且,GeoDaSpace 中变量是按照字母顺序排列的,而在 GeoDa 中变量是按照它们加载到 GUI 中的顺序排列的。

空间滞后系数的 ρ 估计值(0.425 884 5)及其标准误(0.056 955 3)在两个软件设置的精度下是相同的(在更高的精度下两个值略有差别,这是由于迭代估计中存在四舍五入误差),其他系数估计也是相同的。我们需要注意,在 GeoDaSpace 列表中指出了计算的方法,而在 GeoDa 中没有指出计算的方法。

```
SUMMARY OF OUTPUT: SPATIAL LAG MODEL - MAXIMUM LIKELIHOOD ESTIMATION
Data set            : baltim
Spatial Weight      : baltim_q.gal
Dependent Variable  :       PRICE   Number of Observations:     211
Mean dependent var  :      44.3072  Number of Variables   :      11
S.D. dependent var  :      23.5501  Degrees of Freedom    :     200
Lag coeff.   (Rho)  :      0.425885

R-squared           :     0.726908  Log likelihood        :    -832.937
Sq. Correlation     :     -          Akaike info criterion :    1687.87
Sigma-square        :     151.459   Schwarz criterion     :    1724.74
S.E of regression   :      12.3069

-----------------------------------------------------------------------
      Variable       Coefficient    Std.Error       z-value    Probability
-----------------------------------------------------------------------
      W_PRICE        0.4258845     0.05695527     7.477527      0.00000
      CONSTANT       4.367481      4.885862       0.8939017     0.37137
      NROOM          0.7502175     1.059323       0.7082047     0.47882
      NBATH          5.61164       1.749086       3.208326      0.00134
      PATIO          7.049655      2.70953        2.6018        0.00927
      FIREPL         7.72458       2.381079       3.244151      0.00118
      AC             6.123094      2.338753       2.618102      0.00884
      GAR            4.637468      1.69364        2.738166      0.00618
      AGE           -0.1107384     0.05084342    -2.178029      0.02940
      LOTSZ          0.06789793    0.01460569     4.648732      0.00000
      SQFT           0.07935402    0.1630834      0.4865854     0.62655
-----------------------------------------------------------------------

REGRESSION DIAGNOSTICS
DIAGNOSTICS FOR HETEROSKEDASTICITY
RANDOM COEFFICIENTS
TEST                                DF       VALUE         PROB
Breusch-Pagan test                   9      142.7934       0.00000
DIAGNOSTICS FOR SPATIAL DEPENDENCE
SPATIAL LAG DEPENDENCE FOR WEIGHT MATRIX : baltim_q.gal
TEST                                DF       VALUE         PROB
Likelihood Ratio Test                1       44.5721       0.00000
========================== END OF REPORT ==============================
```

图 8.3 GeoDa 中 ML 估计的空间滞后模型结果

```
REGRESSION
----------
SUMMARY OF OUTPUT: MAXIMUM LIKELIHOOD SPATIAL LAG (METHOD = FULL)
----------------------------------------------------------------
Data set            :   baltim.dbf
Weights matrix      :File: baltim_q.gal
Dependent Variable  :       PRICE        Number of Observations:        211
Mean dependent var  :      44.3072       Number of Variables   :         11
S.D. dependent var  :      23.6061       Degrees of Freedom    :        200
Pseudo R-squared    :       0.7271
Spatial Pseudo R-squared:   0.7062
Sigma-square ML     :     151.459        Log likelihood        :   -832.937
S.E of regression   :      12.307        Akaike info criterion :   1687.874
                                         Schwarz criterion     :   1724.745
----------------------------------------------------------------
       Variable      Coefficient      Std.Error      z-Statistic     Probability
       CONSTANT       4.3674844       4.8858623       0.8939025       0.3713741
             AC       6.1230939       2.3387530       2.6181020       0.0088420
            AGE      -0.1107385       0.0508434      -2.1780290       0.0294039
         FIREPL       7.7245808       2.3810788       3.2441516       0.0011780
            GAR       4.6374679       1.6936400       2.7381662       0.0061783
          LOTSZ       0.0678979       0.0146057       4.6487328       0.0000033
          NBATH       5.6116402       1.7490864       3.2083264       0.0013351
          NROOM       0.7502174       1.0593230       0.7082046       0.4788182
          PATIO       7.0496558       2.7095305       2.6017998       0.0092736
           SQFT       0.0793540       0.1630835       0.4865855       0.6265521
        W_PRICE       0.4258845       0.0569553       7.4775248       0.0000000
----------------------------------------------------------------
============================ END OF REPORT =====================
```

图 8.4 GeoDaSpace 中 ML 估计的空间滞后模型结果

如图 8.3 所示，GeoDa 列表中还包含一些模型分析。第一项是近似异方差性的 Breusch-Pagan Test，得到的值是 142.793 4，χ^2 变量的显著性很高，自由度为 9。尽管这是一个粗略的检验结果，但它表明了可能存在异方差性问题。这可能是有问题的，因为 ML 估计的推导中假定了一个恒定的误差方差。因此，这表明 S2SLS 方法更为合适，尤其是运用 White 或者 HAC 鲁棒标准误时。

图 8.3 所示中最后一项检验是 Likelihood Ratio Test，它是基于 $\rho=0$ 的非空假设，并不是关于剩余空间自相关的检验。也就是说，它能替代 ρ 的 Wald 检验（渐近 t 检验），即系数估计值表格中 p 值所表明的。它也能替代 LM_ρ 检验。44.572 1 的值也表明了 χ^2 变量的高显著性，自由度为 1，证明了 Wald 和 LM 检验得出的结论。然而，由于这个检验是基于 ML 估计的结果，它可能会受异方差性的影响。不过，在标准 ML 估计中我们暂时不考虑这一点。

在 GeoDa 中，有一个选项将预测值和残差加载到当前的数据表中，以便在后续的可视化等环节中使用。与 OLS 中的情况相同,这个选项需要勾选 Pred. Val. and Res.框,如图 8.5(a)所示。执行回归后,点击 Save to Table 按钮,弹出一个界面选择变量名,默认的名称如图 8.5(b)所示。在这个例子中,有两种残差,但只列出了约化形式的预测值,LAG_PREDIC 作为默认变量名。当点击 Add Variable 按钮时就会默认生成变量名。Residual 是观测值和粗略预测值之间的差异,而 Prediction Error 是观测值与约化形式的预测值之间的差异。于是,这些变量就添加到数据表中了,如图 8.6 所示。

在 GeoDaSpace 中,创建预测值和残差与之前讲到的相同,即在 Preferences 面板中 Output 选项卡下勾选相应的选项。与 S2SLS 中的情况相同,它提供了四个变量,分别是粗略预测值(ml_predy)及其残差(ml_resid)、约化形式的预测值(ml_predy_e)以及相应的预测误差(ml_e_pred),如图 8.7 所示。预测值和残差的有关内容与 S2SLS 中的相同。

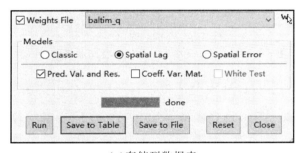

(a)存储到数据表

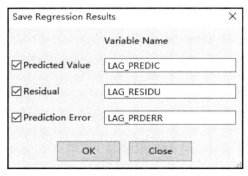

(b)变量命名

图 8.5 GeoDa 中空间滞后预测值与残差

	LAG_PRDERR	LAG_RESIDU	LAG_PREDIC	STATION	PRICE
1	38.0637	39.5958	8.9363	1	47.000000
2	4.0663	3.9125	108.9337	2	113.000000
3	67.2065	63.2636	97.7935	3	165.000000
4	-1.8087	-8.7642	106.1087	4	104.300000
5	-8.9675	-11.6865	71.4675	5	62.500000
6	-18.2283	-23.2342	88.2283	6	70.000000
7	20.3252	15.6180	107.1748	7	127.500000
8	-9.4662	-8.6806	62.4662	8	53.000000
9	4.5489	2.8407	59.9511	9	64.500000
10	26.4682	23.9929	118.5318	10	145.000000

图 8.6　GeoDa 数据表中的预测值与残差

```
IDs,PRICE,ml_predy,ml_resid,ml_predy_e,ml_e_pred
1, 47.0000, 7.4042, 39.5958, 8.9363, 38.0637,
2, 113.0000, 109.0875, 3.9125, 108.9337, 4.0663,
3, 165.0000, 101.7364, 63.2636, 97.7935, 67.2065,
4, 104.3000, 113.0642, -8.7642, 106.1087, -1.8087,
5, 62.5000, 74.1865, -11.6865, 71.4675, -8.9675,
6, 70.0000, 93.2342, -23.2342, 88.2283, -18.2283,
7, 127.5000, 111.8820, 15.6180, 107.1748, 20.3252,
8, 53.0000, 61.6806, -8.6806, 62.4662, -9.4662,
9, 64.5000, 61.6593, 2.8407, 59.9511, 4.5489,
10, 145.0000, 121.0071, 23.9929, 118.5318, 26.4682,
```

图 8.7　GeoDaSpace 数据表中的预测值与残差

8.3　ML 面板高级设置

目前，GeoDaSpace 中对 ML 估计采用两种计算方法。默认的是 Full 方法，它用蛮力来计算行列式和逆矩阵。第二种是基于空间权重矩阵特征值的计算，即 Ord 方法。这个选项可以在 Preferences 面板中 ML 选项卡下进行选择，如图 8.8 所示。在图 8.8(a)中选择的是默认方法，图 8.8(b)中选择的是 Ord 方法。

我们使用图 8.9 中的结果来进行阐述，它是基于 $k=4$ 的最近邻居的空间权重矩阵，与第 7 章中所使用的矩阵相同。正如之前所提到的，GeoDaSpace 中没有矩阵内在对称性的约束条件,我们可以将图 8.9 与第 7 章中的估计结果进行对比。在输出结果的首行标题上,计算方法被列为"ORD"。

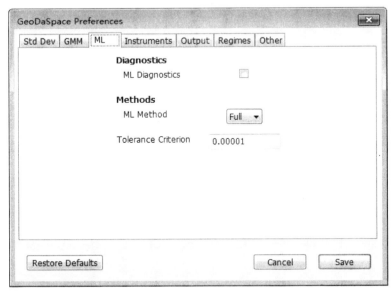

(a)Full 方法(默认)

(b)Ord 方法

图 8.8　**GeoDaSpace 中空间滞后 ML 估计方法**

在前文的 S2SLS 估计值对比中我们加入了 ML 估计值。当时指出,$\hat{\rho}_{\mathrm{ML}}$ 的值比 S2SLS 的值要小得多(分别是 0.345 和 0.48),相应的标准误也比 S2SLS 的值要小。例如,对比图 8.4 中 $\hat{\rho}_{\text{ML}}$ 的标准误(0.056)与表 7.2 中的标准误,其标准误的范围由 0.074 到 0.127。然而我们也可以把它当作一个好的特性,因为 ML 比 S2SLS 更加精确,精度的表达很可能会引起错误。首先,ML 非对称方差的分析结果是基于理想化的非对称设定的,忽略了一些潜在的错误来源,例如非正态性或异方差性。与之相反,S2SLS 的结果是鲁棒的,即使存在这些错误也是有效的。在实践中,我们得出的结论是,在解读 ML 估计结果时要格外谨慎,尤其是当它的值与鲁棒的 S2SLS 估计值不同时。

```
REGRESSION
----------
SUMMARY OF OUTPUT: MAXIMUM LIKELIHOOD SPATIAL LAG (METHOD = ORD)
----------------------------------------------------------------
Data set            : baltim.dbf
Weights matrix      :File: baltim_k4.gwt
Dependent Variable  :     PRICE            Number of Observations:     211
Mean dependent var  :    44.3072           Number of Variables   :      11
S.D. dependent var  :    23.6061           Degrees of Freedom    :     200
Pseudo R-squared    :     0.7057
Spatial Pseudo R-squared:  0.6913
Sigma-square ML     :   163.292            Log likelihood        :  -839.774
S.E of regression   :    12.779            Akaike info criterion :  1701.547
                                           Schwarz criterion     :  1738.418
----------------------------------------------------------------
        Variable    Coefficient     Std.Error     z-Statistic    Probability
----------------------------------------------------------------
        CONSTANT      7.4443663     5.0835159      1.4644129      0.1430812
              AC      6.8624127     2.4216911      2.8337276      0.0046009
             AGE     -0.1274933     0.0527665     -2.4161814      0.0156842
          FIREPL      8.2751991     2.4891073      3.3245650      0.0008856
             GAR      4.1565526     1.7614609      2.3597189      0.0182888
           LOTSZ      0.0751226     0.0150624      4.9874301      0.0000000
           NBATH      5.6161019     1.8094350      3.1037875      0.0019106
           NROOM      0.7035399     1.0995064      0.6398689      0.5222579
           PATIO      7.9811147     2.8080688      2.8422077      0.0044802
            SQFT      0.1064720     0.1694196      0.6284514      0.5297083
         W_PRICE      0.3447891     0.0555589      6.2058261      0.0000000
================================ END OF REPORT =================================
```

图 8.9　使用 k 最近邻的 ML 空间滞后模型结果

第 9 章 GUI 中的空间误差模型的广义矩估计

9.1 模型创建

在 GeoDaSpace 中,空间误差模型的设置与第 5 章中 OLS 的设置相同。如空间滞后模型的例子,必须指定一个空间权重矩阵文件(Model Weights 面板中),但是现在 Model Type 必须选择 Spatial Error,Method 必须选择 GMM(广义矩估计)。在此我们不再重复基本的介绍,具体叙述请参见第 5 章。

基本设置如图 9.1 所示。我们选取美国县级犯罪率数据集的一个子集来阐述空间误差估计。示例数据集中的 south.dbf 文件与 NAT.dbf 文件包含相同的变量,但只包括美国南部的 1 412 个县。这个模型规范与之前使用的很相似,HR90(1990 年的县级犯罪率)作为独立变量,DV90(离婚率)、PS90(人口结构)、RD90(资源匮乏)和 UE90(失业率)作为解释变量。空间权重矩阵符合 Queen 邻接(south_q.gal)。数据集的名称、空间权重矩阵文件、独立变量和解释变量都添加到相应的面板中,如图 9.1 所示。

我们之所以选取这个模型作为案例,是因为它在 OLS 估计的规范检验中显示出了很强的空间误差自相关。尤其是当两种 LM 检验(误差和滞后)都拒绝原假设时,鲁棒检验统计表明空间误差模型是更好的选择。另外,这种规范允许我们将 UE90 作为内生变量来处理,就如之前章节所提到的那样。

下面我们来进行 GM(矩估计)和 GMM 估计方法的比较。空间误差模型的默认估计方法是同质方差的 GMM 估计。我们选择这种估计方法是因为它包含空间自回归系数 λ 的推断。如果要使用原来的 GM 估计方法来达到这一目的,则需要在 Preferences 面板中 GMM 选项卡下进行设置。如图 9.2(a) 所示,默认勾选 Inference on Lambda 选项,这样会调用 GMM 估计方法。如果要选择 GM 估计方法,则不能勾选这个选项(并且要保存设置),如图 9.2(b) 所示。

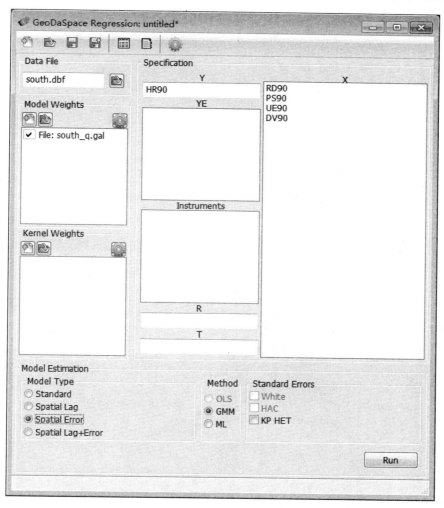

图 9.1　空间误差模型设置界面:GM/GMM

如果不恢复默认并保存,那么新设置的选项就依然有效,后续的操作也是这样。首先,我们来介绍 GM 的设置。

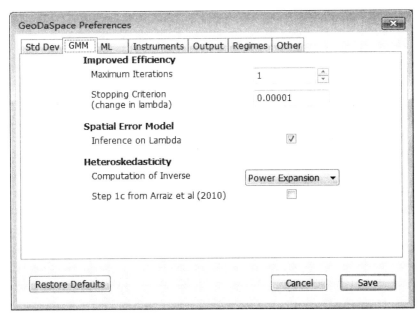

(a) 默认设置（GMM）

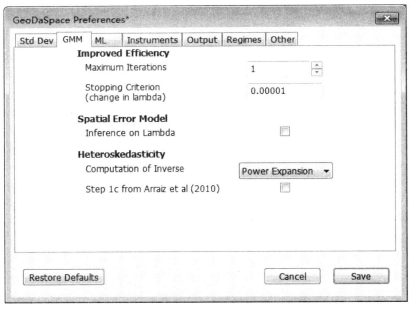

(b) GM

图 9.2　GMM 或 GM 估计方法

9.2 GM 估计

GM 估计的执行方法与前面的方法相同,取消勾选 Inference on Lambda 选项,默认的模型规范如图 9.1 所示,点击 Run 按钮即可,结果如图 9.3 所示。

```
REGRESSION
----------
SUMMARY OF OUTPUT: SPATIALLY WEIGHTED LEAST SQUARES
-----------------------------------------------
Data set            :   south.dbf
Weights matrix      :File: south_q.gal
Dependent Variable  :        HR90      Number of Observations:       1412
Mean dependent var  :      9.5493      Number of Variables   :          5
S.D. dependent var  :      7.0389      Degrees of Freedom    :       1407
Pseudo R-squared    :      0.3066

-----------------------------------------------------------------------
       Variable     Coefficient       Std.Error     z-Statistic     Probability
-----------------------------------------------------------------------
       CONSTANT       6.3386537       1.0155422       6.2416445       0.0000000
           DV90       0.4777216       0.1203677       3.9688512       0.0000722
           PS90       1.8133531       0.2105237       8.6135328       0.0000000
           RD90       4.4326518       0.2318185      19.1212180       0.0000000
           UE90      -0.3985616       0.0772012      -5.1626346       0.0000002
         lambda       0.2604090
-----------------------------------------------------------------------
========================= END OF REPORT =========================
```

图 9.3 空间误差模型:GM

空间加权最小二乘法回归的输出结果与之前的方法格式相同。顶部包含数据集和空间权重矩阵的文件名、独立变量以及一些解释性统计量。其次是拟合度 Pseudo R-Squared,它在本案例中值为 0.306 6。最后是一张表格,内容包括变量名称、系数估计值、标准误差、z 统计量以及相应的 p 值。

λ 的估计值为 0.260 409 0。不出所料,标准误和其他推断统计量都没有给出 λ 的值,因为它在 GM 估计中被处理为多余参数。

在 GeoDaSpace 中,预测值和残差就以常规的方式创建,在 Preferences 面板中 Output 选项卡下勾选相应的选项即可。而在 GM 估计以及本章中的其他空间误差模型中,预测值为 predy,残差为 resid。目前,空间滤波残差并没有包含在标准的输出结果中,但它可以作为 PySAL 回归对象的一部分用于这些方法中。图 9.4 是当前案例的结果。

```
IDs,HR90,predy,resid
54029,0.9461,6.9322,-5.9861,
54009,1.2349,4.7415,-3.5065,
54069,2.6210,9.7169,-7.0958,
54051,4.4616,6.9945,-2.5329,
10003,6.7127,8.1157,-1.4030,
24043,1.6475,7.1821,-5.5345,
24001,3.1134,8.1591,-5.0457,
24015,4.6720,4.8289,-0.1569,
24023,1.1846,5.3564,-4.1718,
24025,3.8434,4.2337,-0.3903,
```

图 9.4　预测值和残差

接下来,我们讨论包含内生变量的 GM 估计。空间加权估计规范也可以应用于包含内生变量的模型中。为了在 GeoDaSpace 中执行该模型,我们需要在 YE 面板中指定内生变量,并在 Instruments 面板中指定相应的工具变量。在本书的案例中,我们仍然使用 UE90 作为内生变量,将 FH90(低于贫困线的家庭所占比例)、GI89(县级基尼指数)、FP89(女性做主的家庭比例)作为工具变量。默认设置如图 9.5 所示。在这个界面中我们无法判断选择的是 GM 还是 GMM 选项,需要查看 Preferences 面板中 GMM 选项卡并确保相应的选项不被勾选(对 GM 估计),如图 9.2(b)所示。

这个模型中估计的过程与之前相同,其产生的结果如图 9.6 所示。在输出结果的底部比图 9.3 中多了几行,列出了内生变量(Instrumented)和工具变量(Instruments),除此之外其布局与图 9.3 完全相同。

λ 的估计值为 0.236 097 4,模型的 Pseudo R-squared 值为 0.281 8。正如之前所提到的,应该谨慎解读拟合度的度量,因为它是基于公式右边观测值的内生变量,而不是基于正确表达的约化形式。在 GM 估计的只有外生性的情况下,标准误和其他统计量都没有多余参数 λ 的值。

另外,我们需注意考虑到 UE90 的内生性对其系数估计的影响。在空间加权最小二乘估计的例子中,这个估计值为 -0.339,而在空间加权两阶段空间最小二乘估计中,系数估计值变为了 -1.141。但它对显著性的影响可以忽略不计,所有的系数估计值都保持高显著性。

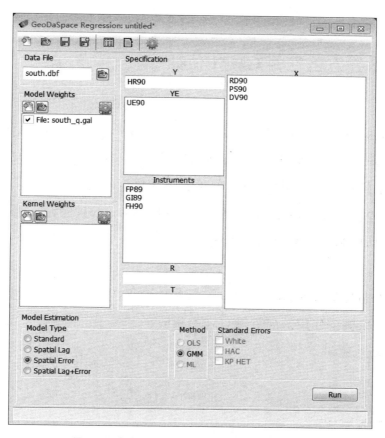

图 9.5 含内生变量的空间误差模型设置:GM

```
REGRESSION
----------
SUMMARY OF OUTPUT: SPATIALLY WEIGHTED TWO STAGE LEAST SQUARES
-------------------------------------------------------------
Data set            :       south.dbf
Weights matrix      :File: south_q.gal
Dependent Variable  :           HR90      Number of Observations:     1412
Mean dependent var  :         9.5493      Number of Variables   :        5
S.D. dependent var  :         7.0389      Degrees of Freedom    :     1407
Pseudo R-squared    :         0.2818

-------------------------------------------------------------------------
     Variable      Coefficient       Std.Error       z-Statistic     Probability
-------------------------------------------------------------------------
     CONSTANT       10.7717841       1.2771988        8.4339137       0.0000000
         DV90        0.4919064       0.1246483        3.9463541       0.0000794
         PS90        2.0455388       0.2190619        9.3377222       0.0000000
         RD90        5.9037130       0.3473996       16.9940125       0.0000000
         UE90       -1.1407122       0.1483842       -7.6875610       0.0000000
       lambda        0.2360974
-------------------------------------------------------------------------
Instrumented: UE90
Instruments: FH90, FP89, GI89
============================ END OF REPORT ============================
```

图 9.6 含内生变量的空间误差模型结果:GM

9.3 包含异方差性的 GMM 估计

正如之前所提到的,实际上空间误差模型 GMM 估计的默认设置并不是 GM 估计,而全都是 GMM 估计。我们刚刚阐述了 GM 估计方法中,需要确认偏好设置中的 GMM 选项已勾选(如果上一次执行的也是 GM 估计方法,则不需要再确认)。如果有必要,我们要 Restore Defaults 并且保存。通常情况下没有这个必要,因为 GM 估计方法主要是用来进行比较的,否则将会被 GMM 估计取代。

异方差通过勾选 Standard Errors 面板中的 KP HET 选项来选择,如图 9.7 所示。这个案例中使用的规范与 GM 的相同。

图 9.7 异方差 GMM 设置

输出结果如图 9.8 所示。其布局与之前的案例有轻微的差异。在 lambda 系数那一行中,也输出了标准误、z 统计量和 p 值。另外,迭代数目设为 1(这是默认设置),并且叙述了是否使用额外的估计步骤,默认设置为 No,如图中所示。

λ 的估计值是 0.314 741 6,与之前的案例相比略微偏高。并且,Pseudo R-squared 值为 0.306 2,也比之前的结果好。与 GM 估计相比,除 DV90 外,标准误都变大了。然而,这并没有影响估计值的显著性,所有的系数都保持高显著性。

```
REGRESSION
---------
SUMMARY OF OUTPUT: SPATIALLY WEIGHTED LEAST SQUARES (HET)
--------------------------------------------------------
Data set            :    south.dbf
Weights matrix      :File: south_q.gal
Dependent Variable  :         HR90          Number of Observations:      1412
Mean dependent var  :       9.5493          Number of Variables    :         5
S.D. dependent var  :       7.0389          Degrees of Freedom     :      1407
Pseudo R-squared    :       0.3062
N. of iterations    :            1          Step1c computed        :        No
--------------------------------------------------------
        Variable     Coefficient     Std.Error     z-Statistic    Probability
--------------------------------------------------------
        CONSTANT       6.2576037     1.0821873       5.7823668      0.0000000
            DV90       0.4811658     0.1198516       4.0146802      0.0000595
            PS90       1.7983276     0.3359957       5.3522335      0.0000001
            RD90       4.4195359     0.3468537      12.7417874      0.0000000
            UE90      -0.3897697     0.0985644      -3.9544664      0.0000767
          lambda       0.3147416     0.0374883       8.3957227      0.0000000
--------------------------------------------------------
========================= END OF REPORT =========================
```

图 9.8 异方差 GMM 结果

9.3.1 估计 λ 时的额外步骤

Arraiz et al.(2010)在阐述 GMM 估计方法时,在初始估计 λ 时包含了一个额外步骤。解决公式 $m = g - \begin{bmatrix} \lambda \\ \lambda^2 \end{bmatrix} = 0$ 的矩条件,得到一个一致的估计后,将执行第二步,使用最优权重的加权非线性最小二乘法(矩条件方差的逆)。在默认程序中,我们会跳过这个额外的步骤,直接进行回归系数的加权最小二乘估计。

要执行这个额外的步骤,我们需要在 Preferences 面板中 GMM 选项卡下勾选相应的选项。如图 9.9(a)所示,Step 1c from Arraiz et al(2010)选项默认不勾选。将其勾选后(并保存)就能执行这个额外的步骤,如图 9.9(b)所示。

估计的过程与之前的相同,输出结果如图 9.10 所示。输出结果中 Step1c computed 结果为 Yes。迭代次数为 1,这是默认的。λ 的估计值只受到了轻微的影响,得到 0.316 144 5(当跳过额外步骤时得到 0.314 741 6)。其他系数的估计值和显著性也同样只受到了轻微的影响。这个结果支持初始和最优解的渐近等价结果。

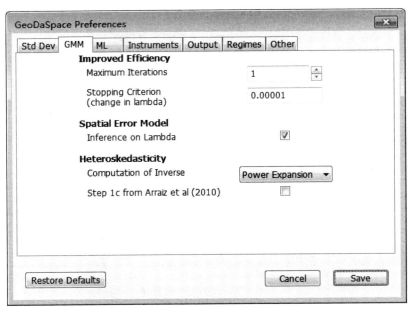

(a) 默认设置

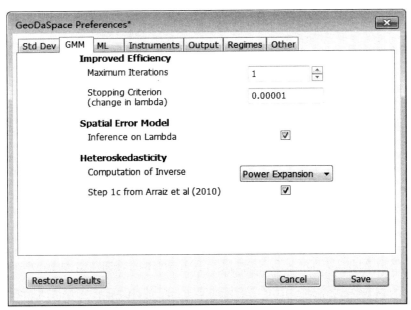

(b) 选择额外步骤

图 9.9　GMM 中 λ 估计的额外步骤

```
REGRESSION
----------
SUMMARY OF OUTPUT: SPATIALLY WEIGHTED LEAST SQUARES (HET)
---------------------------------------------------------
Data set            :    south.dbf
Weights matrix      :File: south_q.gal
Dependent Variable  :         HR90        Number of Observations:      1412
Mean dependent var  :       9.5493        Number of Variables    :         5
S.D. dependent var  :       7.0389        Degrees of Freedom     :      1407
Pseudo R-squared    :       0.3059
N. of iterations    :            1        Step1c computed        :       Yes
-----------------------------------------------------------------------------
       Variable        Coefficient      Std.Error       z-Statistic    Probability
-----------------------------------------------------------------------------
       CONSTANT          6.1903085      1.0826509        5.7177328      0.0000000
           DV90          0.4840327      0.1199034        4.0368561      0.0000542
           PS90          1.7859187      0.3361596        5.3127111      0.0000001
           RD90          4.4088516      0.3472585       12.6961665      0.0000000
           UE90         -0.3824992      0.0986013       -3.8792513      0.0001048
         lambda          0.3161445      0.0374169        8.4492406      0.0000000
-----------------------------------------------------------------------------
============================ END OF REPORT ==================================
```

图 9.10 执行额外步骤的异方差 GMM 结果

9.3.2 迭代估计

Preferences 面板中 GMM 选项卡下最后一个选项是执行的迭代次数。默认是 Drukker et al.(2013)提出的两步估计法,在空间加权回归中将矩方程解的一致性估计作为第二步。如前所述,在估计过程中可以执行多次迭代,每次迭代矩方程都使用更新后的残差向量。

在 Preferences 面板中可以设定最大迭代次数,如图 9.11 所示。第一个界面中[如图 9.11(a)所示]显示的是默认值为 1,第二个界面中[如图 9.11(b)所示]最大迭代次数已改为 10。然而这并不是决定实际迭代次数的唯一因素。因为如果两次迭代中估计值没有显著的改变,则停止迭代。这可以通过 Stopping Criterion 选项来控制,它的值代表在估计 λ 时不再进行迭代的精度改变值,默认值是 0.000 01,在此我们不做改变。点击 Save 保存新的设置。

选择此选项后所得的结果如图 9.12 所示。迭代次数为 5,意味着迭代五次后 λ 的改变小于设定值。λ 的结果为 0.319 134 4,只是略高于非迭代的结果(图 9.8 中的 0.314 741 6)。标准误也略小,但是只在第四位有效数字才显现出来(分别是 0.037 267 1 和 0.037 488 3)。总之,额外的迭代不会对参数估计和估计精度产生实质性的改变,再次支持了在这种情况下初始估计的一致性。

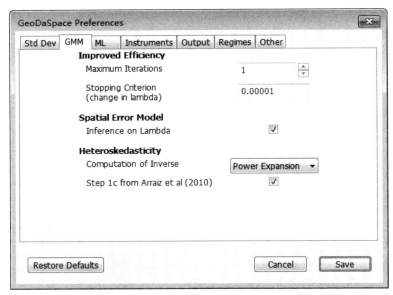

(a)默认设置

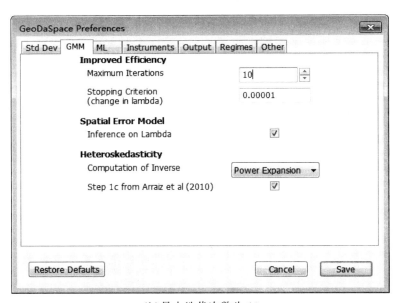

(b)最大迭代次数为 10

图 9.11　迭代次数的选择

```
REGRESSION
----------
SUMMARY OF OUTPUT: SPATIALLY WEIGHTED LEAST SQUARES (HET)
---------------------------------------------------------
Data set            :     south.dbf
Weights matrix      :File: south_q.gal
Dependent Variable  :          HR90      Number of Observations:       1412
Mean dependent var  :        9.5493      Number of Variables   :          5
S.D. dependent var  :        7.0389      Degrees of Freedom    :       1407
Pseudo R-squared    :        0.3053
N. of iterations    :             5      Step1c computed       :        Yes
---------------------------------------------------------
      Variable      Coefficient     Std.Error      z-Statistic     Probability
---------------------------------------------------------
      CONSTANT       6.0484354      1.0837030       5.5812664      0.0000000
      DV90           0.4900934      0.1200190       4.0834659      0.0000444
      PS90           1.7599415      0.3365045       5.2300675      0.0000002
      RD90           4.3869333      0.3481280      12.6014938      0.0000000
      UE90          -0.3672539      0.0986888      -3.7213339      0.0001982
      lambda         0.3191344      0.0372671       8.5634365      0.0000000
---------------------------------------------------------
============================= END OF REPORT =============================
```

图 9.12　迭代次数为 5 的异方差 GMM 结果

9.3.3　包含异方差性和内生变量的 GMM 估计

在包含异方差性的空间误差模型的 GMM 估计中,我们最后再引入内生变量。GUI 中模型创建时的设置与 GM 相同(如图 9.5 所示),唯一不同的是选择了 KP HET 按钮,如图 9.7 所示。

这个模型的结果如图 9.13 所示。在 GM 估计中,考虑到 UE90 的内生性后主要的影响在于它的系数估计值,由图 9.8 中的 -0.3897697 变为了包含内生性后的 -1.1375011。在两种情况下,系数估计值都保持高显著性。λ 的估计值也在本质上发生了变化,由图 9.8 中的 0.314 741 6 变为了包含内生性后的 0.261 624 8,也保持高显著性。当考虑内生性时标准误经常会变大,但是不会影响整体的显著性。

```
REGRESSION
----------
SUMMARY OF OUTPUT: SPATIALLY WEIGHTED TWO STAGE LEAST SQUARES (HET)
-------------------------------------------------------------------
Data set            :   south.dbf
Weights matrix      :File: south_q.gal
Dependent Variable  :       HR90           Number of Observations:      1412
Mean dependent var  :     9.5493           Number of Variables   :         5
S.D. dependent var  :     7.0389           Degrees of Freedom    :      1407
Pseudo R-squared    :     0.2820
N. of iterations    :          1           Step1c computed       :        No

------------------------------------------------------------------------------
       Variable     Coefficient       Std.Error     z-Statistic     Probability
------------------------------------------------------------------------------
       CONSTANT      10.7456340       1.5222725       7.0589425       0.0000000
           DV90       0.4927888       0.1266845       3.8898895       0.0001003
           PS90       2.0357920       0.3491174       5.8312538       0.0000000
           RD90       5.8976659       0.5199311      11.3431685       0.0000000
           UE90      -1.1375011       0.2109871      -5.3913304       0.0000001
         lambda       0.2616248       0.0414083       6.3181770       0.0000000
------------------------------------------------------------------------------
Instrumented: UE90
Instruments: FH90, FP89, GI89
================================ END OF REPORT ================================
```

图 9.13　含内生变量的异方差 GMM 结果

9.4　包含同方差性的 GMM 估计

我们在执行空间误差模型的 GMM 估计时不考虑异方差性。相对于 GM 估计，这一设置的主要优点在于渐进方差-协方差矩阵能用于所有的估计系数，包括 λ（在 GM 估计中 λ 是多余参数，不能用于推断）。

GUI 中模型创建时的设置与 GM 相同，如图 9.1 所示，没有勾选 KP HET 选项。输出结果如图 9.14 所示。

λ 的估计值与使用 GM 估计时相似：分别为图 9.14 中的 0.279 857 2 和图 9.3 中的 0.260 409 0。标准误为 0.035 524 2，显示出高显著性。

我们考虑的最后一个模型设置是在同方差性的情况下引入内生变量，其设置与图 9.5 相同。因为 GM 和 GMM 估计的不同只能在 Preferences 面板中看到，其他方面都是相同的。值得注意的是，一定不能勾选 KP HET 选项。输出结果如图 9.15 所示。

与其他校正内生性的模型一样，主要影响的是系数 UE90 的估计值，在这里得到的值是$-1.140\ 658\ 5$。λ的估计值是$0.243\ 163\ 6$,在所有的GMM估计方法中是最小的,但是比GM估计值略高。然而与之前一样,它对模型系数的整体显著性没有实质性的影响。

```
REGRESSION
----------
SUMMARY OF OUTPUT: SPATIALLY WEIGHTED LEAST SQUARES (HOM)
---------------------------------------------------------
Data set            :    south.dbf
Weights matrix      :File: south_q.gal
Dependent Variable  :       HR90          Number of Observations:     1412
Mean dependent var  :     9.5493          Number of Variables   :        5
S.D. dependent var  :     7.0389          Degrees of Freedom    :     1407
Pseudo R-squared    :     0.3066
N. of iterations    :          1

------------------------------------------------------------------------
       Variable     Coefficient       Std.Error     z-Statistic   Probability
------------------------------------------------------------------------
       CONSTANT       6.3380348       1.0237066       6.1912612     0.0000000
           DV90       0.4777479       0.1210440       3.9468939     0.0000792
           PS90       1.8132381       0.2118595       8.5586829     0.0000000
           RD90       4.4325506       0.2336868      18.9679144     0.0000000
           UE90      -0.3984943       0.0777957      -5.1223182     0.0000003
         lambda       0.2798572       0.0355242       7.8779334     0.0000000
------------------------------------------------------------------------
================================ END OF REPORT ================================
```

图 9.14 同方差 GMM 结果

```
REGRESSION
----------
SUMMARY OF OUTPUT: SPATIALLY WEIGHTED TWO STAGE LEAST SQUARES (HOM)
-------------------------------------------------------------------
Data set            :    south.dbf
Weights matrix      :File: south_q.gal
Dependent Variable  :       HR90          Number of Observations:     1412
Mean dependent var  :     9.5493          Number of Variables   :        5
S.D. dependent var  :     7.0389          Degrees of Freedom    :     1407
Pseudo R-squared    :     0.2818
N. of iterations    :          1

------------------------------------------------------------------------
       Variable     Coefficient       Std.Error     z-Statistic   Probability
------------------------------------------------------------------------
       CONSTANT      10.7713463       1.2834619       8.3924158     0.0000000
           DV90       0.4919212       0.1249985       3.9354165     0.0000831
           PS90       2.0453736       0.2197377       9.3082522     0.0000000
           RD90       5.9036116       0.3489835      16.9165947     0.0000000
           UE90      -1.1406585       0.1491507      -7.6476928     0.0000000
         lambda       0.2431636       0.0389702       6.2397251     0.0000000
------------------------------------------------------------------------
Instrumented: UE90
Instruments: FH90, FP89, GI89
================================ END OF REPORT ================================
```

图 9.15 含内生变量的同方差 GMM 结果

9.5 估计值的比较

在表 9.1 中,我们列出了不同方法下的 λ 估计值、估计标准误和 Pseudo R-Squared,以便于进行比较。该表包含了本章中八种不同方法的变体。为了保证比较的完整性,我们还列出了最大似然(ML)估计的结果,这将在第 10 章中进行详细的介绍。

表 9.1 不同方法下估计值的比较

Method	λ	Standard Error	Pseudo R-Squared
GM	0.260 4		0.306 6
GM Endog	0.236 1		0.281 8
GMM Het	0.314 7	0.037 5	0.306 2
GMM Het 1c	0.316 1	0.037 4	0.305 9
GMM Het Iterated	0.319 1	0.037 3	0.305 3
GMM Het Endog	0.261 6	0.041 4	0.282 0
GMM Hom	0.279 9	0.035 5	0.306 6
GMM Hom Endog	0.243 2	0.039 0	0.281 8
ML	0.299 1	0.037 8	0.305 8

λ 的值域是由内生性 GM 中的 0.236 1 到迭代异方差性 GMM 中的 0.319 1。内生性模型的估计值通常小于未校正内生性的估计值,但是这个差异很小。GM 估计值在内生性和外生性的情况下都是最小的。ML 估计值(0.299 1)略微低于 GMM Het 的值,但是高于其他方法。

标准误的波动比较小,值域是由同方差 GMM 中的 0.035 5 到内生性异方差 GMM 中的 0.041 4。如上面所提到的,在估计 λ 时使用迭代和额外步骤对效率的影响很小。主要在于内生性和外生性之间的差异,前者的标准误总是略高,但这个差异依然很小。有趣的是,ML 估计的标准误(0.037 8)并不是最小的,而是与 GMM Het 外生变量的估计值相一致。

所有模型的拟合度都很相似。外生变量的模型中大约在 0.306，内生变量的模型中大约在 0.28。整体来说，在这个特殊的案例中，异方差性和内生性的校正似乎是有必要的，尽管在实际的模型中这个效果很微弱。另外，这个样本容量足以保持 λ 估计值的渐进特性（一致性），所以通过迭代或额外步骤能获得的信息不多。

第 10 章 GUI 中的空间误差模型的最大似然估计

10.1 模型创建

要阐述 GUI 中空间误差模型的最大似然(ML)估计,我们遵循与第 9 章相同的步骤。我们使用美国南方 1 412 个县的犯罪率数据(包含在 south.dbf 数据集中)。与之前相同,独立变量为 HR90(1990 年的犯罪率),解释变量为 RD90(资源剥夺)、PS90(人口结构)、DV90(离婚率)和 UE90(失业率)。与 GM/GMM 估计不同的是,在这里不允许使用内生性的解释变量。空间权重矩阵基于县之间的 Queen 邻接,就如示例文件 south_q.gal。

在 GeoDa 中,除选择了 Spatial Error 选项外,模型设置与空间滞后模型相同,如图 10.1 所示。在本案例中,还勾选了 Pred. Val. and Res.选项,这样预测值和残差就可以添加到数据表中了。

在 GeoDaSpace 中,除在 Method 面板中选择了 ML 选项外,布局与 GM/GMM 相同(例如图 9.1),如图 10.2 所示。

在两个软件中,点击 Run 按钮,弹出结果窗口。

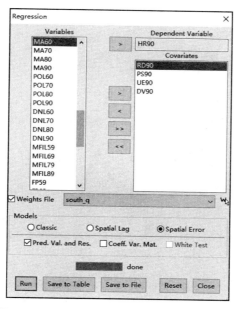

图 10.1　GeoDa 中 ML 空间误差模型设置界面

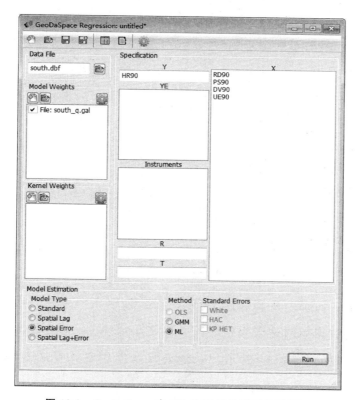

图 10.2　GeoDaSpace 中 ML 空间误差模型设置界面

第 10 章　GUI 中的空间误差模型的最大似然估计

10.2 基本估计结果

GeoDa 和 GeoDaSpace 中的估计结果分别如图 10.3 和图 10.4 所示。两个输出结果格式都与之前的相同,输出了一些描述性统计量、拟合度、估计值和它们的标准误以及相应的 p 值。对于 GeoDa,在输出结果下方还列出了似然比检验和异方差性的 Breusch-Pagan 检验。

```
SUMMARY OF OUTPUT: SPATIAL ERROR MODEL - MAXIMUM LIKELIHOOD ESTIMATION
Data set            : south
Spatial Weight      : south_q.gal
Dependent Variable  :       HR90   Number of Observations: 1412
Mean dependent var  :   9.549293   Number of Variables   :    5
S.D. dependent var  :   7.036358   Degrees of Freedom    : 1407
Lag coeff. (Lambda) :   0.299078

R-squared           :   0.345453   R-squared (BUSE)      :      -
Sq. Correlation     :          -   Log likelihood        :-4471.407067
Sigma-square        :    32.4069   Akaike info criterion :    8952.81
S.E of regression   :     5.6927   Schwarz criterion     :    8979.08

---------------------------------------------------------------------
    Variable      Coefficient     Std.Error     z-value    Probability
---------------------------------------------------------------------
    CONSTANT         6.149225      1.031875     5.959275     0.00000
        RD90         4.40242       0.2355472   18.69018      0.00000
        PS90         1.778371      0.2131787    8.342163     0.00000
        UE90        -0.3780731     0.07838525  -4.823268     0.00000
        DV90         0.4857858     0.121711     3.991306     0.00007
      LAMBDA         0.2990779     0.03781545   7.908879     0.00000
---------------------------------------------------------------------

REGRESSION DIAGNOSTICS
DIAGNOSTICS FOR HETEROSKEDASTICITY
RANDOM COEFFICIENTS
TEST                                      DF       VALUE         PROB
Breusch-Pagan test                         4     523.5007      0.00000

DIAGNOSTICS FOR SPATIAL DEPENDENCE
SPATIAL ERROR DEPENDENCE FOR WEIGHT MATRIX : south_q.gal
TEST                                      DF       VALUE         PROB
Likelihood Ratio Test                      1      52.9575      0.00000
================================ END OF REPORT =====================
```

图 10.3 GeoDa 中 ML 空间误差模型结果

对于 GeoDaSpace,我们选择了 Ord 方法(如输出结果中所列),因为它在计算当前大小的数据集时速度更快。需要在 Preferences 面板中 ML 选项卡下勾选相应的选项,如图 8.8(b)所示。系统会默认使用 Full 方法。两个程序处理的结果相同,所以我们不再显示单独的列表。

```
REGRESSION
----------
SUMMARY OF OUTPUT: MAXIMUM LIKELIHOOD SPATIAL ERROR (METHOD = ORD)
-----------------------------------------------------------------
Data set            :     south.dbf
Weights matrix      :File: south_q.gal
Dependent Variable  :          HR90        Number of Observations:        1412
Mean dependent var  :        9.5493        Number of Variables   :           5
S.D. dependent var  :        7.0389        Degrees of Freedom    :        1407
Pseudo R-squared    :        0.3058
Sigma-square ML     :        32.407        Log likelihood        :    -4471.407
S.E of regression   :         5.693        Akaike info criterion :     8952.814
                                           Schwarz criterion     :     8979.078
-----------------------------------------------------------------
       Variable       Coefficient      Std.Error       z-Statistic     Probability
-----------------------------------------------------------------
       CONSTANT        6.1492254       1.0318746        5.9592760       0.0000000
           DV90        0.4857857       0.1217110        3.9913060       0.0000657
           PS90        1.7783714       0.2131787        8.3421642       0.0000000
           RD90        4.4024202       0.2355472       18.6901843       0.0000000
           UE90       -0.3780732       0.0783852       -4.8232697       0.0000014
         lambda        0.2990777       0.0378155        7.9088741       0.0000000
-----------------------------------------------------------------
========================= END OF REPORT =========================
```

图 10.4　GeoDaSpace 中 ML 空间误差模型结果

GeoDa 和 GeoDaSpace 中的结果相同,只有一些四舍五入带来的误差。需要注意的是,在当前数据集的容量下($n=1\,412$),独立变量的标准误在 GeoDa(常数估计,除以 n)和 GeoDaSpace[无偏估计,除以 $(n-k)$]之间的差异几乎可以忽略不计。$\hat{\lambda}$ 的值为 $0.299\,078$,显示出高显著性(相比于 GM/GMM 估计值和标准误,见 9.5 节)。其他系数的估计值也都具有显著性,与 GM/GMM 估计值相同。

图 10.3 显示的 GeoDa 中的分析表明了存在异方差性。我们使用平方差 GMM 估计证明它,不用 ML 估计方法。似然比检验再次证明了 λ 的高显著性,与我们在渐近 t 检验和 LM_λ 检验中得到的结论一致。

10.3　ML-预测值和残差

在 GeoDa 中,在模型对话框中勾选 Pred. Val. and Res.选项(如图 10.1 所示),就能将预测值和残差添加到数据表中,并进行后续的分析和可视化。点击

Save to Table 按钮,弹出一个对话框,在其中指定预测值和残差的变量名称,如图 10.5 所示。预测值的默认变量名是 ERR_PREDIC,空间滤波残差的是 ERR_RESIDU,预测误差或粗略残差(观测值和预测值的差异,没有任何空间滤波)的是 ERR_PRDERR。相应的值将作为一列数据插入数据表中,如图 10.6 所示。

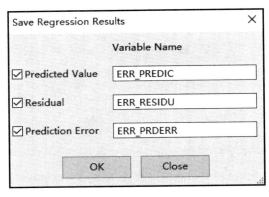

图 10.5 预测值和残差变量命名

	ERR_PRDERR	ERR_RESIDU	ERR_PREDIC	FIPSNO
1	-5.9765	-4.9284	6.9226	54029
2	-3.5043	-1.5538	4.7393	54009
3	-7.0673	-6.1597	9.6883	54069
4	-2.5650	-1.0913	7.0266	54051
5	-1.3002	-0.8710	8.0129	10003
6	-5.4678	-5.3356	7.1153	24043
7	-5.0392	-4.6988	8.1525	24001
8	-0.1182	0.1123	4.7902	24015
9	-4.1861	-3.5067	5.3707	24023
10	-0.3033	-0.2514	4.1466	24025

图 10.6 GeoDa 数据表中的预测值和残差

在 GeoDaSpace 中若想得到相同的结果,就需要勾选 Preferences 面板中 Output 选项卡下的相应选项。然后在对话框中指定的文件中就加入了观测的独立变量值、预测值(ml_predy)和残差(ml_resid),结果如图 10.7 所示。需要注意空间滤波残差目前并不在输出结果之中。

```
IDs, HR90, ml_predy, ml_resid
54029, 0.9461, 6.9226, -5.9765,
54009, 1.2349, 4.7393, -3.5043,
54069, 2.6210, 9.6883, -7.0673,
54051, 4.4616, 7.0266, -2.5650,
10003, 6.7127, 8.0129, -1.3002,
24043, 1.6475, 7.1153, -5.4678,
24001, 3.1134, 8.1525, -5.0392,
24015, 4.6720, 4.7902, -0.1182,
24023, 1.1846, 5.3707, -4.1861,
24025, 3.8434, 4.1466, -0.3033,
```

图 10.7　GeoDaSpace 数据表中的预测值和残差

第 11 章 GUI 中的复合模型

11.1 模型创建

本章我们讨论包含空间滞后因变量和空间自回归误差的模型,综合了第 7 章和第 9 章中估计方法的特性,我们称之为复合模型(Combo Model)。GeoDaSpace 图形用户界面的格式与之前相同,除 Data File 外,我们需要在 Model Weights 面板指定空间权重,而且必须将 Model Type 设为 Spatial Lag+Error。

我们这次使用的案例略微有所不同,如图 11.1 所示,我们使用的是美国 1960 年的县级犯罪率数据,HR60 作为因变量。该数据集包含在县级数据 NAT.dbf 中,空间权重矩阵是基于县之间的一阶 Queen 邻接 nat_queen.gal。图 11.1 中只包含外生性解释变量,有资源剥夺 RD60、人口结构 PS60、离婚率 DV60、非白人家庭比例 BLK60 和失业率 UE60。所有的值都是 1960 年的数据。如界面下方所示,估计方法默认勾选 GMM,Standard Errors 选项勾选 KP HET(注意此处默认不勾选该选项,如图 11.2 所示)。

必须注意复合模型支持空间滞后和空间误差模型中的大部分选项,但不是全部支持。与其他选项一样,它需要在 Preferences 面板中进行选择。

在这个模型中,空间滞后方面最重要的一个选项是:

- 空间滞后解释变量的滞后阶数(空间滞后因变量的工具变量):默认的是一阶,如图 7.14 所示。

需要注意的是,White 和 HAC 的标准误选项在复合模型中是不可用的,因为估计值的标准误取决于模型误差中的空间自回归结构。

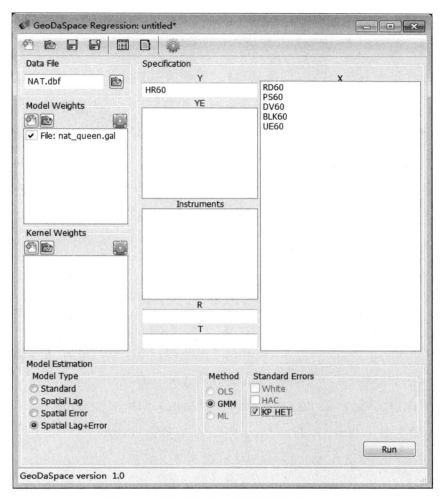

图 11.1 复合模型：只含外生解释变量(HET)

在这个模型中，空间误差方面的一些选项包括：

- 选择 GMM(默认)或 GM 估计，如图 9.2 所示。
- 选择 GMM 估计方法中 λ 估计值的额外步骤(默认无此步骤)，如图 9.9 所示。
- GMM 估计方法中 λ 估计值的迭代次数(默认无迭代)，如图 9.11 所示。

对于这些选项深层次的技术细节，请参阅第 9 章的相关内容。

除 Preferences 界面中设置的选项外，GMM 估计的 Standard Errors 选项是同方差性(默认)或异方差性的(KP HET)。它们都可以在 GUI 下方界面的相应复选框中进行设置(在图 11.1 中选择了 KP HET)。

我们简要总结一下模型建立的结果。原 OLS 估计的结果变为了 0.274。五个解释变量中有三个显示出高显著性,它们的系数值为正(BLK60、DV60 和 RD60)。PS60 不显著,而 UE60 只有微弱的显著性(p 值为 0.059)。空间独立性诊断中 LM_ρ(214.6)和 LM_λ(180.1)的值都显示出高显著性,鲁棒检验表明空间滞后模型为理想的替代($LM_{\rho*} = 34.8, LM_{\lambda*} = 0.4$)。另外,它的非显著性极高(Jarque-Bera 检验 $p = 0.000\,000$),也表现出极高的异方差性(White 检验 $p = 0.000\,000$)。

空间滞后模型的拟合优度有所提高(经典 R^2 和 Pseudo R-squared 度量缺乏可比性),得到空间 Pseudo R-squared 值为 0.284。空间自回归系数为 0.430 7,显著性很高。在 OLS 的结果中,BLK60、DV60 和 RD60 三个变量也具有很高的显著性,PS60 保持非显著。UE60 的显著性受到的影响很小,p 值为 0.047。Anselin-Kelejian 检验统计量的值为 6.24,相应的 p 值为 0.013,表示它保持空间误差自相关。可见,这就是使用复合模型的目的所在。

为了保持完整性,需要注意空间误差模型的 GMM 估计(选择 KP HET 选项,OLS 结果显示出异方差性)相对于 OLS 的拟合度产生了微弱的变化,空间 Pseudo R-squared 值为 0.274。λ 的估计值为 0.378 2,$p = 0.000\,000$,显示出高显著性。除 UE60 以外(它的改变较小,p 值为 0.070),其他参数的显著性从本质上受到了影响。

在实践中,本案例可能不需要执行复合模型,因为重新指定一个回归和/或空间权重可能会删除在空间滞后模型中剩余误差自相关的证据。或者,我们可以执行空间滞后模型,并对标准误使用 HAC 选项,这也能校正剩余误差自相关。然而,这里着重讨论的是 GeoDaSpace 的特性,因此我们继续对复合模型执行估计,而不去细化关心原始设置的问题。

复合模型中除了空间滞后因变量,还包括内生性解释变量。这项设置如图 11.2 所示,与之前的案例相同,失业率 UE60 作为内生变量添加到 YE 面板中。同样,我们将低于贫困线的家庭比例 FP59、县级的基尼指数 GI59 和女性做主的家庭比例 FH60 作为工具变量,添加到 Instruments 面板中。在这个案例中,我们使用标准误的默认选项,而不勾选 KP HET 选项。

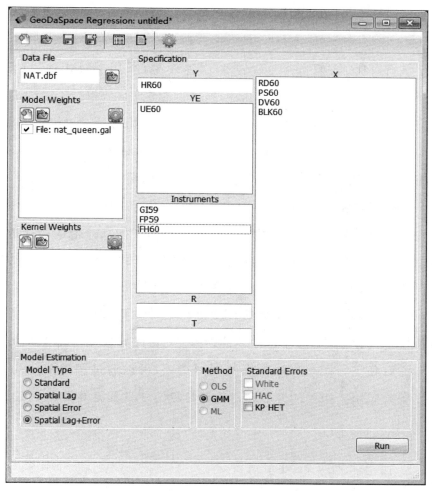

图 11.2 复合模型:含内生解释变量

在这个案例中,我们使用复合模型。我们只总结结果,而不再列出完整的表格,首先来看使用 2SLS 的估计模型。Pseudo R-squared 值为 0.271,拟合度比 OLS 略低。它与 OLS 的主要不同在于 UE60,已经稍微显示出显著性,p 值为 0.034。Anselin-Kelejian 检验统计量的值为 144.3,表现出高显著性,且存在空间自相关。

空间滞后模型的拟合优度略微提高,空间 Pseudo R-squared 值为 0.278。

空间自回归系数为 0.441 2,显著性较高。其他系数的显著性未受影响,主要影响在于 UE60,其 p 值为 0.044。Anselin-Kelejian 检验统计量的值为 6.8,$p = 0.009$,具有显著性,显示存在空间误差自相关。这使得复合模型可以作为可选的模型。

为了进行对比,我们也考虑了空间误差模型,采用 GMM 估计(使用 KP HET 选项)。其 λ 的估计值为 0.362 9,显著性很高,但是相对于空间滞后模型来说拟合度略低。Pseudo R-squared 值为 0.268(相对于之前的 0.278)。与 S2SLS 结果和空间滞后模型的估计值相反,UE60 不再具有显著性,p 值为 0.121。空间误差模型拟合度较好,这使得它比空间滞后模型更有优势,但它仍存在剩余的空间自相关,故仍然不能令人满意。其实,在只有外生解释变量的案例中,复合模型并不一定更有优势。在基本模型中加入其他解释变量,和/或在选择空间权重矩阵时进行细分,可能会得到不同的结果。另外,我们也可以对标准误执行 HAC 选项,这也能校正剩余误差自相关。然而,为了介绍 GeoDaSpace 的特性,我们仍然选择复合模型进行估计。我们将会把我们的讨论限定在默认模型设置上,既允许同方差性误差,又允许异方差性误差。由上述提到的空间滞后和空间误差方法得出的不同选项,可以通过调整 Preferences 面板中的设置来应用。相关的细节和讨论请参见第 7 章和第 9 章。

11.2 复合模型的 GM 估计

我们先来分析使用 GM 估计方法得到的结果。要使用这种方法,就要在 Preferences 面板中 GMM 选项卡下取消勾选 Inference on Lambda 选项,如图 9.2 所示。对于只有外生解释变量的模型,我们使用图 11.1 中 GUI 的设置,但是要取消勾选 KP HET 选项(该选项在 GM 估计中不能使用)。

估计结果如图 11.3 所示。相比于纯空间滞后模型,Pseudo R-squared 值略微提高到 0.285(原来的值为 0.283)。我们已经知道,GM 估计中没有 λ 估计值的推断。它的值是－0.188 4,与在纯空间误差模型中得到的估计值(0.378 2)没有关系,甚至符号都是相反的。相反,自回归系数 ρ 的估计值为0.449 5,是高显著性的,且与纯空间误差模型中得到的值(相比于 0.430 7)非常接近。这表明,包含完全指定的空间自回归误差项的效果是很不显著的(相当于在空间滞后模型中使用的 HAC 标准误的一个混合方法)。鉴于全局推断,它与空间滞后模型的结果只有轻微的不同。主要的不同之处在于 UE60,其 p 值由 0.047 变为了非显著性的 0.087。

```
REGRESSION
----------
SUMMARY OF OUTPUT: SPATIALLY WEIGHTED TWO STAGE LEAST SQUARES
-------------------------------------------------------------
Data set            :   NAT.dbf
Weights matrix      :File: nat_queen.gal
Dependent Variable  :   HR60             Number of Observations:      3085
Mean dependent var  :   4.5041           Number of Variables   :         7
S.D. dependent var  :   5.6497           Degrees of Freedom    :      3078
Pseudo R-squared    :   0.3333
Spatial Pseudo R-squared:  0.2854

------------------------------------------------------------------------------
      Variable      Coefficient       Std.Error     z-Statistic     Probability
------------------------------------------------------------------------------
      CONSTANT       0.3241109       0.2492294       1.3004522       0.1934460
         BLK60       0.0709649       0.0105437       6.7305432       0.0000000
          DV60       0.6157709       0.0980317       6.2813471       0.0000000
          PS60       0.1056478       0.0843697       1.2522008       0.2104967
          RD60       0.8086625       0.1400977       5.7721323       0.0000000
          UE60       0.0527934       0.0308956       1.7087671       0.0874941
        W_HR60       0.4495031       0.0652376       6.8902409       0.0000000
        lambda      -0.1884266
------------------------------------------------------------------------------
Instrumented: W_HR60
Instruments: W_BLK60, W_DV60, W_PS60, W_RD60, W_UE60
============================ END OF REPORT ==================================
```

图 11.3 只含外生解释变量的 GM 复合模型结果

与之前相同,我们可以指定预测值和残差的输出文件,通过勾选 Preferences 面板中 Output 选项卡下的相应选项。该文件包含 ID 变量、观测因变量和 predy、resid、predy_e、e_predy,与空间滞后模型相似。具体细节请参见第 7 章,在本章中我们不再讨论其他模型的处理方法。

对含有外生和内生解释变量的复合模型执行 GM 估计的结果如图 11.4 所示。这要通过如图 11.2 中 GUI 的设置来完成。仍然要记住 GM 估计中不能勾选 KP HET 选项(该选项在 Preferences 面板中 GMM 选项卡下选择)。

```
REGRESSION
----------
SUMMARY OF OUTPUT: SPATIALLY WEIGHTED TWO STAGE LEAST SQUARES
-----------------------------------------------------------
Data set            :     NAT.dbf
Weights matrix      :File: nat_queen.gal
Dependent Variable  :        HR60          Number of Observations:        3085
Mean dependent var  :      4.5041          Number of Variables   :           7
S.D. dependent var  :      5.6497          Degrees of Freedom    :        3078
Pseudo R-squared    :      0.3328
Spatial Pseudo R-squared:  0.2812
-----------------------------------------------------------------------------
        Variable     Coefficient      Std.Error     z-Statistic     Probability
-----------------------------------------------------------------------------
        CONSTANT      -0.0618162      0.3505032      -0.1763642      0.8600079
           BLK60       0.0703360      0.0108268       6.4964399      0.0000000
            DV60       0.5411868      0.1009337       5.3618036      0.0000001
            PS60       0.0636171      0.0911780       0.6977245      0.4853495
            RD60       0.6903681      0.1485215       4.6482704      0.0000033
            UE60       0.1276860      0.0688647       1.8541563      0.0637168
          W_HR60       0.4818021      0.0610440       7.8926964      0.0000000
          lambda      -0.1901571
-----------------------------------------------------------------------------
Instrumented: UE60, W_HR60
Instruments: FH60, FP59, GI59, W_BLK60, W_DV60, W_FH60, W_FP59, W_GI59,
             W_PS60, W_RD60
============================== END OF REPORT ================================
```

图 11.4　含内生解释变量的 GM 复合模型结果

估计值与外生模型中的值略有不同,但是它们的空间参数极为相似。λ 的估计值为 -0.1902,又是一个负值,且与包含内生解释变量的空间误差模型的度量不相关。ρ 的值为 0.4818,显著性很高,且其绝对值比外生变量模型中的值 (0.4495) 略高。主要的影响还是在 UE60 的估计值上,得到的 p 值为 0.064。空间 Pseudo R-squared 值略小于外生模型,为 0.281(相对于外生模型中的 0.285,纯空间滞后模型中的 0.284)。

总之,似乎空间误差参数的 GM 估计值对纯空间滞后模型的改善并没有意义(尤其是当后者使用 HAC 标准误时)。我们仍要记住 OLS 结果表现出强异方差性。这很重要,因为 GM 估计与异方差性不相符。另外,由于 GM 估计没有提供 λ 估计值的推断,它只能用来进行对照说明。在实际应用中,我们往往更多使用 GMM 估计方法。

11.3 复合模型的 GMM 估计

11.3.1 外生解释变量

复合模型的 GMM 估计是默认方法。如果之前在偏好设置中改为了 GM 估计(即不勾选 Inference on Lambda 选项),则需要重置默认。如果偏好设置没有更改过,则不需要做任何改变。

外生变量模型的估计使用了图 11.1 中的设置。首先,我们来考虑同方差性的情况,结果如图 11.5 所示。要得到这个结果,我们一定不能勾选 GUI 中的 KP HET 选项,这也是默认的设置。

```
REGRESSION
----------
SUMMARY OF OUTPUT: SPATIALLY WEIGHTED TWO STAGE LEAST SQUARES (HOM)
----------
Data set            :       NAT.dbf
Weights matrix      :File: nat_queen.gal
Dependent Variable  :          HR60      Number of Observations:         3085
Mean dependent var  :        4.5041      Number of Variables   :            7
S.D. dependent var  :        5.6497      Degrees of Freedom    :         3078
Pseudo R-squared    :        0.3333
Spatial Pseudo R-squared:    0.2854
N. of iterations    :             1

------------------------------------------------------------------------------
       Variable     Coefficient       Std.Error     z-Statistic     Probability
------------------------------------------------------------------------------
       CONSTANT       0.3239850       0.2364887       1.3699807       0.1706929
          BLK60       0.0709563       0.0103216       6.8745561       0.0000000
           DV60       0.6158838       0.0969425       6.3530825       0.0000000
           PS60       0.1056035       0.0804090       1.3133301       0.1890717
           RD60       0.8086410       0.1364000       5.9284534       0.0000000
           UE60       0.0527400       0.0295573       1.7843270       0.0743705
         W_HR60       0.4495694       0.0652271       6.8923719       0.0000000
         lambda      -0.2729182       0.1021516      -2.6716980       0.0075469
------------------------------------------------------------------------------
Instrumented: W_HR60
Instruments: W_BLK60, W_DV60, W_PS60, W_RD60, W_UE60
================================ END OF REPORT ================================
```

图 11.5 只含外生解释变量的 GMM 复合模型结果(HOM)

相比于 GM 估计,GMM 估计最大的不同在于 λ 估计值的变化。在这里,

其结果为 -0.2729，具有高显著性，$p=0.008$。这个值的绝对值比 GM 估计中的值（-0.1884）大 50%。ρ 估计值的差异没有那么明显，为 0.4496，与 GM 估计中的值（0.4495）几乎相同，且保持高显著性。空间 Pseudo R-squared 值为 0.285，与 GM 估计中得到的值相同。同样，UE60 也不再具有显著性（$p=0.07$）。也就是说，使用 GMM 估计而非 GM 估计的主要影响在于 λ 系数。

最后，我们来考虑勾选 KP HET 选项后的 GMM 估计。在实践中，我们通常选用这种方法，因为横截面数据通常都具有高度的异方差性。如果这种异方差性确实存在，就如 OLS 估计诊断出的结果所示，那么 GM 和同方差 GMM 中的 λ 估计值就会不一致。在图 11.6 的结果中也表现出了这一点。λ 估计值是 -0.4383，与之前的值有很大的不同。该值仍然是负值，且其绝对值是三种方法中最大的。它的显著性仍然很高，$p=0.0000077$。ρ 的估计值为 0.4483，比之前的值略小，但是保持很高的显著性（$p=0.0000000$）。有趣的是，ρ 和 λ 的绝对值几乎是相等的，只是它们的符号相反。空间自回归误差系数的负号表示具有空间异质性，它与之前证明存在异方差性的证据是相容的。在实际应用中，很多情况下都会出现误差系数为负值，而滞后系数为正值且高显著性的现象。在这种情况下，空间滞后模型中的 HAC 方法同样能分析出空间异质性，尽管目前仍然缺乏对这些方法相对属性的深入了解。模型的拟合度不受估计方法的影响，空间 Pseudo R-squared 值仍为 0.2853。系数 UE60 的估计值也保持非显著，$p=0.06$。

11.3.2 外生和内生解释变量

要在包含外生和内生解释变量的复合模型中使用 GMM 估计，我们需要按照图 11.2 中的布局来设置。其中展示的是同方差的情况，标准误默认不勾选 KP HET 选项。其结果如图 11.7 所示。

在外生模型中，GMM 估计方法的主要影响在于 λ 的估计值，它由 GM 中的 -0.1902 变为同方差 GMM 中的 -0.3105。其显著性仍然很高，$p=0.002$。拟合度 Pseudo R-squared 值不变，为 0.281（因此它也小于外生模型中的拟合

```
REGRESSION
----------
SUMMARY OF OUTPUT: SPATIALLY WEIGHTED TWO STAGE LEAST SQUARES (HET)
-------------------------------------------------------------------
Data set            :     NAT.dbf
Weights matrix      :File: nat_queen.gal
Dependent Variable  :        HR60      Number of Observations:     3085
Mean dependent var  :      4.5041      Number of Variables   :        7
S.D. dependent var  :      5.6497      Degrees of Freedom    :     3078
Pseudo R-squared    :      0.3333
Spatial Pseudo R-squared:  0.2853
N. of iterations    :           1      Step1c computed       :       No
-------------------------------------------------------------------

           Variable    Coefficient    Std.Error    z-Statistic    Probability
-------------------------------------------------------------------
           CONSTANT     0.3264431     0.2256289      1.4468142      0.1479490
              BLK60     0.0711234     0.0122398      5.8108400      0.0000000
               DV60     0.6136830     0.1071702      5.7262456      0.0000000
               PS60     0.1064660     0.1016379      1.0475035      0.2948674
               RD60     0.8090534     0.1532549      5.2791348      0.0000001
               UE60     0.0537745     0.0287134      1.8728001      0.0610960
             W_HR60     0.4482870     0.0719587      6.2297823      0.0000000
             lambda    -0.4383045     0.0979689     -4.4739149      0.0000077
-------------------------------------------------------------------
Instrumented: W_HR60
Instruments: W_BLK60, W_DV60, W_PS60, W_RD60, W_UE60
=========================== END OF REPORT =========================
```

图 11.6 只含外生解释变量的 GMM 复合模型结果(HET)

```
REGRESSION
----------
SUMMARY OF OUTPUT: SPATIALLY WEIGHTED TWO STAGE LEAST SQUARES (HOM)
-------------------------------------------------------------------
Data set            :     NAT.dbf
Weights matrix      :File: nat_queen.gal
Dependent Variable  :        HR60      Number of Observations:     3085
Mean dependent var  :      4.5041      Number of Variables   :        7
S.D. dependent var  :      5.6497      Degrees of Freedom    :     3078
Pseudo R-squared    :      0.3328
Spatial Pseudo R-squared:  0.2812
N. of iterations    :           1
-------------------------------------------------------------------

           Variable    Coefficient    Std.Error    z-Statistic    Probability
-------------------------------------------------------------------
           CONSTANT    -0.0617938     0.3188267     -0.1938164      0.8463197
              BLK60     0.0703134     0.0103875      6.7690271      0.0000000
               DV60     0.5412369     0.0977580      5.5365000      0.0000000
               PS60     0.0635952     0.0851447      0.7469065      0.4551200
               RD60     0.6902893     0.1403672      4.9177379      0.0000009
               UE60     0.1275722     0.0631550      2.0199859      0.0433848
             W_HR60     0.4819608     0.0602250      8.0026721      0.0000000
             lambda    -0.3104618     0.0989503     -3.1375537      0.0017036
-------------------------------------------------------------------
Instrumented: UE60, W_HR60
Instruments: FH60, FP59, GI59, W_BLK60, W_DV60, W_FH60, W_FP59, W_GI59,
             W_PS60, W_RD60
=========================== END OF REPORT =========================
```

图 11.7 含内生解释变量的 GMM 复合模型结果(HOM)

度,尽管在严格意义上这两种度量是没有可比性的)。ρ 的估计值为 0.482 0,它本质上未发生改变(相比于 0.481 8),并且保持高显著性($p=0.000\,000\,0$)。有趣的是,系数 UE60 变为了轻微显著,$p=0.04$。

最后一种方法包含异方差,要勾选 GUI 中的 KP HET 选项来完成。若不勾选,则模型的设置就如图 11.2 所示。输出的结果如图 11.8 所示。

```
REGRESSION
----------
SUMMARY OF OUTPUT: SPATIALLY WEIGHTED TWO STAGE LEAST SQUARES (HET)
----------
Data set            :   NAT.dbf
Weights matrix      :File: nat_queen.gal
Dependent Variable  :   HR60         Number of Observations:      3085
Mean dependent var  :   4.5041       Number of Variables   :         7
S.D. dependent var  :   5.6497       Degrees of Freedom    :      3078
Pseudo R-squared    :   0.3328
Spatial Pseudo R-squared: 0.2810
N. of iterations    :   1            Step1c computed       :        No

----------
      Variable     Coefficient     Std.Error     z-Statistic    Probability
----------
      CONSTANT     -0.0622402      0.3447555     -0.1805344     0.8567330
         BLK60      0.0707237      0.0111402      6.3485286     0.0000000
          DV60      0.5402806      0.1044551      5.1723732     0.0000002
          PS60      0.0639946      0.0894662      0.7152939     0.4744275
          RD60      0.6916849      0.1395608      4.9561544     0.0000007
          UE60      0.1296600      0.0692818      1.8714876     0.0612775
        W_HR60      0.4790831      0.0645823      7.4181827     0.0000000
        lambda     -0.4644452      0.0926202     -5.0145115     0.0000005
----------
Instrumented: UE60, W_HR60
Instruments: FH60, FP59, GI59, W_BLK60, W_DV60, W_FH60, W_FP59, W_GI59,
             W_PS60, W_RD60
================================ END OF REPORT ================================
```

图 11.8 含内生解释变量的 GMM 复合模型结果(HET)

我们找到了与外生模型中十分相似的模式,说明异方差性的调整是有必要的。λ 的估计值为 $-0.464\,4$,其绝对值在三种方法中是最大的。它具有很高的显著性($p=0.000\,000\,5$)且绝对值与 ρ 的估计值 0.479 1 大致相等。后者也具有很高的显著性。模型的拟合度 Pseudo R-squared 值不变,为 0.281。而系数 UE60 仍然是非显著的,$p=0.06$。ρ 和 λ 的估计值大致相等,符号相反,意味着公式 $(I-\rho w)^{-1}(I-\lambda w)^{-1}=I+(\rho+\lambda)w+[(\rho+\lambda)^2-\rho\lambda]w^2+\cdots$ 中单位矩阵 I 之后的第一项趋近于零,否定了一阶邻居的影响。二阶邻居的影响($-\lambda\rho$)变为了正值,这是由于系数的符号相反。

与之前相同,考虑内生性的主要影响在于系数 UE60 的估计值,最后也没显示出显著性。同样,负的空间误差自相关也表明了空间异质性,可以在 HAC 标准误的滞后规范中进行处理。

11.3.3 估计值的比较

在表 11.1 中,我们总结了所有相关的估计值和标准误,对所选方法的结果给出了一个最终的概述。对于每个只含外生解释变量和同时包含外生和内生解释变量的模型,我们展示了纯空间滞后模型、纯空间误差模型(含异方差性)和复合模型中三种方法得到的结果。

表 11.1 三种方法估计值的比较

方法	ρ	St. Err.	λ	St. Err.	R^2
外生解释变量					
Lag	0.430 7	0.066 2			0.284
Error-HET			0.378 2	0.031 0	0.274
Combo GM	0.449 5	0.065 2	−0.188 4		0.285
Combo GMM-HOM	0.449 6	0.065 4	−0.272 9	0.102 2	0.285
Combo GMM-HET	0.448 3	0.072 0	−0.438 3	0.098 0	0.285
外生和内生解释变量					
Lag	0.441 2	0.063 1			0.278
Error-HET			0.362 9	0.032 8	0.268
Combo GM	0.481 8	0.061 0	−0.190 2		0.281
Combo GMM-HOM	0.482 0	0.060 2	−0.310 5	0.099 0	0.281
Combo GMM-HET	0.479 1	0.064 6	−0.464 4	0.092 6	0.281

正如之前所提到的,主要的不同在于不同方法的 λ 系数。然而纯空间误差模型的结果是正值,具有显著性,复合模型中的值是负值。复合模型中三种方法的值也有所差异,可能是受到异方差性的影响。由于异方差性,复合 GM 和复合同方差 GMM 方法得到的 λ 估计值是不可信的。系数的负值可能表明它主要捕捉空间异质性。相反,在纯空间误差模型中系数反映的是整体的空间自相关,是正值,而空间异质性可能被异方差性捕捉。

ρ 的估计值在不同的方法中以及在纯空间滞后模型和复合模型之间都很接近。在复合模型中，三种方法的值大体上是相等的，比纯空间滞后模型中的估计值略大。

各种方法对模型系数（表中未列出）的主要影响在于 UE60。其估计值在 OLS 估计的模型中表现出微弱的显著性，在 S2SLS 估计的模型中也表现出一定的显著性。然而，在不同的空间模型之间，p 值在 0.05 处上下波动，没有强有力的证据表明显著性。这也解释了为什么它的结果在外生变量模型和内生变量模型中差别不大。因为内生性归因于 UE60，它缺乏显著性，会限制由内生性引起的有偏效应。

总的来说，复合模型没有表现出很强的优势。这也证实了我们选择模型的总体策略，即选择简单的模型。在很多情况下（包括我们的案例），当原模型中增加了额外的变量，或者重新设置了空间权重时，将不再适合使用复合模型。

特别地，复合模型中 λ 系数在处理时需要格外谨慎。它不一定指向空间溢出的一个有意义的模式，但在某些情况下也能校正剩余空间异质性。在某种程度上，这样的结果是一个精细的模型参数（包括 ρ）的估计，这可能是有益的，但其他影响可以用一个简单的模型来完成，例如 HAC 标准误。

下篇 基于 Python 的空间计量分析库:PySAL

第 12 章　PySAL 软件简介与安装

我们将要讨论的 spreg 模块是 PySAL 软件的一部分功能,它是一个用 Python 语言开发的用于做空间分析的开源跨平台对象库。这个库并没有图形用户界面,所以其用户主要应该是那些习惯于使用命令行界面的程序员。到现在,这个库包含了如下功能:读入及导出数据、创建空间权重对象及对其的操作、空间数据分析、空间动力系统分析、空间回归分析等。我们进行空间计量经济学计算,需要用到 weights 和 spreg 两个模块。

下面我们介绍 PySAL spreg 的下载与安装。PySAL 作为一个 Python 模型,需要按照以下过程进行安装,在接下来的安装与使用过程中,我们假设读者具有一定的 Python 语言基础,可以进行基本 Python 程序的安装与使用。

到目前为止,最简便的安装 PySAL 的方式是从 Continuum Analytics (http://www.continuum.io/)下载基于 Python 开发的完整的软件:Anaconda Distribution。软件里不仅含有 Python、IPython 等,还继承了很多 Python 扩展包,其中就包括 PySAL 及其一系列需要用到的包,如 numpy 与 scipy。这种方法的优点就是简单,但安装的扩展包较多,占用空间较多。使用 Anaconda Distribution 安装 PySAL 时,需通过使用 Conda 更新 PySAL 命令获取 PySAL 的最新版本。

GeoDa 中心软件下载网址(https://spatial.uchicago.edu/software)提供了另外一种安装 PySAL 的方法:

• 从 Python 的包索引(python package index)中下载安装最新官方版本的源代码形成软件包,网址为 https://pypi.python.org/pypi/PySAL。当然,我们也可以在电脑终端通过命令下载 PySAL-1.x.x.tar.gz。

• 我们也可以在 https://sourceforge.net/projects/pysal/files/上下载压

缩的 zip 或者 tar.gz 格式的安装文件。

• 还可以在 GitHub 网站（https://github.com/pysal/pysal）上下载最新版本 PySAL。

• 对于 Windows 用户，可以在 https://sourceforge.net/projects/pysal/files/上下载 PySAL-1.x.x.win32.exe。

安装过程结束后，打开 Python 程序，导入 PySAL 模块，在打开的 Python 程序命令行中输入如下代码：

```
>>> import pysal
>>> pysal.open.check()
```

如果程序安装正确，那么将会出现程序所能支持的文件格式列表，其结果如下所示：

```
PySAL File I/O understands the following file extensions:
Ext: '.shp', Modes: ['r', 'wb', 'w', 'rb']
Ext: '.mtx', Modes: ['r', 'w']
Ext: '.swm', Modes: ['r', 'w']
Ext: '.mat', Modes: ['r', 'w']
Ext: '.shx', Modes: ['r', 'wb', 'w', 'rb']
Ext: '.stata_text', Modes: ['r', 'w']
Ext: '.geoda_txt', Modes: ['r']
Ext: '.dbf', Modes: ['r', 'w']
Ext: '.dat', Modes: ['r', 'w']
Ext: '.gwt', Modes: ['r', 'w']
Ext: '.gal', Modes: ['r', 'w']
Ext: '.arcgis_text', Modes: ['r', 'w']
Ext: '.kwt', Modes: ['r', 'w']
Ext: '.wk1', Modes: ['r', 'w']
Ext: '.arcgis_dbf', Modes: ['r', 'w']
Ext: '.geobugs_text', Modes: ['r', 'w']
Ext: '.csv', Modes: ['rU', 'r', 'U', 'Ur']
```

```
Ext: '.wkt', Modes: ['r']
```

如果程序给出错误信息,例如"module not found",那么需要对 PySAL 的支持程序(numpy、scipy)进行安装或对 Python 程序路径进行调整,使得 Python 程序可以找到安装的 PySAL 模型。具体安装细节可参考 GeoDa 中心的软件安装教程。

第 13 章　PySAL 和 spreg 计算包的基本原理

在使用 PySAL 的回归模型之前,我们需要安装 Python 及相应的支持程序,在 Python 中进行空间回归分析时,所有程序代码通常以导入 numpy 与 pysal 模块为开始,如下所示。

>>> import numpy as np
>>> import scipy

为简单起见,我们在执行的每一个命令之前使用标准的 Python 提示符 ">>>",如果想在交互式环境中使用这些命令,例如 IPython,那么提示符将会发生变化。在接下来的章节中,我们会大致描述 PySAL 的基本逻辑以及进行空间回归分析之前的准备工作。特定的空间回归模型的具体操作详见下文各个章节。

13.1　PySAL spreg 的逻辑原理

为使用 spreg 进行空间计量经济学分析,首先要导入 PySAL 程序包,然后使用 Python 的标准连接符执行回归模型中的特定功能,程序命令行代码如下所示:

>>> model = pysal.moduleName.functionName(arguments and options)

在空间计量经济学分析中,命令行的一般步骤如下所示:

- 导入 numpy;
- 导入 scipy;

- 使用 PySAL FileIO 模型创建一个数据库对象；
- 从数据库对象中导入各个数据变量；
- 将数据变量转换为 numpy 可以识别的向量或者矩阵；
- 调用回归用户类创建回归对象；
- 输出结果或者从回归对象中提取相关属性。

例如，假设因变量已经转换为 numpy 中的数组 y，解释变量已经转换为 numpy 中的数组 x，那么一个基础的 OLS 估计对象就可创建如下：

```
>>> model = pysal.spreg.OLS(y,x)
```

在输入子模块时可以实现对子模块名称的简写，通过这种方式可以避免在命令行中输入全部的模块名称。

此外，读者可以通过使用别名的方式使得函数调用过程中缩短模块的名称符号。例如，一般使用 ps 作为 pysal 的别名，使用 np 作为 numpy 的别名：

```
>>> import numpy as np
>>> import pysal as ps:
```

这样，调用基本的 OLS 估计时，代码变为：

```
>>> model = ps.spreg.OLS(y,x)
```

同理，执行所有的 numpy 的相关命令时，可以使用 np 功能代替 numpy 功能。

在接下来的章节中，更多具体的程序细节与详尽的图例将会逐渐出现，首先，就是要将数据基础文件中的变量转换为 numpy 格式的数组。

13.2 样本数据录入

在 GeoDaSpace 或 GeoDa 这种有用户界面的软件中，所有的操作基本上在后台进行处理，各种模型及算法已经集成在软件中，用户只需要进行软件的操作。而在 PySAL 中，每一个步骤必须非常明确地键入才能够执行。正如在上一节中所描述的那样,这个执行过程包括数据库对象的创建,从数据库中抽取单个变量的数据,然后把单个变量的数据转换为 numpy 数组。

对于初学者来讲,程序代码看上去非常困难,但是每一次回归运算时的代码基本相同,因此用户可以很快地熟悉其中的相关代码。为证明这个过程,我们使用与前面章节中相同的模型进行示范,使用 NAT.dbf 作为基础数据集,HR90 作为因变量,RD90 与 UE90 作为解释变量。

程序的最开始要导入 numpy 与 pysal 模块,根据 Python 的编程习惯,我们使用 np 代替 numpy。

```
>>> import numpy as np
>>> import pysal
```

第一步是使用 PySAL FileIO open 命令打开数据集,创建数据库对象。假设数据集 NAT.dbf 位于当前的工作目录中,数据库对象 db 通过以下方式进行创建:

```
>>> db = pysal.open('NAT.dbf','r')
```

如果数据来自 pysal examples 数据目录,那么数据路径可以表示为以下形式:

```
>>> db = pysal.open(pysal.examples.get_path('NAT.dbf'),'r')
```

在本书接下来的各个章节中一般采用这种方式进行数据的读取。

数据库对象含有许多重要的属性,包括样本的数量(len)、变量的名称列表(header),可以使用标准的 Python 代码来获取这些属性信息。通常情况下,对数据库对象进行头文件信息的检查是非常有必要的,可以避免数据中的输入错误(命令行对输入错误无法修正):

```
>>> len(db)
3085
>>> db.header
[u'NAME', u'STATE_NAME', u'STATE_FIPS', u'CNTY_FIPS', u'FIPS', u'STFIPS',
u'COFIPS', u'FIPSNO', u'SOUTH', u'HR60', u'HR70', u'HR80', u'HR90', u'HC60',
u'HC70', u'HC80', u'HC90', u'PO60', u'PO70', u'PO80', u'PO90', u'RD60',
```

```
u'RD70', u'RD80', u'RD90', u'PS60', u'PS70', u'PS80', u'PS90', u'UE60',
u'UE70', u'UE80', u'UE90', u'DV60', u'DV70', u'DV80', u'DV90', u'MA60',
u'MA70', u'MA80', u'MA90', u'POL60', u'POL70', u'POL80', u'POL90', u'DNL60',
u'DNL70', u'DNL80', u'DNL90', u'MFIL59', u'MFIL69', u'MFIL79', u'MFIL89',
u'FP59', u'FP69', u'FP79', u'FP89', u'BLK60', u'BLK70', u'BLK80', u'BLK90',
u'GI59', u'GI69', u'GI79', u'GI89', u'FH60', u'FH70', u'FH80', u'FH90']
```

第二步是从数据库对象中抽取感兴趣的变量,这个步骤使用到了头文件列表(header list)中的变量名以及 PySAL 中的 by_col 命令,例如因变量 HR90 就可以通过以下代码获取:

```
>>> hr90= db.by_col('HR90')
```

得到的结果是一个 Python 列表,为使其可以在 PySAL 的回归功能中使用,仍需要将其转换为一个 numpy 的数组,为保证数组是 $n\times 1$ 维的,可以使用 numpy 的 reshape 功能将数组转换为合适的维数。同时使用 array 与 reshape 功能,实现列表(list)到数组(array)的转换,代码如下所示:

```
>>> y= np.array(hr90).reshape((len(db),1))
```

为确保数组的维数正确,我们查看数组的 shape 属性:

```
>>> y.shape
(3085, 1)
```

作为 reshape 的替代功能,读者可使用转置(T)功能得到想要维数的数组,具体操作如下所示。

我们用相同的方法处理解释变量 RD90 与 UE90,但现在,我们使用 numpy 中的 array、by_col 以及 T 共同实现,结果如下所示:

```
>>> rd90= np.array([db.by_col('RD90')]).T
>>> rd90.shape
(3085, 1)
>>> ue90= np.array([db.by_col('UE90')]).T
>>> ue90.shape
(3085, 1)
```

最后,所有的解释变量需要合并到同一个数组 x 中,此时可以使用 numpy

中的 hstack 功能：

```
>>> x= np.hstack((rd90,ue90))
>>> x.shape
(3085, 2)
```

当解释变量的数量较多时，使用上一种方法显得非常烦琐，还有另外一种非常有效的方法可以充分利用 Python 中的列表。首先，创建一个所需的解释变量名称的列表，然后，通过这个解释变量名称列表创建所需要的解释变量数组 x。例如，我们创建一个含有 RD90 与 UE90 作为解释变量的名称列表，然后通过如下方式将其转换为具有正确维数的 numpy 数组：

```
>>> x_names= ['RD90','UE90']
>>> x1= np.array([db.by_col(var) for var in x_names]).T
>>> x1.shape
(3085, 2)
```

在程序的第二行中，我们使用到了 Python 的一个循环功能，[db.by_col(var) for var in x_names]，在这个过程中，通过遍历 x_names 中的每一个解释变量名称来获取数据，并同时创建了一个大的完整的解释变量 numpy 数组。这是 Python 中常用的将复杂的解释变量转换为 numpy 数组的方法。

总的来讲，上述全部过程可以通过如下步骤来完成：

```
>>> import numpy as np
>>> import pysal
>>> db = pysal.open(pysal.examples.get_path('NAT.dbf'),'r')
>>> y= np.array([db.by_col('HR90')]).T
>>> x_names= ['RD90','UE90']
>>> x1= np.array([db.by_col(var) for var in x_names]).T
```

此时，numpy 数组 y 与 x 已经准备完成，我们在后面的章节中可以将其输入 spreg 的各种回归模型中去。

第 14 章 PySAL 中的邻接权重矩阵

GeoDaSpace 是 PySAL 打包的产物，它并没有包含 PySAL 模块的所有功能。在命令行环境下，PySAL weights 模块里的各项功能都可以通过调整其各项参数和选项来实现。相比之下，虽然二者建立在相同代码的基础之上，但是 GeoDaSpace 可用的选项被限制在最常用的范围内。

PySAL spreg 模块的回归估计运算是建立在 Python scipy 模块的稀疏矩阵格式基础之上的。在 PySAL 中，有两种不同的空间权重数据结构都被支持为 Python 类，第一种是空间权重对象 w，它主要依靠字典这种数据结构存储点 ID 以及相关的权重；另一种是稀疏空间权重对象 WSP，它依靠 scipy 稀疏数组存储空间权重矩阵。

spreg 中的回归函数会把空间权重对象视作一个参数，在内部把它转化为稀疏数组的形式。为了完善我们的讨论，我们简要介绍这两种不同的数据结构。但是出于实践与应用的考虑，我们主要考察一般的空间权重对象 w。

我们先来讨论这两种不同的承载空间权重对象的数据结构。首先我们应该确保 numpy 和 pysal 模块已经导入：

```
>>> import numpy as py
>>> import pysal
```

14.1 空间权重对象

作为用户，我们很少自己直接手动生成空间权重对象，一般是从 shape 文件生成或者从已有的 gal 文件中读取。但是，一旦生成了空间权重对象，我们就应该准确地理解它的各项属性。在 PySAL 中创建一个空间权重对象实际上就是创建一个字典数据结构。

为了详细地探讨这种数据结构，我们考察一个九宫格，从左上至右下依次编号为 0—8，再添加一个孤立点 9，一共 10 个观测点。我们首先创建 neighbors 字典如下：

>>> neighbors= {0:[3,1],1:[0,4,2],2:[1,5],3:[0,6,4],4:[1,3,7,5],5:[2,4,8],6:[3,7],7:[4,6,8],8:[5,7],9:[]}

上述字典按照方格邻接与否给出了各个观测点邻接点的编号。为了生成一个空间权重对象，完整的命令如下：

>>> w= pysal.W(neighbors,weights= None,id_order= None,silent_island_warning= False)

在这四个参数中，只有 neighbors 字典是强制必须有的参数，其余可选参数为：

- weights：一个字典，它的 key 为观测点的 ID，值是一个包含各个邻接点权重的列表；这里如果给出权重字典，则每个观测点的权重列表需要与之前每个观测点的邻接点 ID 列表顺序保持一致。
- id_order：一个可选的包含观测点 ID 顺序的列表。
- silent_island_warning：孤立点警示是否需要关闭；默认值是 False，即有孤立点警示。

一般情况下，各个邻接点的权重应该相等，均为 1.0，所以上述对列表顺序的要求就显得没有那么必要了。如果没有明确 weights 字典，则默认值为 1.0。id_order 选项对确保权重值和观测点 ID 一一准确对应有着重要作用。因为 Python 的字典数据结构本身是无序的，而其默认的顺序为对字典中的 keys 按字典序排序，在某些时候，这样不指名顺序会导致混乱。一般最稳妥的做法还是要明确 id_order。在实际操作中，这一步一般可以借助调用数据集中本身就有的 ID 来完成。

我们现在举例说明。首先，我们用默认的方法生成一个空间权重对象，只考虑唯一的强制参数 neighbors 字典：

>>> w1= pysal.W(neighbors)
WARNING: there is one disconnected observation (no neighbors)
Island id: [9]

和我们所预料的一样，它生成了一个警示信息，提示我们观测点 9 是没有邻接点的(孤立点)。我们现在考察空间权重对象 $w1$ 的三个最重要的属性：观测点个数 n，空间权重字典 weights，观测点 ID 的顺序列表 id_order。

在我们的案例中：

>>> w1.n
10
>>> w1.weights
{0:[1.0, 1.0], 1:[1.0, 1.0, 1.0], 2:[1.0, 1.0], 3:[1.0, 1.0, 1.0], 4:[1.0, 1.0, 1.0, 1.0], 5:[1.0, 1.0, 1.0], 6:[1.0, 1.0], 7:[1.0, 1.0, 1.0], 8:[1.0, 1.0], 9:[]}
>>> w1.id_order
[0, 1, 2, 3, 4, 5, 6, 7, 8, 9]

我们可以看到，默认的权重是 1.0，它们按照 ID 的字典序排列，与 id_order 是相同的。在这个例子中，恰好和我们创建邻接字典时的键入顺序是相同的，但这只是个巧合，它们二者并无关系。为了说明这个问题，我们换个键入顺序来创建邻接字典：

>>> neighbors1= {9:[],0:[3,1],3:[0,6,4],6:[3,7],1:[0,4,2],4:[1,3,7,5],7:[4,6,8],2:[1,5],5:[2,4,8],8:[5,7]}
>>> w1a= pysal.W(neighbors1)
WARNING: there is one disconnected observation (no neighbors)
Island id: [9]

我们再查看其权重字典会发现它与我们的键入顺序不一致而与之前一样仍成字典序排列：

>>> w1a.weights
{0:[1.0, 1.0], 1:[1.0, 1.0, 1.0], 2:[1.0, 1.0], 3:[1.0, 1.0, 1.0], 4:[1.0,

1.0, 1.0, 1.0], 5:[1.0,1.0,1.0], 6:[1.0,1.0], 7:[1.0,1.0,1.0], 8:[1.0, 1.0], 9:[]}

>>> w1a.id_order

[0, 1, 2, 3, 4, 5, 6, 7, 8, 9]

我们现在尝试自己赋权重,创建一个行标准化的权重字典:

>>> myweights= {0:[0.5,0.5],
    1:[0.3333,0.3333,0.3333],
    2:[0.5,0.5],
    3:[0.3333,0.3333,0.3333],
    4:[0.25,0.25,0.25,0.25],
    5:[0.3333,0.3333,0.3333],
    6:[0.5,0.5],
    7:[0.3333,0.3333,0.3333],
    8:[0.5,0.5],
    9:[]}

利用这个权重字典以及最先创建的邻接字典,我们可以再生成一个新的空间权重对象 $w2$：

>>> w2= pysal.W(neighbors,weights= myweights)

WARNING: there is one disconnected observation (no neighbors)

Island id: [9]

>>> w2.weights

{0: [0.5, 0.5], 1: [0.3333, 0.3333, 0.3333], 2: [0.5, 0.5], 3: [0.3333, 0.3333, 0.3333], 4: [0.25, 0.25, 0.25, 0.25], 5: [0.3333, 0.3333, 0.3333], 6: [0.5, 0.5], 7: [0.3333, 0.3333, 0.3333], 8: [0.5, 0.5], 9: []}

我们再赋予一个列方向的 ID 顺序列表：

>>> order_id= [9,0,3,6,1,4,7,2,5,8]

>>> w3= pysal.W(neighbors,weights= myweights,id_order= order_id)

>>> w3.weights

{0: [0.5, 0.5], 1: [0.3333, 0.3333, 0.3333], 2: [0.5, 0.5], 3: [0.3333, 0.3333, 0.3333], 4: [0.25, 0.25, 0.25, 0.25], 5: [0.3333, 0.3333, 0.3333], 6: [0.5, 0.5],

7: [0.3333, 0.3333, 0.3333], 8: [0.5, 0.5], 9: []}

>>> w3.id_order

[9, 0, 3, 6, 1, 4, 7, 2, 5, 8]

显而易见，权重字典的顺序依然是字典序，而 id_order 的顺序则发生了变化。最后，我们尝试把参数 silent_island_warning 设为 True：

>>> w4= pysal.W(neighbors,weights= myweights,id_order= order_id,silent_island_warning= True)

运行后发现没有警示信息，我们可以查看这个属性：

>>> w4.silent_island_warning

True

我们接下来考察空间权重对象 w 的其他属性，w 共有 37 项不同的属性，其中包括我们之前讨论过的 4 项，其余属性我们在这里简要地按顺序分组讨论，大致分为 4 组：

- 空间权重对象的基本描述；
- 空间权重的统计特征；
- 变形函数；
- 统计检验与回归估计中会用到的辅助变量。

第一部分属性为基本描述（我们利用空间权重对象 $w3$ 作为例子）。

- id2i：一个由观测值 ID 和顺序列表一一对应生成的字典；

>>> w3.id2i

{0: 1, 1: 4, 2: 7, 3: 2, 4: 5, 5: 8, 6: 3, 7: 6, 8: 9, 9: 0}

- id_order_set：用于查看是否赋予顺序列表，默认值是 False；

>>> w3.id_order_set

True

- neighbor_offsets：一个新的邻接字典，其中邻接点的 ID 为 id_order 中的编号；

>>> w3.neighbor_offsets

{0: [2, 4], 1: [1, 5, 7], 2: [4, 8], 3: [1, 3, 5], 4: [4, 2, 6, 8], 5: [7, 5, 9], 6:

[2, 6], 7: [5, 3, 9], 8: [8, 6], 9: []}

- transform：指出当前的权重值类型,默认设置为"O";

>>> w3.transform

'O'

- transformations：一个新字典,其中 key 为 transform,值为相应的权重矩阵(也是一个权重字典);这里会出现以前所有进行过的权重类型变换,方便我们回溯之前的计算结果。

>>> w3.transform= 'B'

>>> w3.transformations

{'B': {0: [1.0, 1.0], 1: [1.0, 1.0, 1.0], 2: [1.0, 1.0], 3: [1.0, 1.0, 1.0],

4: [1.0, 1.0, 1.0, 1.0], 5: [1.0, 1.0, 1.0], 6: [1.0, 1.0],

7: [1.0, 1.0, 1.0], 8: [1.0, 1.0], 9: []},

'O': {0: [0.5, 0.5], 1: [0.3333, 0.3333, 0.3333], 2: [0.5, 0.5],

3: [0.3333, 0.3333, 0.3333], 4: [0.25, 0.25, 0.25, 0.25],

5: [0.3333, 0.3333, 0.3333], 6: [0.5, 0.5], 7: [0.3333, 0.3333, 0.3333],

8: [0.5, 0.5], 9: []}

第二部分属性为空间权重的统计特征。

- asymmetries：一个包含不对称观测点对 ID 的列表,如果 i 与 j 相邻,但是 j 与 i 不相邻,则会出现 $[i,j]$;

>>> w3.asymmetries

[]

- cardinalities：一个包含各个观测点邻接点数的字典;

>>> w3.cardinalities

{0: 2, 1: 3, 2: 2, 3: 3, 4: 4, 5: 3, 6: 2, 7: 3, 8: 2, 9: 0}

- histogram：一个由数对组成的列表,其中数对的第一个数为邻接点数,第二个数为对应的观测点个数;

>>> w3.histogram

[(0, 1), (1, 0), (2, 4), (3, 4), (4, 1)]

- islands：一个孤立点 ID 的列表;

```
>>> w3.islands
[9]
```

- max_neighbors:邻接点个数的最大值;

```
>>> w3.max_neighbors
4
```

- mean_neighbors:邻接点个数的平均值;

```
>>> w3.mean_neighbors
2.3999999999999999
```

- min_neighbors:邻接点个数的最小值,有孤立点自然为 0;

```
>>> w3.min_neighbors
0
```

- nonzero:$n \times n$ 权重矩阵中非 0 位置的数量;

```
>>> w3.nonzero
24
```

- pct_nonzero:权重矩阵中非 0 位置的百分比(不显示百分号);

```
>>> w3.pct_nonzero
24.0
```

- sd:邻接点数的标准误。

```
>>> w3.sd
1.019803902718557
```

第三部分属性为变形函数,它们主要被用来把空间权重对象从一种格式转化为另一种格式。

- asymmetry:用来计算 asymmetries 属性的函数,返回非对称列表,或一个空列表;

```
>>> w3.asymmetry()
[]
```

- full:从空间权重信息创建一个完整的 numpy 数组,其中第一个位置是空间权重矩阵,第二个位置是 id_order 列表;注意,这里的空间权重矩阵的节点顺序是按照 id_order 来排序的,而不是默认的字典序;

```
>>> w3.full()
(array([[ 0.,  0.,  0.,  0.,  0.,  0.,  0.,  0.,  0.,  0.],
        [ 0.,  0.,  1.,  0.,  1.,  0.,  0.,  0.,  0.,  0.],
        [ 0.,  1.,  0.,  1.,  0.,  1.,  0.,  0.,  0.,  0.],
        [ 0.,  0.,  1.,  0.,  0.,  0.,  1.,  0.,  0.,  0.],
        [ 0.,  1.,  0.,  0.,  0.,  1.,  0.,  1.,  0.,  0.],
        [ 0.,  0.,  1.,  0.,  1.,  0.,  1.,  0.,  1.,  0.],
        [ 0.,  0.,  0.,  1.,  0.,  1.,  0.,  0.,  0.,  1.],
        [ 0.,  0.,  0.,  0.,  1.,  0.,  0.,  0.,  1.,  0.],
        [ 0.,  0.,  0.,  0.,  0.,  1.,  0.,  1.,  0.,  1.],
        [ 0.,  0.,  0.,  0.,  0.,  0.,  1.,  0.,  1.,  0.]]),
 [9, 0, 3, 6, 1, 4, 7, 2, 5, 8])
```

如果我们只需要第一项也就是空间权重矩阵的 numpy 数组：

```
>>> w3.full()[0]
array([[ 0.,  0.,  0.,  0.,  0.,  0.,  0.,  0.,  0.,  0.],
       [ 0.,  0.,  1.,  0.,  1.,  0.,  0.,  0.,  0.,  0.],
       [ 0.,  1.,  0.,  1.,  0.,  1.,  0.,  0.,  0.,  0.],
       [ 0.,  0.,  1.,  0.,  0.,  0.,  1.,  0.,  0.,  0.],
       [ 0.,  1.,  0.,  0.,  0.,  1.,  0.,  1.,  0.,  0.],
       [ 0.,  0.,  1.,  0.,  1.,  0.,  1.,  0.,  1.,  0.],
       [ 0.,  0.,  0.,  1.,  0.,  1.,  0.,  0.,  0.,  1.],
       [ 0.,  0.,  0.,  0.,  1.,  0.,  0.,  0.,  1.,  0.],
       [ 0.,  0.,  0.,  0.,  0.,  1.,  0.,  1.,  0.,  1.],
       [ 0.,  0.,  0.,  0.,  0.,  0.,  1.,  0.,  1.,  0.]])
```

- get_transform：一个返回当前权重类型的函数，与 transform 属性类似；

```
>>> w3.get_transform()
'B'
```

- set_transform：一个设置权重类型的函数，与给 transform 属性赋值类似；

```
>>> w3.transform= 'B'
```

```
>>> w3.set_transform("R")
WARNING:  9  is an island (no neighbors)
>>> w3.transform
'R'
```

- sparse：空间权重对象的实质内容，包含空间权重矩阵 numpy 数组，它可以被调用为 numpy 数组，但不是一个稀疏空间权重对象；

```
>>> w3.sparse
<10x10 sparse matrix of type '< type 'numpy.float64'> '
    with 24 stored elements in Compressed Sparse Row format>
```

- towsp：一个把普通空间权重对象转化为稀疏空间权重对象（WSP 类）的函数，返回值不仅是 spicy 那样的稀疏空间权重对象，而且是一个带有各种属性的权重对象。

```
>>> w3.towsp()
<pysal.weights.weights.WSP object at 0x05342BF0>
```

第四部分属性为一些辅助变量，这里列出一些用来进行回归和统计检验的辅助变量，虽然在实际运算中没有必要把它们算出来，但是对教学分析可能会有所帮助。

- diagW2：矩阵 WW 的对角线元素；

```
>>> w3.diagW2
array([ 0., 0.33333333, 0.41666667, 0.33333333, 0.41666667, 0.33333333,
0.41666667, 0.33333333, 0.41666667, 0.33333333])
```

- diagWtW：矩阵 $W'W$ 的对角线元素；

```
>>> w3.diagWtW
array([ 0., 0.22222222, 0.5625, 0.22222222, 0.5625, 0.44444444, 0.5625,
0.22222222, 0.5625, 0.22222222])
```

- diagWtW_WW：矩阵 $W'W+WW$ 的对角线元素；

```
>>> w3.diagWtW_WW
array([ 0., 0.55555556, 0.97916667, 0.55555556, 0.97916667, 0.77777778,
0.97916667, 0.55555556, 0.97916667, 0.55555556])
```

- s0:空间权重矩阵的元素之和(本例中因为观测点 9 是孤立点,那一行元素之和为 0,剩余行为 1,故所有元素之和为 9);

>>> w3.s0

9.0

- trcW2:矩阵 WW 的迹;

>>> w3.trcW2

3.333333333333333

- trcWtW:矩阵 WtW 的迹;

>>> w3.trcWtW

3.583333333333333

- trcWtW_WW:矩阵 $WW+W'W$ 的迹。

>>> w3.trcWtW_WW

6.916666666666667

接下来,我们简要介绍第二种空间权重对象——稀疏空间权重类 WSP。这个空间权重对象一般应用于底层程序,我们通常不需要特定地将其生成。为了完善起见,我们在这里将它的生成与属性作简要讨论。

我们可以用一般空间权重对象 w 的 towsp 属性函数,这里我们再给出一种直接创建 WSP 对象的方法:

>>> ws= pysal.WSP(sparse,id_order= None)

它的两个参数分别为:

- sparse:一个 scipy 稀疏数组格式的矩阵,这是一个强制必须有的参数(赋予 WSP 的稀疏数组可以是任何稀疏格式的 scipy 数组);
- id_order:可选参数,可以附加一个 id_order 列表。

我们仍然使用之前的一般空间权重对象 $w3$ 作为例子来说明:

>>> sparsemat= w3.sparse

>>> sparsemat

< 10x10 sparse matrix of type '< type 'numpy.float64'> '
    with 24 stored elements in Compressed Sparse Row format>

```
>>> sparseW= pysal.weights.WSP(sparsemat,id_order= order_id)
>>> sparseW
<pysal.weights.weights.WSP object at 0x05342A90>
```

当然在实际操作中,我们肯定会选用第一种方法来创建 WSP 对象,即先生成一般空间权重对象,再使用 towsp 函数;而 pysal.weights.WSP2W 函数也可以将 WSP 空间权重对象转化为一般空间权重对象 w。

WSP 对象一共只有四个属性,我们举例说明:

```
>>> sparseW.id_order
[9, 0, 3, 6, 1, 4, 7, 2, 5, 8]
>>> sparseW.n
10
>>> sparseW.s0
9.0
>>> sparseW.trcWtW_WW
6.916666666666667
```

而其余空间权重对象 w 的数十项属性,WSP 对象均不具有,例如:

```
>>> sparseW.transform
Traceback (most recent call last):
  File "< pyshell# 77> ", line 1, in < module>
    sparseW.transform
AttributeError: 'WSP' object has no attribute 'transform'
```

14.2 从 shape 文件生成空间邻接权重对象

基于多边形邻接关系的空间权重对象可以直接由 ESRI shape 文件生成,PySAL 目前支持的权重对象有 Queen 型、Rook 型以及高阶邻接型,下面我们依次讨论。

在 PySAL 中,Queen 邻接权重对象是通过用户函数 queen_from_shapefile

创建的。这个函数唯一的强制参数是 shape 文件的文件名(包括.shp)。如果该文件不在当前运行的目录下,则其路径名称也必须被明确指出。完整的代码为:

>>> w= pysal.queen_from_shapefile(shapefile,idVariable= None,sparse= False)

可选的参数如下:

• idVariable:在一个与 shape 文件相关联的 dbf 文件中,明确多边形区域 ID 的变量;

• sparse:确定是生成一般空间权重对象 w 还是生成稀疏空间权重对象 WSP,默认为 False(生成一般空间权重对象)。

这个函数返回一个一般空间权重对象,如果把 sparse 设为 True,则返回一个稀疏空间权重对象。这两个对象的各项属性我们在前面已经详细讨论。在此我们使用 PySAL 样本数据举例说明:

>>> wq= pysal.queen_from_shapefile(pysal.examples.get_path('NAT.shp'), idVariable= 'FIPSNO')
>>> wq
< pysal.weights.weights.W object at 0x05458B30>

需要注意到,从 shape 文件创建的空间权重对象的权重类型默认为二进制型(只有 0 或者 1),我们在查看 transform 属性时也不能看到,因为类型初始化为'O':

>>> wq.transform
'O'

但是我们可以查看一下权重取值:

>>> wq.weights[27077]
[1.0, 1.0, 1.0]

因此,我们用 shape 文件创建好空间权重对象之后,一定要按照我们自己的需求把权重类型转换为我们需要的类型,一般做行标准化处理:

>>> wq.transform= 'R'

```
>>> wq.weights[27077]
[0.3333333333333333, 0.3333333333333333, 0.3333333333333333]
```

当我们把 sparse 选项设为 True 时，会生成一个稀疏空间权重对象 WSP：

```
>>> wqsparse = pysal.queen_from_shapefile(pysal.examples.get_path
('NAT.shp'),idVariable='FIPSNO',sparse=True)
>>> wqsparse
<pysal.weights.weights.WSP object at 0x025B9290>
```

此时的权重类型依然是二进制型：

```
>>> wqsparse.s0
18168.0
```

当类型是行标准化型时，s0 的值应该为观测点总数，在这里是 3 085：

```
>>> wqsparse.n
3085
```

因为 WSP 对象没有 transform 等用于转化权重类型的属性，我们最好先生成一个 "R" 型的一般空间权重对象，再将其用 towsp 转化为 WSP 对象，这样既方便又准确。

对于 Rook 型空间邻接权重对象，创建它的代码和 Queen 型几乎完全一致，我们在这里给出其完整命令，不做过多赘述：

```
>>> w=pysal.rook_from_shapefile(shapefile,idVariable=None,sparse=
False)
```

14.3 从矩形方格生成空间邻接权重对象

在模拟实验中，我们经常会用到矩形方格或者六边形网格结构，PySAL 提供了直接从矩形方格生成空间邻接权重对象的功能。因为矩形方格结构的观测点及其邻接性质是显而易见的，我们只需要规定其规模大小即可，使用用户函数 lat2w 完成：

```
>>> wgrid= pysal.lat2W(nrows= 5,ncols= 5,rook= True,id_type= 'int')
```

这个函数返回一个一般空间权重对象，如果没有任何参数输入，则会返回一个 5×5 的网格所对应的空间权重对象，即一个 25×25 的空间权重矩阵。它的四个参数及默认值如下：

- nrows：网格中的行数，默认为 5；
- ncols：网格中的列数，默认为 5；
- rook：邻接类型，默认为 True，也就是 Rook 型；
- id_type：观测点 ID 变量的类型，可以是以 0 为开始的整数（'int'），或者是以 0.0 为开始的浮点数（'float'），也可以是以 'id0' 为开始的字符串（'string'）。

我们用这种方式创建本章初给出的九宫格的例子（分别用整数、浮点数和字符串作为观测点 ID）：

首先是整数 ID：

```
>>> w3x3= pysal.lat2W(3,3)
>>> w3x3.weights
{0:[1.0, 1.0], 1:[1.0, 1.0, 1.0], 2:[1.0, 1.0], 3:[1.0, 1.0, 1.0], 4:[1.0, 1.0, 1.0, 1.0], 5:[1.0, 1.0, 1.0], 6:[1.0, 1.0], 7:[1.0, 1.0, 1.0], 8:[1.0, 1.0]}
```

其次是浮点数 ID：

```
>>> w3x3f= pysal.lat2W(3,3,id_type= 'float')
>>> w3x3f.weights
{0.0:[1.0, 1.0], 1.0:[1.0, 1.0, 1.0], 2.0:[1.0, 1.0], 3.0:[1.0, 1.0, 1.0], 4.0:[1.0, 1.0, 1.0, 1.0], 5.0:[1.0, 1.0, 1.0], 6.0:[1.0, 1.0], 7.0:[1.0, 1.0, 1.0], 8.0:[1.0, 1.0]}
```

最后是字符串 ID：

```
>>> w3x3s= pysal.lat2W(3,3,id_type= 'string')
>>> w3x3s.weights
{'id8':[1.0, 1.0], 'id6':[1.0, 1.0], 'id7':[1.0, 1.0, 1.0], 'id4':[1.0, 1.0,
```

1.0, 1.0], 'id5': [1.0, 1.0, 1.0], 'id2': [1.0, 1.0], 'id3': [1.0, 1.0, 1.0], 'id0': [1.0, 1.0], 'id1': [1.0, 1.0, 1.0]}

一个类似的用于生成六边形网格空间权重对象的函数是 PySAL.hexlat2W，读者可以参照软件在线使用手册自行学习使用。

14.4 分块权重

一种特殊的邻接权重是分块权重，也就是把整个区域分成若干个块，在块内部的各个观测点均相邻，而与其所属块之外的观测点均不相邻。在 PySAL 中，利用 regime_weights 函数可以创建这样的空间权重对象：

>>> wreg= pysal.regime_weights(regimes)

其中，只有一个参数 regimes，它是一个列表或者一个 numpy 数组，把每一个观测点对应为一个块。

区分这些块的标识可以是数值型的，也可以是字符型的；可以是某些整数或浮点数，也可以是某些字符串。这样生成的空间权重对象也默认是二进制型的权重值。我们举例说明：

>>> regimes= [1,1,1,1,1,2,2,2,2,2,3,3,3,3,3]
>>> wreg= pysal.regime_weights(regimes)
PendingDepricationWarning: regime_weights will be renamed toblock_weights in PySAL 2.0
>>> wreg.neighbors
{0:[1, 2, 3, 4], 1:[0, 2, 3, 4], 2:[0, 1, 3, 4], 3:[0, 1, 2, 4], 4:[0, 1, 2, 3], 5:[6, 7, 8, 9], 6:[5, 7, 8, 9], 7:[5, 6, 8, 9], 8:[5, 6, 7, 9], 9:[5, 6, 7, 8], 10:[11, 12, 13, 14], 11:[10, 12, 13, 14], 12:[10, 11, 13, 14], 13:[10, 11, 12, 14], 14:[10, 11, 12, 13]}

我们通过 neighbors 字典可以看出，块内均相邻，而块与块之间完全不相邻。

14.5 高阶权重

当我们获得了一般空间权重对象 w 后,也可以非常简单地获得高阶空间权重对象。在 PySAL 中,我们使用 higher_order 函数可以完成创建:

```
>>> w_high= pysal.higher_order(w,k= 2)
```

其中,w 是一个必须参数,它应该是一个已经创建好的一般空间权重对象(不是稀疏空间权重对象 WSP);k 是邻接的阶数,默认值为 2。我们需要注意,这里生成的高阶空间权重对象不会自动地包含低阶空间权重对象,也没有这个参数可以选择,我们需要使用 PySAL 中的 w_union 函数来完成合并,完整命令为:

```
>>> w_combined= pysal.w_union(w1,w2,silent_island_warning= False)
```

其中,第一、第二个参数就是两个一般空间权重对象(非 WSP),可选的参数是孤立点警示。该函数返回一个有二进制型权重值的新的一般空间权重对象,其中邻接点是两个矩阵的并。由此可见,如果我们需要使用高阶空间权重对象,则需要一步一步地把低阶的各个空间权重对象全部生成并且融合,这样才能获得一个完整的高阶空间权重对象。我们拿二阶举例:

```
>>> wq= pysal.queen_from_shapefile(pysal.examples.get_path('NAT.shp'),
idVariable= 'FIPSNO')
```

生成二阶空间权重对象:

```
>>> wq2= pysal.higher_order(wq,k= 2)
```

把一阶和二阶权重对象进行融合:

```
>>> wq2include= pysal.w_union(wq,wq2)
```

我们查看 neighbors 字典的特定值来检查融合结果:

```
>>> wq.neighbors[53019]
[53065, 53047, 53043]
>>> wq2.neighbors[53019]
```

[53073, 53063, 53057, 53025, 53075, 53001, 53051, 53017, 53007]

>>> wq2include.neighbors[53019]

[53025, 53057, 53065, 53063, 53001, 53007, 53073, 53043, 53047, 53017, 53075, 53051]

这样的结果是显而易见的。

14.6 空间滞后变量的生成

在 PySAL 中，我们可以创建空间滞后变量，它是利用 scipy 模块中的稀疏矩阵乘法完成的，这都发生在用户函数 lag_spatial 的底层，其完整命令为：

>>> wy= pysal.lag_spatial(w,y)

其中，两个参数均是强制必须参数，分别为一个 n 维空间权重对象和一个包含 k 个变量的 $n \times k$ 维 numpy 数组。函数返回一个 $n \times k$ 的 numpy 数组。

我们利用第 2 章已经介绍的方法将数据从 dbf 文件中导出为 numpy 数组，并创建一组空间滞后变量：

>>> db = pysal.open(pysal.examples.get_path('NAT.dbf'),'r')

>>> v_names= ['HR60','HR70']

>>> v= np.array([db.by_col(var) for var in v_names]).T

当我们确保之前生成的 wq 空间权重对象是行标准化权重值之后，使用 lag_spatial 函数生成空间滞后变量：

>>> wq.transform

'O'

>>> wq.transform= 'r'

>>> vlag= pysal.lag_spatial(wq,v)

我们可以确认新生成的 numpy 数组的维数是否正确：

>>> vlag.shape

(3085, 2)

我们也可以查看数组最初的几行内容：

```
>>> vlag[:3]
array([[ 0.9486541 ,  0.        ],
       [ 2.50965874,  2.22872694],
       [ 1.39193892,  1.74019933]])
```

第 15 章 PySAL 中的距离权重矩阵

在底层程序中,PySAL 通过一个 numpy 数组中的 (x,y) 坐标创建距离权重,但是若干用户类掩盖了这一点,它们使得 PySAL 可以在 shape 文件上直接执行运算从而生成空间距离权重对象。PySAL 可以运算而生成空间距离权重对象的 shape 文件可以是点文件也可以是多边形文件,可以是投影过的也可以是未经投影的。对于上述各种情况,均分别有各种特定的 PySAL 用户类可以解决。

在本章中,我们只讨论一些距离权重对象特有的属性,对于一些邻接权重对象也有的普遍属性、形式转化、空间滞后变量的构造等问题,希望读者可以自行查阅上一章内容,并推广应用于距离权重对象上即可。

为了更好地演示 PySAL 的这项功能,我们也使用 PySAL 自带的样本数据集 baltim.shp,它是由一些投影点的数据构成的。

最后,我们必须提醒读者注意,虽然距离度量仅仅定义在点与点之间,但是 PySAL 针对多边形文件创建距离权重时定义两个多边形中心之间的距离为两个多边形的距离。这个过程是完全处于底层中的,PySAL 用户完全不需要输入其他更多相关的参数。

15.1 从 shape 文件生成空间距离权重对象

15.1.1 k 最近邻二元权重

一个 k 最近邻空间权重对象是调用用户类 knnW_from_shapefile 来生成

的,这个用户类中唯一的强制参数是一个 shape 文件的路径。完整地调用这个用户类的命令是:

>>> wknn= pysal.knnW_from_shapefile(shapefile,k= 2,p= 2,idVariable= None,radius= None)

其余几个选择性参数是:

- k:最近邻居的个数,默认值是 2;
- p:距离度量的方幂次数,默认值是 2,符合欧几里得距离的定义;
- idVariable:点变量的编号,它必须包含于 dbf 文件并且与 shape 文件一致;
- radius:地球的半径,用于计算两点之间的弧距。

在我们的例子中,我们选取 baltim.shp 为 shape 文件,设置最近邻居个数为 4,并明确 STATION 为点变量的编号,完整的命令为:

>>> wk4= pysal.knnW_from_shapefile(pysal.examples.get_path('baltim.shp'),k= 4,idVariable= 'STATION')

我们可以键入如下命令来检查点的编号、权重的取值以及邻居的编号:

>>> wk4.id_order[:3]

[1, 2, 3]

>>> wk4.weights[1]

[1.0, 1.0, 1.0, 1.0]

>>> wk4.neighbors[1]

[96, 16, 90, 133]

我们一定要注意到这里的权重是 0-1 二进制的,为了能够直接在空间回归中使用,必须进行行标准化:

>>> wk4.transform= 'r'

>>> wk4.weights[1]

[0.25, 0.25, 0.25, 0.25]

如果我们要使用曼哈顿距离度量来获得 4 最近邻二元权重对象,就需要加入额外的参数 $p=1$,如下:

```
>>> wk4m = pysal.knnW_from_shapefile(pysal.examples.get_path
('baltim.shp'),k=4,p=1,idVariable='STATION')
```

我们通过检查 1 点和 2 点的邻居可以发现会有所不同：

```
>>> wk4m.neighbors[1]
[96, 90, 16, 133]
>>> wk4.neighbors[2]
[5, 4, 7, 185]
>>> wk4m.neighbors[2]
[5, 4, 15, 7]
```

这个用户类也可以用来计算以弧距为度量的 k 最近邻二元权重对象，我们稍后进行讨论。

最后，我们应该注意到，如果两个或以上个点与同一个点之间的距离相等，那么这会使得 k 最近邻居的选取出现麻烦。因为 k 一旦确定，则处在边界上的多个距离相等的点就会有一些点不能被选进邻居集合之中，一种解决方案是增大 k 的值，但是这并不总能很令人满意地解决一些问题。在上述出现问题的情况里，一般不建议使用 k 最近邻空间权重对象。

15.1.2 距离范围二元权重

在处理投影点并采取欧几里得距离度量的情况下，生成一个基于距离范围的二元权重矩阵需要经过两个步骤。第一步先要计算一个范围下界，使得每一个点都会有至少一个邻居，也就是要确定每一个点与其最近邻居的距离的最大值；这一步要用到用户类 min_threshold_dist_from_shapefile。第二步需要利用上一步生成的下界值作为一个参数，调用用户类 threshold_binaryW_from_shapefile 真正生成权重对象。

用户类 min_threshold_dist_from_shapefile 只有一个强制参数，也就是 shape 文件的路径，完整的命令为：

```
>>> mdist=pysal.min_threshold_dist_from_shapefile(shapefile,radius=None,p=2)
```

其中两个可选的参数为:
- radius:地球半径,用于计算弧距;
- p:距离度量的方幂次数,默认值为 2,与欧几里得距离度量相符(当 $p=1$ 时为曼哈顿距离),但当 radius 确定时,p 的赋值便不再起作用。

用户类 threshold_binaryW_from_shapefile 有两个强制参数,一个是 shape 文件的路径,另一个是距离下界值,完整的命令为:

```
>>> wd= pysal.threshold_binaryW_from_shapefile(shapefile,threshold,p=
2,idVariable= None,radius= None)
```

其中三个可选的参数为:
- radius:地球半径,用于计算弧距;
- p:距离度量的方幂次数,默认值为 2,与欧几里得距离度量相符(当 $p=1$ 时为曼哈顿距离),但当 radius 确定时,p 的赋值便不再起作用;
- idVariable:点变量的编号,它必须包含于 dbf 文件并且与 shape 文件一致。

我们用 baltim.shp 作为 shape 文件来给出实际例子。第一步的命令如下:

```
>>> mdist= pysal.min_threshold_dist_from_shapefile(pysal.examples.get_
path('baltim.shp'))
>>> print mdist
21.3190056053
```

第二步的命令中利用上面定义的 mdist 对象为距离下界参数,如:

```
>>> wd= pysal.threshold_binaryW_from_shapefile(pysal.examples.get_path
('baltim.shp'),mdist)
WARNING: there is one disconnected observation (no neighbors)
Island id: [101]
>>> wd= pysal.threshold_binaryW_from_shapefile(pysal.examples.get_path
('baltim.shp'),mdist+ 1)
```

这样得到的权重对象包含 0-1 二进制权重值。由于我们没有定义点变量的具体编号,系统默认会用自然数序列编号,从 0 开始,如下:

```
>>> wd
<pysal.weights.Distance.DistanceBand object at 0x05312C90>
>>> wd.n
211
>>> wd.id_order[:3]
[0, 1, 2]
>>> wd.weights[0][:5]
[1, 1, 1, 1, 1]
```

为了加入点变量的具体编号,我们需要在调用用户类时对 idVariable 参数赋值,如:

```
>>> wdid= pysal.threshold_binaryW_from_shapefile(pysal.examples.get_path('baltim.shp'),mdist+ 1,idVariable= "STATION")
```

正如我们所料想的那样,点变量的编号从 1,而不是原来未明确编号时的 0 开始了,与我们赋给点的编号序列相一致:

```
>>> wdid.id_order[:3]
[1, 2, 3]
```

为了使我们生成的权重对象转变成为行标准化形式,我们必须明确地设置其形式属性为"R"型,如下:

```
>>> wdid.transform= 'r'
>>> wdid.weights[1][:5]
[0.018867924528301886, 0.018867924528301886, 0.018867924528301886, 0.018867924528301886, 0.018867924528301886]
```

15.1.3 倒数距离权重

倒数距离权重对象与上述距离范围二元权重对象类似,同样需要通过两个步骤来生成。第一步与上文是相同的,我们需要使得每一个点都会有至少一个邻居,也就是要确定每一个点与其最近邻居的距离的最大值;第二步,我们需要调用用户类 threshold_continuousW_from_shapefile 来生成具体权重对象,该用户类有两个强制参数,其一是 shape 文件的路径,其二是距离下界的值,完整的命令如下：

```
>>> wdinv= pysal.threshold_continuousW_from_shapefile(shapefile,threshold,p= 2,alpha= -1,idVariable= None,radius= None)
```

其中四个可选的参数为：

- radius:地球半径,用于计算弧距；
- p:距离度量的方幂次数,默认值为 2,与欧几里得距离度量相符（当 $p=1$ 时为曼哈顿距离），但当 radius 确定时,p 的赋值便不再起作用；
- idVariable:点变量的编号,它必须包含于 dbf 文件并且与 shape 文件一致；
- alpha:计算相反距离权重值时的方幂次数,默认值为 -1。

我们在例子中仍然运用之前生成的距离下界对象(mdist)为用户类中的参数赋值,同时也将观测点编号赋值为列表 STATION,命令如下：

```
>>> wdinv= pysal.threshold_continuousW_from_shapefile(pysal.examples.get_path('baltim.shp'),mdist+ 1,idVariable= 'STATION')
```

我们目前利用的是默认的 alpha 值(-1),相反距离权重值计算如下：

```
>>> wdinv.weights[1][:3]
[0.057259833431386825, 0.077037121577134535, 0.10101525445522107]
```

我们可以通过对 alpha 赋值的改变来确定任意相反距离权重的方幂,例如我们生成重力权重（二次幂的相反距离权重）,alpha$=-2.0$,命令如下：

```
>>> wdinv2= pysal.threshold_continuousW_from_shapefile(pysal.examples.get_path('baltim.shp'),mdist+ 1,alpha= - 2.0,idVariable= 'STATION')
```

查看权重值的一部分：

```
>>> wdinv2.weights[1][:3]
[0.0032786885245901648, 0.0059347181008902071, 0.01020408163265306]
```

我们容易看到,这些权重值恰好是上面相反距离权重的平方。

15.1.4 弧距

针对投影点（坐标）之间的距离,PySAL 默认使用欧几里得距离度量进行计算。然而,当 shape 文件是由未经投影的点组成的,也就是只有精确到 0.1 的经纬度坐标时,如果继续使用欧几里得距离度量,那就显得很不合适,取而代之的是进行弧距的计算。

在 PySAL 中,这个过程我们只需要对 radius 参数进行赋值就可以了,这个参数的默认值是空缺。这个参数实际上就是给地球半径赋值,因为我们将在圆弧距离计算的过程中用到它。当然,任意的数值都可以被输入,但是有两个推荐大家输入的值,分别是地球赤道处的以英里为单位的半径长和以千米为单位的半径长,这两个值毫无疑问也是近似值,因为地球表面比起标准球面要复杂得多,但是基本上也足够用了。这两个值存储在 PySAL 的常数库中,以英里为单位的是 pysal.cg.RADIUS_EARTH_MILES,以千米为单位的是 pysal.cg.RADIUS_EARTH_KM。

接下来我们举例说明,考虑计算 NAT.dbf 中的最小阈值距离,在这个例子中,点坐标是精确到 0.1 的经纬度坐标,我们调用与之前完全相同的阈值计算用户类,但是给 radius 参数赋以英里为单位的赤道处地球半径的值,命令如下:

```
>>> dist2= pysal.min_threshold_dist_from_shapefile(pysal.examples.get_path('NAT.shp'),radius= pysal.cg.RADIUS_EARTH_MILES)
>>> dist2
90.865247381472884
```

这个结果的单位是英里,为了实用起见,我们并不需要这么多位小数,并且我们看到,这和我们在 GeoDa 和 GeoDaSpace 中的距离范围对话框中算出的值是完全一样的。

15.2 核权重对象的生成

PySAL 对每一个核用户类均可生成可变带宽和固定带宽这两种核权重对象(在 GeoDaSpace 中,只能生成可变带宽的核权重对象),我们涉及的五种核函数在本章第一节中有所介绍,但是其中的 Epanechnikov 核函数在 PySAL 中的代码是 quadratic。空间核权重对象不仅可以从 shape 文件生成,也可以从包含点坐标的 numpy 数组生成,在此我们只介绍前者。

GeoDaSpace 支持生成可变带宽的核权重对象,核函数的带宽取决于我们取点的最近邻居的阶数 k,对于每一个不同的点,带宽恰好是该点到它的 k 阶最近邻居的距离。

我们要生成可变带宽空间核权重对象的用户类,其唯一一个强制性参数是 shape 文件的路径,完整的命令为:

```
>>> wk= pysal.adaptive_kernelW_from_shapefile(shapefile,bandwidths=
None,k= 2,function= "triangular",idVariable= None,radius= None,diagonal=
False)
```

其中可选参数有:

- bandwidths:一个数组,它包含针对每一个点的明确的带宽,如果没有明确指出,那么 k 将会被用来计算每个点的带宽;
- k:最近邻居的阶数,它被用来计算可变带宽,默认值是 2;
- function:五个核函数之一(triangular, uniform, quadratic, quartic, gaussian),其中默认值是 triangular;
- idVariable:点变量的编号,它必须包含于 dbf 文件并且与 shape 文件一致;
- radius:地球半径,用于计算弧距;
- diagonal:用于确定权重矩阵中对角线元素取值的一个选项,其默认值取按照核函数计算出的真实值(diagonal=False);在 HAC 估计中,对角线的值必须是 1.0,我们需要明确赋值为 diagonal=True。

我们仍然以 baltim.shp 这个投影点数据为例,spreg 的 HAC 估计中需要最少的邻居数量大于等于样本数的三次方根,这个数在 GeoDaSpace 中是系统帮忙计算的,但是在 PySAL 中,我们需要自己计算样本数的三次方根(取整),并在用户类的参数设置中自行明确其赋值。当 $n=211$ 时,其三次方根应该至少是 6，k 至少取 6。在这里我们采用默认的核函数（triangular）、欧几里得距离度量并且不对点变量附加编号，具体的命令如下：

>>> kw1= pysal.adaptive_kernelW_from_shapefile(pysal.examples.get_path('baltim.shp'),k= 6)

我们可以查看第一个点的核权重如下：

>>> kw1.weights[0]

[1.0, 0.29289328952412363, 0.12294206839876398, 0.0880073449393135, 0.056907799290817906, 0.007237830111578081, 9.99999900663795e-08]

我们必须清楚地意识到，对于任意数据，用 triangular 核函数生成的核权重矩阵的对角线元素一定是 1，这是由 triangular 函数的特性决定的。当我们选用其他核函数时，不能保证出现同样的情况，比如，我们取 gaussian 核函数：

>>> kw2= pysal.adaptive_kernelW_from_shapefile(pysal.examples.get_path('baltim.shp'),k= 6,function= 'gaussian',idVariable= "STATION")

我们查看第一个观测点的权重值：

>>> kw2.weights[1]

[0.3989422804014327, 0.31069657591175387, 0.2715649773742695, 0.26320980303601943, 0.255725677138998, 0.2437220368780333, 0.2419707487162134]

为了确保我们生成的核权重对象能够用于 HAC 估计，我们需要给参数 diagonal 赋值为 True 以确保生成的核权重对象的对角线元素均为 1.0，命令如下：

>>> kw3= pysal.adaptive_kernelW_from_shapefile(pysal.examples.get_path('baltim.shp'),k= 6,function= 'gaussian',idVariable= "STATION",diagonal= True)

查看第一个点的核权重则有：

>>> kw3.weights[1]

[1.0, 0.31069657591175387, 0.2715649773742695, 0.26320980303601943, 0.255725677138998, 0.2437220368780333, 0.2419707487162134]

与其他生成空间权重对象的用户类一样，如果需要进行弧距的计算，则只需要对参数 radius 进行合理的赋值即可。

用户类 kernelW_from_shapefile 可以生成固定带宽的空间核权重对象,这个固定的带宽则是所有点中与其各自 k 阶最近邻居距离值的最大值。与可变带宽的用户类类似,这个用户类的强制必需参数也只有 shape 文件的路径,完整的命令如下:

>>> kwfix= pysal.kernelW_from_shapefile(shapefile,k= 2,function= "triangular",idVariable= None,fixed= True,radius= None,diagonal= False)

这里唯一需要注意的参数是 fixed,默认值是 True,如果设置为 False,则这个用户类和之前可变带宽空间核权重对象用户类没有任何区别。

我们运用同样的数据库来展示可变带宽和固定带宽的区别,具体命令如下:

>>> kw4= pysal.kernelW_from_shapefile(pysal.examples.get_path('baltim.shp'),k= 6,idVariable= "STATION")

这里使用默认的核函数 triangular。因为固定带宽所用的带宽值是最大 6 阶最近邻居的距离,也就是说,如果某一个点的 6 阶最近邻居的距离非常远,那么这个固定带宽值也会非常大。比如说,第一个点原本在可变带宽空间核权重对象中只有 6 个非 0 权重,现在在固定带宽中却有了 115 个非 0 权重,如下:

>>> len(kw4[1])

115

第 16 章　PySAL spreg 中的普通最小二乘估计

因为 GeoDaSpace 是基于 PySAL 编写的界面化程序,所以在 GeoDaSpace 中可以实现的每一类回归模型、各种不同的估计方法以及各个检验统计量均可以利用 PySAL 中的 spreg 模块通过编程实现。为了在 PySAL 中展示普通最小二乘(OLS)回归过程,首先我们简要回顾基本的准备工作,然后介绍主要的 OLS 回归命令;之后,我们针对不同的检验和不同的强标准误选项进行详细介绍。

16.1　回归运算的准备工作

在开始回归运算之前,首先应该把需要的变量数据从数据库中调出并以可识别、可运算的形式(numpy 数组)录入,这部分命令在之前已经详细地介绍过。在这里,我们利用的样本数据库是 baltim.shp。像之前一样,我们一定要在最初执行 import numpy 和 import pysal 的命令,之后打开样本数据库,从中提取一个因变量和一组解释变量;之后分别将它们转化为 numpy 数组 y 和 x。具体操作如下:

```
>>> import numpy as np
>>> import pysal
>>> db= pysal.open(pysal.examples.get_path("baltim.dbf"),'r')
>>> y_name= "PRICE"
>>> y= np.array([db.by_col(y_name)]).T
```

```
>>> x_names = ['NROOM','NBATH','PATIO','FIREPL','AC','GAR','AGE',
'LOTSZ','SQFT']
>>> x= np.array([db.by_col(var) for var in x_names]).T
```

我们可以运用下面的操作检查数组矩阵的维数：

```
>>> y.shape
(211, 1)
>>> x.shape
(211, 9)
```

为了做空间相关性检验，在这里提前确定一个空间权重对象以便后面调用。我们先从样本数据(baltim.shp)中生成一个 k 邻接权重对象，其中 $k=4$：

```
>>> w= pysal.knnW_from_shapefile(pysal.examples.get_path('baltim.shp'),
k= 4,idVariable= 'STATION')
```

在这里需要注意，PySAL spreg 与前两种界面化软件的不同之处之一是，在这里系统不会自动把邻接权重对象做行标准化处理。事实上，我们必须亲自把刚刚生成的二进制形式的权重对象转化成空间相关性检验可用的行标准化对象。

```
>>> w.transform= 'r'
```

为了可以进行带有 HAC 标准误的回归运算，我们还需要生成一个核权重对象。在这里我们仍然选取与之前相同的样本数据，生成一个以 12 个最近邻居为标准的可变带宽三角核权重对象：

```
>>> kw= pysal.adaptive_kernelW_from_shapefile(pysal.examples.get_path
('baltim.shp'),k= 12,idVariable= 'STATION')
```

至此，我们做好了所有进行 OLS 所必需的准备工作。

16.2 普通最小二乘命令

在 PySAL 中，我们可以在使用用户类进行 OLS 模型回归的同时，进行统计检验。在底层程序中，用户类的命令将调用其他功能或函数进行真正的计算

(在本章最后,我们会给出一些可以看到的底层函数的例子,读者可以查阅源代码及其他相关资料获得更深入的认识)。

spreg.OLS用户类中numpy数组y和x是两个强制参数,其余所有参数均是可选择的;除非我们特别地指定其取值,否则其会按默认的取值来执行运算。一个完整的spreg.OLS命令应该包括如下内容:

```
>>> ols_full= pysal.spreg.OLS(y,x,w= None,robust= None,gwk= None,
    sig2n_k= True,nonspat_diag= True,spat_diag= False,moran= False,
    white_test= False,vm= False,name_y= None,name_x= None,
    name_w= None,name_gwk= None,name_ds= None)
```

可选择参数及其默认值如下:

- w:为了做空间相关性检验的空间权重对象,默认为无权重对象(从而也不做空间相关性检验);

- robust:这个选项决定是否在回归运算中计算强标准误,robust='white'或者robust='hac',默认为无强标准误;

- gwk:为了做有HAC强标准误的回归运算所需要的核权重对象(robust='hac'),默认为无核权重对象(从而也没有HAC强标准误);

- sign2n_k:这个选项决定如何计算残差的方差,默认是用无偏估计方法,用自由度($n-k$,这是默认值sign2n_k=True)来除残差的平方和;当有sign2n_k=False时,应用ML估计方法,用样本数除残差的平方和;这个选项同时也决定是否对怀特标准误用$n/(n-k)$做重新调节(默认是做重新调节);

- nonspat_diag:这个选项决定是否做一些非空间的检验(包括多重共线性、正态性以及异方差性),默认值是True,这些非空间检验是计算的;

- spat_diag:空间相关性检验,默认是没有空间相关性检验,当我们取spat_diag=True时,会进行空间相关性检验,这也意味着我们需要一个空间权重对象w;

- moran:这个选项决定是否进行Moran's I检验(空间自相关性),默认是不进行的,所以为了获得这个统计量我们必须自己明确设定moran=True;

- white_test:这个选项决定是否计算怀特检验(异方差性),默认是不计算的,所以我们为了获得这个统计量必须自己明确设定 white_test=True;
- vm:这个选项决定是否在正常回归结果的输出中附加整个系数方差-协方差矩阵,默认是不附加这个矩阵的(这个矩阵是一定会计算的,选项只是决定是否在结果中直接输出这个矩阵);
- name_y:一个字符串,包含因变量 y 的名称,默认是没有明确的名称;
- name_x:一组字符串变量,包含所有解释变量 x 的名称,用户必须自己确保名称顺序和 x 数组的顺序对应正确,默认是没有明确的名称序列;
- name_w:空间权重对象的名称,默认是无名称;
- name_gwk:核权重对象的名称,默认是没有核权重对象的名称;
- name_ds:数据库的描述,默认是没有数据库的描述。

16.3　普通最小二乘对象

我们执行 spreg.OLS 命令就会生成一个回归对象,这个回归对象包括许多属性,其中包括估计的结果以及各种检验的结果与统计量的值,也包括一些对其他后续运算很有用处的中间结果。我们为了说明 OLS 对象,考虑最基本的回归对象,也就是之前执行的只利用 y 和 x 两个强制参数的对象。

>>> ols1= pysal.spreg.OLS(y,x)

这个操作把 OLS 的计算结果全部附加在了回归对象 ols1 上。我们运用 Python 的 dir 命令来查看这个回归对象 ols1 都有哪些属性:

>>> dir(ols1)

['__class__', '__delattr__', '__dict__', '__doc__', '__format__', '__getattribute__', '__hash__', '__init__', '__module__', '__new__', '__reduce__', '__reduce_ex__', '__repr__', '__setattr__', '__sizeof__', '__str__', '__subclasshook__', '__summary', '__weakref__', '_cache', 'aic', 'ar2', 'betas', 'breusch_pagan', 'f_stat', 'jarque_bera', 'k', 'koenker_bassett', 'logll', 'mean_y', 'mulColli', 'n', 'name_ds', 'name_gwk', 'name_w', 'name_x', 'name_y', 'predy', 'r2', 'robust', 'schwarz', 'sig2', 'sig2ML', 'sig2n', 'sig2n_k', 'std_err', 'std_y', 'summary', 't_stat', 'title', 'u', 'utu', 'vm', 'x', 'xtx', 'xtxi', 'y']

这些属性包括回归对象 ols1 的如下特征,在这里我们省略掉那些已经在上一节介绍过的键入参数:

- n:样本数量;
- k:解释变量的个数,这其中包括一个常数项;
- mean_y:因变量的平均值;
- std_y:因变量的标准误;
- betas:$k \times 1$ 数组,估计的系数;
- std_err:$k \times 1$ 数组,估计的标准误差;
- t_stat:一组数组,每一个估计的系数所对应的 t 统计量和相应的 p 值;
- vm:$k \times k$ 的系数的方差-协方差矩阵;
- u:$n \times 1$ 数组,OLS 的残差;
- predy:$n \times 1$ 数组,预测值(predicted value);
- utu:残差的平方和;
- sig2:无偏估计的残差方差(与 sig2n_k 相同);
- sig2ML:ML 估计的残差方差(与 sig2n 相同);
- r2:R^2;
- ar2:校正过的 R^2;
- f_stat:回归的 F 统计量;
- logll:极大对数似然估计值;
- aic:AIC 准则;
- schwarz:施瓦茨准则;
- mulColli:多重共线性指数;
- jarque_bera:一个字典集,其中包括 Jarque-Bera 检验结果、'jb'统计量、'pvalue'相应的 p 值、'df'自由度;

- breusch_pagan：一个字典集，其中包括 Breusch-Pagan 检验结果、'bp'统计量、'pvalue'相应的 p 值、'df'自由度；
- koenker_bassett：一个字典集，其中包括 Koenker-Bassett 检验结果、'kb'统计量、'pvalue'相应的 p 值、'df'自由度；
- white：一个字典集，其中包括 White 检验结果、'wh'统计量、'pvalue'相应的 p 值、'df'自由度；
- lm_error：一个数组，包括 LM-error 检验结果、统计量与 p 值；
- lm_lag：一个数组，包括 LM-lag 检验结果、统计量与 p 值；
- rlm_error：一个数组，包括强 LM-error 检验结果、统计量与 p 值；
- rlm_lag：一个数组，包括强 LM-lag 检验结果、统计量与 p 值；
- lm_sarma：一个数组，包括 LM-sarma 检验结果、统计量与 p 值；
- moran_res：一个数组，包括 Moran's I 检验结果、统计量与 p 值；
- xtx：一个 $k \times k$ 矩阵，$X'X$；
- xtxi：一个 $k \times k$ 矩阵，$X'X$-1；

以上每一个 OLS 回归对象的属性均可以单独地调用，例如我们可以像下面这样提取估计得到的系数：

```
>>> ols1.betas
array([[ 23.26999634],
       [  0.22249352],
       [  5.64840507],
       [ 10.33587549],
       [ 11.17272765],
       [  7.85416373],
       [  5.40206849]
       [ -0.21345497],
       [  0.09490639],
       [  0.18775621]])
```

需要注意的是，betas 这个对象在内部存储的顺序和我们看到的这个数组的顺序可能有所区别。在内部，betas 的存储顺序是与解释变量数组 x 保持一致的；但是当我们调用这个数组时，这些估计系数是与解释变量的字母表排序相一致的。

逐个单独地提取 OLS 回归对象的属性可能会对一些后续运算有所帮助，但是整体来说它并不是一个实用而方便的做法。属性 summary 提供了一个现成的更实用的方法，它和 GeoDaSpace 类似地以表格方式列出了几乎所有主要的回归结果。我们举例说明，以 ols1 为例，我们执行 print ols1.summary 的操作便可以获得相应的结果，如图 16.1 所示，这里的回归结果与使用 GeoDa 或 GeoDaSpace 所得的结果完全相同。

```
REGRESSION
----------
SUMMARY OF OUTPUT: ORDINARY LEAST SQUARES
-----------------------------------------
Data set            :    unknown
Weights matrix      :       None
Dependent Variable  :    dep_var          Number of Observations:       211
Mean dependent var  :    44.3072          Number of Variables   :        10
S.D. dependent var  :    23.6061          Degrees of Freedom    :       201
R-squared           :     0.6500
Adjusted R-squared  :     0.6343
Sum squared residual:  40960.463          F-statistic           :   41.4718
Sigma-square        :    203.783          Prob(F-statistic)     :  3.24e-41
S.E. of regression  :     14.275          Log likelihood        :  -855.223
Sigma-square ML     :    194.125          Akaike info criterion :  1730.446
S.E of regression ML:    13.9329          Schwarz criterion     :  1763.965

-----------------------------------------------------------------------------
       Variable     Coefficient      Std.Error     t-Statistic     Probability
-----------------------------------------------------------------------------
       CONSTANT     23.2699963      5.2241658       4.4542989       0.0000140
          var_1      0.2224935      1.2279277       0.1811943       0.8563976
          var_2      5.6484051      2.0182820       2.7986204       0.0056318
          var_3     10.3358755      3.1202987       3.3126350       0.0010966
          var_4     11.1727277      2.7323132       4.0891094       0.0000626
          var_5      7.8541637      2.7024343       2.9063292       0.0040671
          var_6      5.4020685      1.9636140       2.7510848       0.0064824
          var_7     -0.2134550      0.0573535      -3.7217456       0.0002568
          var_8      0.0949064      0.0165355       5.7395480       0.0000000
          var_9      0.1877562      0.1890598       0.9931047       0.3218530
-----------------------------------------------------------------------------

REGRESSION DIAGNOSTICS
MULTICOLLINEARITY CONDITION NUMBER          20.609

TEST ON NORMALITY OF ERRORS
TEST                            DF        VALUE          PROB
Jarque-Bera                      2      429.933        0.0000

DIAGNOSTICS FOR HETEROSKEDASTICITY
RANDOM COEFFICIENTS
TEST                            DF        VALUE          PROB
Breusch-Pagan test               9      167.792        0.0000
Koenker-Bassett test             9       39.197        0.0000
================================ END OF REPORT =============================
```

图 16.1　ols1 的标准输出结果图表

图 16.1 中并没有给出解释变量的名称,这样的结果信息含量很低,不利于我们进一步分析回归结果。因此,我们应该养成好习惯,在用 PySAL spreg 做 OLS 回归时,添加上之前所讨论的两个参数 name_y 和 name_x。为了确保我们在生成解释变量数组 x 时的顺序与 name_x 一致,我们最好定义 x_name 变量,用它从样本数据库中提取解释变量数据来生成数组,随后在做 spreg.OLS 回归时,在参数的设置里令 name_y＝y_name 及 name_x＝x_name,即可确保定义的名称变量的准确一致性。类似地,我们一般也会明确数据库以及其他任何使用过或将要使用的空间权重对象的名称,这样会使我们更方便地输出信息含量更高的结果图表。

16.4　OLS 与怀特检验

在默认的 spreg.OLS 命令中,不会计算针对异方差性的怀特检验。为了获得这个统计量,在键入 spreg.OLS 命令时,必须明确地将参数 white_test 设置为 True。像上面所建议的那样,我们给数据库、因变量和解释变量分别都赋予相应的名称,具体命令如下:

> > > ols2= pysal.spreg.OLS(y,x,white_test= True,name_y= y_name,name_x= x_names,name_ds= 'baltim.shp')

> > > print ols2.summary

结果如图 16.2 所示。与之前的结果(图 16.1)进行对比,我们容易看出有两个比较重要的不同之处:第一,针对异方差性的怀特检验的结果在结果输出图表的最下面有所显示;第二,我们得到的对回归系数的估计值现在已经按照解释变量名称的字母表排序排列了,所以数值的顺序与之前结果中的顺序不同。虽然这是一个很小的细节,但是我们一定记得回归对象(如 ols.betas)的这种类似的小特点,从而在单独利用这些对象时避免出错。最后,我们注意到,数据库的名称也出现在了结果输出图表的最上部。

```
REGRESSION
----------
SUMMARY OF OUTPUT: ORDINARY LEAST SQUARES
-----------------------------------------
Data set            :    baltim.shp
Weights matrix      :         None
Dependent Variable  :        PRICE    Number of Observations:         211
Mean dependent var  :      44.3072    Number of Variables   :          10
S.D. dependent var  :      23.6061    Degrees of Freedom    :         201
R-squared           :       0.6500
Adjusted R-squared  :       0.6343
Sum squared residual:    40960.463    F-statistic           :     41.4718
Sigma-square        :      203.783    Prob(F-statistic)     :     3.24e-41
S.E. of regression  :       14.275    Log likelihood        :    -855.223
Sigma-square ML     :      194.125    Akaike info criterion :    1730.446
S.E of regression ML:      13.9329    Schwarz criterion     :    1763.965

      Variable     Coefficient      Std.Error     t-Statistic     Probability
      CONSTANT     23.2699963       5.2241658      4.4542989       0.0000140
         NROOM      0.2224935       1.2279277      0.1811943       0.8563976
         NBATH      5.6484051       2.0182820      2.7986276       0.0056318
         PATIO     10.3358755       3.1202987      3.3124635       0.0010966
        FIREPL     11.1727277       2.7323132      4.0891094       0.0000626
            AC      7.8541637       2.7024343      2.9063292       0.0040671
           GAR      5.4020685       1.9636140      2.7510848       0.0064824
           AGE     -0.2134550       0.0573535     -3.7217456       0.0002568
         LOTSZ      0.0949064       0.0165355      5.7395064       0.0000000
          SQFT      0.1877562       0.1890598      0.9931047       0.3218530

REGRESSION DIAGNOSTICS
MULTICOLLINEARITY CONDITION NUMBER     20.609
TEST ON NORMALITY OF ERRORS
TEST                      DF         VALUE           PROB
Jarque-Bera                2       429.933         0.0000

DIAGNOSTICS FOR HETEROSKEDASTICITY
RANDOM COEFFICIENTS
TEST                      DF         VALUE           PROB
Breusch-Pagan test         9       167.792         0.0000
Koenker-Bassett test       9        39.197         0.0000

SPECIFICATION ROBUST TEST
TEST                      DF         VALUE           PROB
White                     51       164.335         0.0000
================================ END OF REPORT =====================================
```

图 16.2 ols2 的标准结果输出图表

16.5 OLS 与空间相关性检验

通过设置不同的 spreg.OLS 回归命令的参数,我们可以获得空间相关性的检验结果。我们需要改变 spat_diag 为 True,明确地给出一个空间权重对象 w(名称为 name_w),并且如果需要的话,把 moran 参数也设置为 True。在下面的例子中,我们这样设置参数:

```
>>> ols3= pysal.spreg.OLS(y,x,w= w,spat_diag= True,moran= True,name_y= y
_name,name_x= x_names,name_w= 'baltim_k4',name_ds= 'baltim.shp')
```

```
>>> print ols3.summary
```

结果如图 16.3 所示。

```
REGRESSION
----------
SUMMARY OF OUTPUT: ORDINARY LEAST SQUARES
-----------------------------------------
Data set            :   baltim.shp
Weights matrix      :   baltim_k4
Dependent Variable  :        PRICE    Number of Observations :      211
Mean dependent var  :      44.3072    Number of Variables    :       10
S.D. dependent var  :      23.6061    Degrees of Freedom     :      201
R-squared           :       0.6500
Adjusted R-squared  :       0.6343
Sum squared residual:    40960.463    F-statistic            :  41.4718
Sigma-square        :      203.783    Prob(F-statistic)      : 3.24e-41
S.E. of regression  :       14.275    Log likelihood         : -855.223
Sigma-square ML     :      194.125    Akaike info criterion  : 1730.446
S.E of regression ML:      13.9329    Schwarz criterion      : 1763.965

----------------------------------------------------------------------
     Variable     Coefficient      Std.Error     t-Statistic  Probability
----------------------------------------------------------------------
     CONSTANT     23.2699963       5.2241658      4.4542989    0.0000140
        NROOM      0.2224935       1.2279277      0.1811943    0.8563976
        NBATH      5.6484051       2.0182820      2.7986204    0.0056318
        PATIO     10.3358755       3.1202987      3.3124635    0.0010966
       FIREPL     11.1727277       2.7323132      4.0891094    0.0000626
           AC      7.8541637       2.7024343      2.9063292    0.0040671
          GAR      5.4020685       1.9636140      2.7510848    0.0064824
          AGE     -0.2134550       0.0573535     -3.7217456    0.0002568
        LOTSZ      0.0949064       0.0165355      5.7395480    0.0000000
         SQFT      0.1877562       0.1890598      0.9931047    0.3218530
----------------------------------------------------------------------

REGRESSION DIAGNOSTICS
MULTICOLLINEARITY CONDITION NUMBER         20.609

TEST ON NORMALITY OF ERRORS
TEST                              DF       VALUE            PROB
Jarque-Bera                        2     429.933           0.0000

DIAGNOSTICS FOR HETEROSKEDASTICITY
RANDOM COEFFICIENTS
TEST                              DF       VALUE            PROB
Breusch-Pagan test                 9     167.792           0.0000
Koenker-Bassett test               9      39.197           0.0000

DIAGNOSTICS FOR SPATIAL DEPENDENCE
TEST                            MI/DF      VALUE            PROB
Moran's I (error)               0.1073      2.648          0.0081
Lagrange Multiplier (lag)          1       30.912          0.0000
Robust LM (lag)                    1       28.466          0.0000
Lagrange Multiplier (error)        1        5.442          0.0197
Robust LM (error)                  1        2.996          0.0835
Lagrange Multiplier (SARMA)        2       33.908          0.0000

================================ END OF REPORT ================================
```

图 16.3　ols3 的标准结果输出图表

16.6　OLS 与怀特标准误

如果要获得对回归标准误的在异方差条件下的强估计,那么我们需要把参

数 robust 从默认值重新明确设置为非默认值'white'。在下面的例子中,我们这样设置参数:

```
>>> ols4= pysal.spreg.OLS(y,x,robust= 'white',name_y= y_name,name_x= x_names,name_ds= 'baltim.shp')
>>> print ols4.summary
```

回归结果会给出一组新的标准误差,以及其相应的 t 统计量和 p 值,如图 16.4 所示。

```
REGRESSION
----------
SUMMARY OF OUTPUT: ORDINARY LEAST SQUARES
-----------------------------------------
Data set             :    baltim.shp
Weights matrix       :          None
Dependent Variable   :         PRICE    Number of Observations:       211
Mean dependent var   :       44.3072    Number of Variables   :        10
S.D. dependent var   :       23.6061    Degrees of Freedom    :       201
R-squared            :        0.6500
Adjusted R-squared   :        0.6343
Sum squared residual:      40960.463    F-statistic           :   41.4718
Sigma-square         :       203.783    Prob(F-statistic)     :  3.24e-41
S.E. of regression   :        14.275    Log likelihood        :  -855.223
Sigma-square ML      :       194.125    Akaike info criterion :  1730.446
S.E of regression ML:         13.9329   Schwarz criterion     :  1763.965

White Standard Errors
------------------------------------------------------------------------
       Variable      Coefficient      Std.Error     t-Statistic   Probability
------------------------------------------------------------------------
       CONSTANT      23.2699963       6.5488415      3.5532997     0.0004741
          NROOM       0.2224935       1.3934904      0.1596663     0.8733042
          NBATH       5.6484051       2.4995696      2.2597511     0.0249092
          PATIO      10.3358755       4.1978783      2.4621665     0.0146520
         FIREPL      11.1727277       3.0235003      3.6952957     0.0002831
             AC       7.8541637       3.1147472      2.5216055     0.0124581
            GAR       5.4020685       3.2537312      1.6602688     0.0984196
            AGE      -0.2134550       0.1082717     -1.9714745     0.0500417
          LOTSZ       0.0949064       0.0260489      3.6433902     0.0003425
           SQFT       0.1877562       0.2099744      0.8941860     0.3722918
------------------------------------------------------------------------

REGRESSION DIAGNOSTICS
MULTICOLLINEARITY CONDITION NUMBER           20.609

TEST ON NORMALITY OF ERRORS
TEST                         DF        VALUE           PROB
Jarque-Bera                   2       429.933          0.0000

DIAGNOSTICS FOR HETEROSKEDASTICITY
RANDOM COEFFICIENTS
TEST                         DF        VALUE           PROB
Breusch-Pagan test            9       167.792          0.0000
Koenker-Bassett test          9        39.197          0.0000
================================ END OF REPORT =========================
```

图 16.4 ols4 的标准结果输出图表

我们为了获得未重新调节的怀特标准误,需要把参数 sig2n_k 重新设置为 False(因为默认值为 True,并且做重新调节):

>>> ols5= pysal.spreg.OLS(y,x,robust= 'white',sig2n_k= False,name_y= y_name,name_x= x_names,name_ds= 'baltim.shp')

>>> print ols5.summary

这样我们就获得了第二种怀特标准误的估计结果,如图 16.5 所示。

```
REGRESSION
----------
SUMMARY OF OUTPUT: ORDINARY LEAST SQUARES
-----------------------------------------
Data set            :      baltim.shp
Weights matrix      :            None
Dependent Variable  :           PRICE    Number of Observations:         211
Mean dependent var  :         44.3072    Number of Variables    :          10
S.D. dependent var  :         23.6061    Degrees of Freedom     :         201
R-squared           :          0.6500
Adjusted R-squared  :          0.6343
Sum squared residual:       40960.463    F-statistic            :     41.4718
Sigma-square        :         194.125    Prob(F-statistic)      :    3.24e-41
S.E. of regression  :          13.933    Log likelihood         :    -855.223
Sigma-square ML     :         194.125    Akaike info criterion  :    1730.446
S.E of regression ML:         13.9329    Schwarz criterion      :    1763.965

White Standard Errors
------------------------------------------------------------------------------
       Variable     Coefficient       Std.Error     t-Statistic     Probability
------------------------------------------------------------------------------
       CONSTANT      23.2699963       6.3917721       3.6406174       0.0003459
          NROOM       0.2224935       1.3600685       0.1635899       0.8702183
          NBATH       5.6484051       2.4396191       2.3152815       0.0216067
          PATIO      10.3358755       4.0971951       2.5226710       0.0124216
         FIREPL      11.1727277       2.9509837       3.7861028       0.0002020
             AC       7.8541637       3.0400421       2.5835707       0.0104876
            GAR       5.4020685       3.1756927       1.7010678       0.0904767
            AGE      -0.2134506       0.1056749      -2.0199209       0.0447190
          LOTSZ       0.0949064       0.0254242       3.7329217       0.0002464
           SQFT       0.1877562       0.2049383       0.9161595       0.3606811
------------------------------------------------------------------------------

REGRESSION DIAGNOSTICS
MULTICOLLINEARITY CONDITION NUMBER           20.609

TEST ON NORMALITY OF ERRORS
TEST                       DF        VALUE           PROB
Jarque-Bera                 2       429.933         0.0000

DIAGNOSTICS FOR HETEROSKEDASTICITY
RANDOM COEFFICIENTS
TEST                       DF        VALUE           PROB
Breusch-Pagan test          9       167.792         0.0000
Koenker-Bassett test        9        39.197         0.0000
================================ END OF REPORT ================================
```

图 16.5　ols5 的标准结果输出图表

16.7 OLS 与 HAC 标准误

与上节类似，为了获得 HAC 标准误的估计结果，我们需要把参数 robust 设置为 'hac'，并且需要明确地给定一个核权重对象 gwk（并在 name_gwk 处附有名称，如命名为 baltim_tri_k12）。完整的命令如下：

>>> ols6= pysal.spreg.OLS(y,x,robust= 'hac',gwk= kw,name_y= y_name,name_x= x_names,name_gwk= 'baltim_tri_k12',name_ds= 'baltim.shp')

>>> print ols6.summary

结果如图 16.6 所示。

```
REGRESSION
----------
SUMMARY OF OUTPUT: ORDINARY LEAST SQUARES
-----------------------------------------
Data set            :   baltim.shp
Weights matrix      :         None
Dependent Variable  :        PRICE    Number of Observations:         211
Mean dependent var  :      44.3072    Number of Variables   :          10
S.D. dependent var  :      23.6061    Degrees of Freedom    :         201
R-squared           :       0.6500
Adjusted R-squared  :       0.6343
Sum squared residual:    40960.463    F-statistic           :     41.4718
Sigma-square        :      203.783    Prob(F-statistic)     :     3.24e-41
S.E. of regression  :       14.275    Log likelihood        :    -855.223
Sigma-square ML     :      194.125    Akaike info criterion :    1730.446
S.E of regression ML:      13.9329    Schwarz criterion     :    1763.965

HAC Standard Errors; Kernel Weights: baltim_tri_k12
----------------------------------------------------------------------
       Variable    Coefficient      Std.Error    t-Statistic   Probability
----------------------------------------------------------------------
       CONSTANT     23.2699963      6.7557589      3.4444682     0.0006964
          NROOM      0.2224935      1.3841624      0.1607424     0.8724578
          NBATH      5.6484051      2.4853389      2.2726901     0.0241027
          PATIO     10.3358755      4.4904057      2.3017687     0.0223729
         FIREPL     11.1727277      2.9682469      3.7640830     0.0002194
             AC      7.8541637      3.2786034      2.3955822     0.0175113
            GAR      5.4020685      3.5732508      1.5118078     0.1321534
            AGE     -0.2134550      0.1067463     -1.9996471     0.0468849
          LOTSZ      0.0949064      0.0251785      3.7693418     0.0002151
           SQFT      0.1877562      0.1867878      1.0051843     0.3160167
----------------------------------------------------------------------

REGRESSION DIAGNOSTICS
MULTICOLLINEARITY CONDITION NUMBER        20.609
TEST ON NORMALITY OF ERRORS
TEST                          DF        VALUE          PROB
Jarque-Bera                    2       429.933        0.0000

DIAGNOSTICS FOR HETEROSKEDASTICITY
RANDOM COEFFICIENTS
TEST                          DF        VALUE          PROB
Breusch-Pagan test             9       167.792        0.0000
Koenker-Bassett test           9        39.197        0.0000
========================= END OF REPORT ==============================
```

图 16.6 ols6 的标准结果输出图表

16.8 单独获取底层函数

正如最初所介绍的那样,在 PySAL 中,我们使用的用户类包含多个函数以及类,正是这些函数和类执行完成了我们需要的估计和各种各样的检验任务。这些函数可以被单独获取,以便我们进行一些后续的模拟实验。这些用户类的调用方式基本类似:给这个用户类一个(可能带有一些非基本参数的)回归对象,它会运算并返回相应的结果,结果也是一个对象(一般是一个数组或者字典)。

我们来尝试调用空间相关性检验用户类,单独地用这个用户类来对一个回归对象进行空间相关性的检验。这个用户类是 diagnostics_sp.LMtests,它有两个参数:一个是回归对象,另一个是空间权重对象。具体执行方式如下:

>>> vw= pysal.spreg.diagnostics_sp.LMtests(ols1,w)

这个结果对象(vw)包括五个属性:lme,lml,rlme,rlml 及 sarma;每一个属性均是一个数组,包括相应的统计量大小和 p 值。如检验空间误差自相关性的 LM_λ 统计量就可以被提取,如下:

>>> vw.lme

(5.2825246195980231, 0.0215404925054027877)

而空间滞后统计量 LM_ρ 也可以被提取:

>>> vw.lml

(31.407013776711235, 2.0922374390102738e-08)

我们会发现,这里给出的结果都是非常精确的,这是 Python 的默认精确度,我们可以运用 python formatting 命令进行调整。

第 17 章 PySAL spreg 中的两阶段最小二乘估计

类似于上一章中介绍普通最小二乘(OLS)的顺序,本章先概述所需的准备工作,再结合具体的例子加以详细说明。与上一章不同的是,我们会在命令参数中直接明确地附上因变量和解释变量的名称以及对数据库的描述。

17.1 回归运算的准备工作

与 OLS 一样,最初我们还是要先输入 numpy 和 pysal 两个模块,从数据库中提取变量并转化为 numpy 数组,同时依照需要生成空间权重对象和核权重对象。其主要不同在于,我们需要把解释变量中的外生变量、内生变量和工具变量分别生成为 numpy 数组而不是简单的 y 和 x。

我们使用 NAT.dbf 这个 pysal 样本数据作为例子。在这个例子中,因变量 y 是 HR90,外生解释变量 x 是 RD90、MA90、PS90,内生解释变量 yend 是 UE90,工具变量 q 是 FH90、FP89、GI89。我们使用一阶 Queen 邻接权重矩阵作为空间权重对象,以基于最近的 20 个邻居生成的可变带宽的三角核权重矩阵为空间核权重对象。像之前一样,我们用如下系列命令完成回归前的准备工作。

输入模块打开数据库:

```
>>> import numpy as np
>>> import pysal
>>> db= pysal.open(pysal.examples.get_path('NAT.dbf'),'r')
```

因变量(y)：

```
>>> y_name='HR90'
>>> y= np.array([db.by_col(y_name)]).T
```

外生解释变量(x)：

```
>>> x_names=['RD90','MA90','PS90']
>>> x= np.array([db.by_col(var) for var in x_names]).T
```

内生解释变量(yend)：

```
>>> yend_names=['UE90']
>>> yend= np.array([db.by_col(var) for var in yend_names]).T
```

工具变量(q)：

```
>>> q_names=['FH90','FP89','GI89']
>>> q= np.array([db.by_col(var) for var in q_names]).T
```

为了空间相关性检验而创建的空间权重对象：

```
>>> w= pysal.queen_from_shapefile(pysal.examples.get_path('NAT.shp'), idVariable="FIPSNO")
>>> w.transform= 'r'
```

核权重对象：

```
>>> kw= pysal.adaptive_kernelW_from_shapefile(pysal.examples.get_path('NAT.shp'), k = 20, radius = pysal.cg.RADIUS_EARTH_MILES, idVariable = 'FIPSNO')
```

17.2 两阶段最小二乘命令

为了完成两阶段最小二乘回归(2SLS)，spreg设计有一个类似于OLS的用户类：spreg.TSLS。它的强制参数包括numpy数组y,x, yend和q，也就是因变量、外生解释变量、内生解释变量和工具变量。其他参数都是选择性设置的，当我们没有明确设置时，均取默认值。下面是一个完整的包括所有参数的

spreg.TSLS 命令：

>>> twosls_full= pysal.spreg.TSLS(y,x,yend,q,w= None,robust= None,gwk= None,sig2n_k= False,spat_diag= False,vm= False,name_y= None,name_x= None,name_yend= None,name_q= None,name_w= None,name_gwk= None,name_ds= None)

选择性设置的参数及其默认值如下：

- w：为了做空间相关性检验的空间权重对象，默认为无权重对象（从而也不做空间相关性检验）；
- robust：这个选项决定是否在回归运算中计算强标准误，robust='white'或者robust='hac'，默认为无强标准误；
- gwk：为了做有 HAC 强标准误的回归运算所需要的核权重对象（robust='hac'），默认为无核权重对象（从而也没有 HAC 强标准误）；
- sign2n_k：这个选项决定如何计算残差的方差，与 OLS 不同的是，这里默认是一致估计方法，用样本数来除残差的平方和（sign2n_k=False）；
- spat_diag：空间相关性检验，默认是没有空间相关性检验，当我们取 spat_diag=True 时，会进行空间相关性检验，这也意味着我们需要一个空间权重对象 w；
- vm：这个选项决定是否在正常回归结果的输出中附加整个系数方差-协方差矩阵，默认是不附加这个矩阵的（这个矩阵是一定会计算的，选项只是决定是否在结果中直接输出这个矩阵）；
- name_y：一个字符串，包含因变量 y 的名称，默认是没有明确的名称；
- name_x：一组字符串变量，包含所有解释变量 x 的名称，用户必须自己确保名称顺序和 x 数组的顺序对应正确，默认是没有明确的名称序列；
- name_yend：一组字符串变量，包含所有内生解释变量 yend 的名称，用户必须自己确保名称顺序和 yend 数组的顺序对应正确，默认是没有明确的名称序列；
- name_q：一组字符串变量，包含所有工具变量 q 的名称，用户必须自己

确保名称顺序和 q 数组的顺序对应正确,默认是没有明确的名称序列;
- name_w:空间权重对象的名称,默认是无名称;
- name_gwk:核权重对象的名称,默认是没有核权重对象的名称;
- name_ds:数据库的描述,默认是没有数据库的描述。

17.3 两阶段最小二乘对象

一个 spreg.TSLS 命令就会生成一个回归对象,和 OLS 一样,这个回归对象包括大量属性,其中包括估计的结果以及各种检验的结果与统计量的值,也包括一些可用于其他计算的中间结果。为了清晰明了地解释这个对象,我们用之前创建好的 y,x,yend 和 q 来创建一个最基本的回归对象。因为我们之前提取数据转换成 numpy 数组的时候已经写好了 y_name,x_names,yend_names,q_names 这几个字符串组,我们不妨在参数中就加上它们,以提高我们输出结果的信息含量。

>>> reg1= pysal.spreg.TSLS(y,x,yend,q,name_y= y_name,name_x= x_names, name_yend= yend_names,name_q= q_names,name_ds= "NAT.dbf")

这个命令把所有的回归运算及可能的统计检验结果全部附加给了 reg1 这个回归对象,成为 reg1 的属性,利用 Python 中我们已经很熟悉的 dir 命令来查看 reg1 的所有属性:

>>> dir(reg1)
['_doc_', '_init_', '_module_', '_summary', '_cache', 'betas', 'h', 'hth', 'hthi', 'htz', 'k', 'kstar', 'mean_y', 'n', 'name_ds', 'name_gwk', 'name_h', 'name_q', 'name_w', 'name_x', 'name_y', 'name_yend', 'name_z', 'pfora1a2', 'pr2', 'predy', 'q', 'robust', 'sig2', 'sig2n', 'sig2n_k', 'std_err', 'std_y', 'summary', 'title', 'u', 'utu', 'varb', 'vm', 'x', 'y', 'yend', 'z', 'z_stat', 'zthhthi']

大部分属性都和 OLS 回归对象中的属性含义相同。在此我们着重指出那

些与 OLS 回归对象不同的属性,这其中不包括我们键入命令时输入的参数:
- k:所有被估计的参数总个数,包括常数项,也包括内生变量;
- kstar:内生变量的个数;
- z:$n \times k$ 数组,解释变量的样本数据数组,包括内生变量和外生变量;
- h:$n \times h$ 数组,工具变量的样本数据数组,包括外生变量和工具变量;
- pr2:伪 R^2;
- z_stat:类似于 OLS 中的 t_stat,是一个数组表,包括 z 统计量的值和相应的 p 值;
- ak_test:一个数组,包括 Anselin-Kelejian 检验的统计量值和相应的 p 值;
- name_z:一个列表,包括所有外生变量和内生变量的名称;
- name_h:一个列表,包括所有工具变量的名称,其中包括所有外生变量和工具变量;
- hth:$h \times h$ 数组,H'H;
- hthi:$h \times h$ 数组,H'H-1;
- varb:$k \times k$ 数组,Z'H(H'H)-1H'Z;
- zthhthi:$k \times h$ 数组,Z'H(H'H)-1。

与之前的情况相同,回归对象的每一个属性均可以被单独地调用。例如,系数的估计值数组包含于属性 betas 中,我们这样调用:

```
>>> reg1.betas
array([[ 15.64555155],
       [  5.72924882],
       [ -0.09837584],
       [  1.8770506 ],
       [ -0.91445539]])
```

我们仍然需要注意,betas 中对估计系数的排序方式和 x 数组中的变量顺序是一致的,与标准结果图表中输出的以变量名称字母表排序为顺序的系数不同。

与 OLS 相似,为了实用与方便,我们可以通过 print(打印)回归对象,即 summary(print reg1.summary)得到一个标准结果输出图表,如图 17.1 所示。

```
REGRESSION
----------
SUMMARY OF OUTPUT: TWO STAGE LEAST SQUARES
------------------------------------------
Data set            :      NAT.dbf
Weights matrix      :         None
Dependent Variable  :         HR90      Number of Observations:        3085
Mean dependent var  :       6.1829      Number of Variables   :           5
S.D. dependent var  :       6.6414      Degrees of Freedom    :        3080
Pseudo R-squared    :       0.3570

------------------------------------------------------------------------------------
        Variable     Coefficient       Std.Error     z-Statistic     Probability
------------------------------------------------------------------------------------
        CONSTANT      15.6455516       1.3545018      11.5507796       0.0000000
            RD90       5.7292488       0.2129126      26.9089171       0.0000000
            MA90      -0.0983758       0.0299492      -3.2847583       0.0010207
            PS90       1.8770506       0.1070934      17.5272273       0.0000000
            UE90      -0.9144554       0.0986831      -9.2665854       0.0000000

Instrumented: UE90
Instruments: FH90, FP89, GI89
=============================== END OF REPORT =======================================
```

图 17.1   reg1 的标准结果输出图表

17.4 两阶段最小二乘的两个阶段

正如上文所介绍的那样,2SLS 可以由两个 OLS 回归得到。为了清楚地说明这个关系,我们首先用外生解释变量(x)和工具变量(q)合成的大的解释变量数组(bigx)来回归内生解释变量(yend);然后,我们用上一步回归的预测值来代替内生解释变量,把它和外生解释变量合成新的解释变量数组用(newx)来回归因变量(y)。

为了完成第一步,我们需要把 x 和 q 合成一个新的解释变量数组(bigx),创建这个数组需要用到 np.hstack 命令:

```
>>> bigx= np.hstack((x,q))
```

然后,我们用 bigx 数组来对 yend 做第一次 OLS 回归,并提取这一次回归

的预测值为 $y2$：

> > > step1= pysal.spreg.OLS(yend,bigx)

> > > y2= step1.predy

至此，我们还需要把 $y2$ 与 x 合并成新的解释变量数组（newx）：

> > > newx= np.hstack((x,y2))

最后，我们用 newx 来回归 y 完成第二次 OLS 回归：

> > > step2= pysal.spreg.OLS(y,newx)

我们键入命令 print step2.summary 获得最终结果，如图 17.2 所示。我们首先可以看到，按上述两步骤得到的对系数的估计与之前的结果一致，但是标准误、t 统计量和 p 值会有一些不同。

```
REGRESSION
----------
SUMMARY OF OUTPUT: ORDINARY LEAST SQUARES
-----------------------------------------
Data set            :       unknown
Weights matrix      :          None
Dependent Variable  :       dep_var    Number of Observations:     3085
Mean dependent var  :        6.1829    Number of Variables   :        5
S.D. dependent var  :        6.6414    Degrees of Freedom    :     3080
R-squared           :        0.4027
Adjusted R-squared  :        0.4019
Sum squared residual:      81252.812   F-statistic           :   519.1009
Sigma-square        :       26.381    Prob(F-statistic)      :         0
S.E. of regression  :        5.136    Log likelihood         :  -9422.964
Sigma-square ML     :       26.338    Akaike info criterion  :  18855.928
S.E of regression ML:       5.1321    Schwarz criterion      :  18886.100

      Variable     Coefficient      Std.Error     t-Statistic    Probability
------------------------------------------------------------------------
      CONSTANT     15.6455516       1.2962099     12.0702300      0.0000000
         var_1     5.7292488        0.2037498     28.1190386      0.0000000
         var_2    -0.0983758        0.0286603     -3.4324773      0.0006060
         var_3     1.8770506        0.1024846     18.3154447      0.0000000
         var_4    -0.9144554        0.0944362     -9.6833132      0.0000000
------------------------------------------------------------------------

REGRESSION DIAGNOSTICS
MULTICOLLINEARITY CONDITION NUMBER          30.224

TEST ON NORMALITY OF ERRORS
TEST                          DF        VALUE           PROB
Jarque-Bera                    2      56513.324        0.0000

DIAGNOSTICS FOR HETEROSKEDASTICITY
RANDOM COEFFICIENTS
TEST                          DF        VALUE           PROB
Breusch-Pagan test             4       1350.019        0.0000
Koenker-Bassett test           4        120.991        0.0000
============================== END OF REPORT ==============================
```

图 17.2 step2 的标准结果输出图表

这是因为上述第二步中对残差、方差的估计方法并不是准确的 2SLS 对残差、方差的估计方法，如果要得到正确的估计，则需要在第二步 OLS 回归计算其预测值时使用最初的解释变量的取值而不是第一步的结果。

17.5　2SLS 与空间相关性检验

我们要获得 Anselin-Kelejian 检验的结果必须明确地给定一个空间权重对象(w)，并在输入命令时对 spat_diag 赋值为 True，最好给权重对象也附加一个名称。我们做空间相关性检验的完整命令如下：

```
>>> reg2=pysal.spreg.TSLS(y,x,yend,q,w=w,spat_diag=True,name_y=y_name,name_x=x_names,name_yend=yend_names,name_q=q_names,name_ds="NAT.dbf",name_w="NAT_queen.gal")
>>> print reg2.summary
```

结果如图 17.3 所示。

17.6　2SLS 与怀特标准误

如果要获得对回归标准误的在异方差条件下的强估计，那么我们需要把参数 robust 从默认值重新明确设置为非默认值'white'，如下：

```
>>> reg3=pysal.spreg.TSLS(y,x,yend,q,robust="white",name_y=y_name,name_x=x_names,name_yend=yend_names,name_q=q_names,name_ds="NAT.dbf")
>>> print reg3.summary
```

结果如图 17.4 所示。

```
REGRESSION
----------
SUMMARY OF OUTPUT: TWO STAGE LEAST SQUARES
------------------------------------------
Data set            :   NAT.dbf
Weights matrix      :   NAT_queen.gal
Dependent Variable  :   HR90            Number of Observations:   3085
Mean dependent var  :   6.1829          Number of Variables   :      5
S.D. dependent var  :   6.6414          Degrees of Freedom    :   3080
Pseudo R-squared    :   0.3570

-----------------------------------------------------------------------
        Variable     Coefficient    Std.Error     z-Statistic    Probability
-----------------------------------------------------------------------
        CONSTANT     15.6455516     1.3545018     11.5507796     0.0000000
           RD90       5.7292488     0.2129126     26.9089171     0.0000000
           MA90      -0.0983758     0.0299492     -3.2847583     0.0010207
           PS90       1.8770506     0.1070934     17.5272273     0.0000000
           UE90      -0.9144554     0.0986831     -9.2665854     0.0000000
-----------------------------------------------------------------------
Instrumented: UE90
Instruments: FH90, FP89, GI89

DIAGNOSTICS FOR SPATIAL DEPENDENCE
TEST                        MI/DF       VALUE         PROB
Anselin-Kelejian Test         1        124.415       0.0000
============================= END OF REPORT =============================
```

图 17.3　reg2 的标准结果输出图表

```
REGRESSION
----------
SUMMARY OF OUTPUT: TWO STAGE LEAST SQUARES
------------------------------------------
Data set            :   NAT.dbf
Weights matrix      :   None
Dependent Variable  :   HR90            Number of Observations:   3085
Mean dependent var  :   6.1829          Number of Variables   :      5
S.D. dependent var  :   6.6414          Degrees of Freedom    :   3080
Pseudo R-squared    :   0.3570

White Standard Errors
-----------------------------------------------------------------------
        Variable     Coefficient    Std.Error     z-Statistic    Probability
-----------------------------------------------------------------------
        CONSTANT     15.6455516     1.5393092     10.1640082     0.0000000
           RD90       5.7292488     0.3053397     18.7635242     0.0000000
           MA90      -0.0983758     0.0316213     -3.1110577     0.0018642
           PS90       1.8770506     0.1688432     11.1171261     0.0000000
           UE90      -0.9144554     0.1384631     -6.6043272     0.0000000
-----------------------------------------------------------------------
Instrumented: UE90
Instruments: FH90, FP89, GI89
============================= END OF REPORT =============================
```

图 17.4　reg3 的标准结果输出图表

17.7　2SLS 与 HAC 标准误

与上节类似，为了获得 HAC 标准误的估计结果，我们需要把参数 robust 设置为'hac'，并且需要明确地给定一个核权重对象 gwk。我们利用已经定义好的空间核权重对象 kw，键入完整的命令如下：

```
>>> reg4= pysal.spreg.TSLS(y,x,yend,q,robust= "hac",gwk= kw,name_y= y_name,name_x= x_names,name_yend= yend_names,name_q= q_names,name_gwk= "nat_k20_triang.kwt",name_ds= "NAT.dbf")
>>> print reg4.summary
```

结果如图 17.5 所示。

```
REGRESSION
----------
SUMMARY OF OUTPUT: TWO STAGE LEAST SQUARES
------------------------------------------
Data set            :       NAT.dbf
Weights matrix      :          None
Dependent Variable  :          HR90    Number of Observations:       3085
Mean dependent var  :        6.1829   Number of Variables   :          5
S.D. dependent var  :        6.6414   Degrees of Freedom    :       3080
Pseudo R-squared    :        0.3570

HAC Standard Errors; Kernel Weights: nat_k20_triang.kwt
-------------------------------------------------------------------------
       Variable     Coefficient       Std.Error     z-Statistic    Probability
-------------------------------------------------------------------------
       CONSTANT      15.6455516       1.6405678      9.5366688      0.0000000
           RD90       5.7292488       0.3304847     17.3358973      0.0000000
           MA90      -0.0983758       0.0341965     -2.8767776      0.0040176
           PS90       1.8770506       0.1982054      9.4702289      0.0000000
           UE90      -0.9144554       0.1429221     -6.3982775      0.0000000
-------------------------------------------------------------------------
Instrumented: UE90
Instruments:  FH90, FP89, GI89
================================ END OF REPORT =========================================
```

图 17.5　reg4 的标准结果输出图表

第 18 章 PySAL spreg 中的空间滞后模型的空间两阶段最小二乘估计

与之前章节类似,我们在这里先简要介绍做空间两阶段最小二乘(S2SLS)回归运算的准备工作,之后用一些例子来说明这一模型的诸多可变选项。我们使用 baltim.dbf 作为无内生性的空间滞后模型的样本数据库,以 NAT.dbf 为有内生性的空间滞后模型的样本数据库。我们在本章例子中选取使用的变量与在 GeoDaSpace 中所选取的完全相同。

18.1 回归运算的准备工作

由于我们选取的因变量、解释变量、空间权重对象以及空间核权重对象都和第 16 章中 OLS 回归模型的例子完全相同,因此建立因变量 numpy 数组、解释变量 numpy 数组等命令也是完全一致的,请读者参见第 16 章的准备工作,在此不再重复。

在完成类似 OLS 的准备工作后,我们应该有一个因变量 numpy 数组 y、一个解释变量 numpy 数组 x、一个空间权重对象 w 和一个空间核权重对象 kw12。同时,我们还应该有一个因变量字符串列表 y_name、一个解释变量字符串列表 x_names、一个空间权重对象名称 name_w=baltim_k4 和数据库描述 name_ds=baltim。

18.2 GM_Lag 命令

我们用来估计空间滞后模型的 PySAL 用户类是一个 S2SLS 回归用户类 spreg.GM_Lag,它的强制必需参数包括因变量 numpy 数组 y 和解释变量 numpy 数组 x 以及一个空间权重对象 w。一个完整的 spreg.GM_Lag 命令如下:

```
>>> s2sls_full= pysal.spreg.GM_Lag(y,x,yend= None,q= None,
    w= w,w_lags= 1,lag_q= True,spat_diag= False,robust= None,
    gwk= None,sig2n_k= False,vm= False,name_y= None,name_x= None,
    name_yend= None,name_q= None,name_w= None,
    name_gwk= None,name_ds= None)
```

其他可选参数及其默认值为:
- yend:内生解释变量数组(如果存在,则 q 也成为强制必需参数),默认是 None;
- q:工具变量数组(当 yend 存在时,它是强制必需参数),默认是 None;
- w:空间权重对象;
- w_lags:在创建空间滞后解释变量(WX)作为工具变量时,所取的邻接权重矩阵的阶数,默认值是 1,也就是取 WX(若赋值为 2,则取 WX 与 W2X 为工具变量);
- lag_q:是一个决定空间滞后解释变量(Wq)是否包含于整体的工具变量 q 中的选项,默认是 True,也就是包含;
- robust:这个选项决定是否在回归运算中计算强标准误,robust = 'white'或者 robust='hac',默认是无强标准误;
- gwk:为了做有 HAC 强标准误的回归运算所需要的核权重对象(robust='hac'),默认是无核权重对象(从而也没有 HAC 强标准误);

- sign2n_k：这个选项决定如何计算残差的方差；与 2SLS 类似，默认是用一致估计方法，用样本数来除残差的平方和（sign2n_k=False）；
- spat_diag：空间相关性检验，默认是没有空间相关性检验，当我们取 spat_diag=True 时，会进行空间相关性检验，这也意味着我们需要一个空间权重对象 w；
- vm：这个选项决定是否在正常回归结果的输出中附加整个系数方差-协方差矩阵，默认是不附加这个矩阵的（这个矩阵是一定会计算的，选项只是决定是否在结果中直接输出这个矩阵）；
- name_y：一个字符串，包含因变量 y 的名称，默认是没有明确的名称；
- name_x：一组字符串变量，包含所有解释变量 x 的名称，用户必须自己确保名称顺序和 x 数组的顺序对应正确，默认是没有明确的名称序列；
- name_yend：一组字符串变量，包含所有内生解释变量 yend 的名称，用户必须自己确保名称顺序和 yend 数组的顺序对应正确，默认是没有明确的名称序列；
- name_q：一组字符串变量，包含所有工具变量 q 的名称，用户必须自己确保名称顺序和 q 数组的顺序对应正确，默认是没有明确的名称序列；
- name_w：空间权重对象的名称，默认是无名称；
- name_gwk：核权重对象的名称，默认是没有核权重对象的名称；
- name_ds：数据库的描述，默认是没有数据库的描述。

18.3 GM_Lag 对象

与其他回归模型一样，spreg.GM_Lag 命令会运算生成一个回归对象。这个对象具有包括估计结果、标准误在内的许多属性，这其中也包括一些对后续计算或有帮助的中间结果。

同样地，我们在这里用最简单的命令生成一个回归对象：利用最开始所做的准备工作,y 和 x 分别为因变量和解释变量,一阶邻接权重对象 w 为空间权重对象,除对变量、权重对象、数据库附加名称外(这样方便与 GeoDaSpace 中的结果进行对照),其他参数均取默认值。上述参数和第 16 章进行 OLS 回归时所用的是同一组数据,相应的命令如下:

```
>>> reg1= pysal.spreg.GM_Lag(y,x,w= w,name_y= y_name,name_x= x_names,
name_w= 'baltim_k4',name_ds= 'baltim')
```

这个过程把计算的结果全部附加给了 reg1 这个回归对象,我们可以用 Python 的 dir 命令来查看其中的内容:

```
>>> dir(reg1)
['_class_', '_delattr_', '_dict_', '_dir_', '_doc_', '_eq_', '_format_',
'_ge_', '_getattribute_', '_gt_', '_hash_', '_init_', '_init_subclass_',
'_le_', '_lt_', '_module_', '_ne_', '_new_', '_reduce_', '_reduce_ex_',
'_repr_', '_setattr_', '_sizeof_', '_str_', '_subclasshook_', '_summary',
'_weakref_', '_cache', 'betas', 'e_pred', 'h', 'hth', 'hthi', 'htz', 'k',
'kstar', 'mean_y', 'n', 'name_ds', 'name_gwk', 'name_h', 'name_q', 'name_w',
'name_x', 'name_y', 'name_yend', 'name_z', 'pfora1a2', 'pr2', 'pr2_e',
'predy', 'predy_e', 'q', 'rho', 'robust', 'sig2', 'sig2n', 'sig2n_k',
'std_err', 'std_y', 'summary', 'title', 'u', 'utu', 'varb', 'vm', 'x', 'y',
'yend', 'z', 'z_stat', 'zthhthi']
```

大部分 spreg.GM_Lag 回归对象的属性和 OLS 是类似的,和 2SLS 更为相似。在这里只简要介绍那些不同之处:

- betas:一个 $k\times 1$ 的数组,包括回归运算对系数的估计值,空间自相关系数是它的最后一项,也就是 betas[-1];
- e_pred:一个 $n\times 1$ 的数组,它是由公式 $[\hat{e}=y-\hat{y}=y-(I-\hat{\rho}W)^{-1}X\hat{\beta}]$ 计算得到的残差值,它与一般标准方法 $[e=y-(\hat{\rho}Wy+X\hat{\beta})]$ 计算得来的残差 u 有一定的区别;
- predy_e:一个 $n\times 1$ 的数组,它是由公式 $[(I-\hat{\rho}W)^{-1}X\hat{\beta}]$ 计算得到的预测值,与之相对的是 predy,其预测值按照公式 $(\hat{\rho}Wy+X\hat{\beta})$ 计算得到;

- pr2：由 y 和上述 predy 计算得到的伪 R^2；
- pr2_e：由 y 和上述 predy_e 计算得到的伪 R^2。

类似地，上述所有的属性均可以被单独地提取应用，例如我们提取系数估计数组 betas 如下：

```
>>> reg1.betas
array([[ 1.32765782],
       [ 0.88946746],
       [ 5.60361648],
       [ 7.07098446],
       [ 7.15528549],
       [ 6.47909448],
       [ 3.67515267],
       [-0.09426859],
       [ 0.0674761 ],
       [ 0.07505512],
       [ 0.47805226]])
```

大部分结果依然包含在回归对象的 summary 属性中，我们通过 print reg1.summary 命令来获得一个如图 18.1 所示的标准结果图表。像之前反复强调的那样，标准结果图表中估计系数的排序和 betas 属性中的排序并不一致（前者按照名称的字母表排序，而后者按照 x_names 列表本身的顺序排序）。

在 GeoDaSpace 中，我们通过在 Preference 面板中调整空间滞后模型解释变量所采用的空间邻接矩阵阶数（w_lags），而在 spreg 中，这个参数正如我们之前所提到的，默认值为 1。我们为了获得更高阶或称之为更准确的回归结果，可以更改 w_lags 参数。例如，我们更改 w_lags 参数的赋值为 2，命令为：

```
>>> reg2= pysal.spreg.GM_Lag(y,x,w= w,w_lags= 2,name_y= y_name,name_x= x_names,name_w= 'baltim_k4',name_ds= 'baltim')
```

这个回归对象的标准结果图表如图 18.2 所示；类似地，当我们更改 w_lags 参数的赋值为 3 时，我们也可以得到如图 18.3 所示的结果图表。

```
REGRESSION
----------
SUMMARY OF OUTPUT: SPATIAL TWO STAGE LEAST SQUARES
--------------------------------------------------
Data set            :      baltim
Weights matrix      :      baltim_k4
Dependent Variable  :      PRICE        Number of Observations :    211
Mean dependent var  :     44.3072       Number of Variables    :     11
S.D. dependent var  :     23.6061       Degrees of Freedom     :    200
Pseudo R-squared    :      0.7064
Spatial Pseudo R-squared:  0.6856

------------------------------------------------------------------------
     Variable       Coefficient     Std.Error     z-Statistic   Probability
------------------------------------------------------------------------
     CONSTANT        1.3276578      5.7718694     0.2300222     0.8180746
        NROOM        0.8894675      1.1026083     0.8066940     0.4198428
        NBATH        5.6036165      1.8043761     3.1055700     0.0018991
        PATIO        7.0709845      2.8348494     2.4943069     0.0126203
       FIREPL        7.1552855      2.5203968     2.8389519     0.0045262
           AC        6.4790945      2.4253311     2.6714268     0.0075530
          GAR        3.6751527      1.7756639     2.0697344     0.0384772
          AGE       -0.0942686      0.0544832    -1.7302327     0.0835887
        LOTSZ        0.0674761      0.0153788     4.3875982     0.0000115
         SQFT        0.0750551      0.1699164     0.4417178     0.6586934
      W_PRICE        0.4780523      0.0738868     6.4700639     0.0000000
------------------------------------------------------------------------
Instrumented: W_PRICE
Instruments: W_AC, W_AGE, W_FIREPL, W_GAR, W_LOTSZ, W_NBATH, W_NROOM,
             W_PATIO, W_SQFT
================================ END OF REPORT =========================
```

图 18.1 reg1 的标准结果输出图表

现在从实践出发,重新回顾一下之前对某个解释变量对因变量的直接、非直接和总体影响的讨论。我们利用这个例子来展示回归对象是如何被运用以获得新的更进一步的结果的(这些结果很可能不在 GeoDaSpace 和 PySAL spreg 自动生成的结果图表中)。

一个解释变量的变化对因变量直接、非直接以及总体的影响,并没有出现在 S2SLS 回归的标准结果中。但是我们通过对 spreg.GM_Lag 回归对象的 betas 属性略加应用,便可以自行计算出它。我们从 reg1 的 betas 数组出发,可以获得除空间自回归系数 rho 之外的系数估计值(它是 betas 的一个子向量,只是不包括其最后一项):

```
REGRESSION
----------
SUMMARY OF OUTPUT: SPATIAL TWO STAGE LEAST SQUARES
--------------------------------------------------
Data set            :     baltim
Weights matrix      :     baltim_k4
Dependent Variable  :        PRICE                Number of Observations:         211
Mean dependent var  :      44.3072                Number of Variables    :          11
S.D. dependent var  :      23.6061                Degrees of Freedom     :         200
Pseudo R-squared    :       0.7061
Spatial Pseudo R-squared:   0.6845

------------------------------------------------------------------------------------
       Variable     Coefficient       Std.Error     z-Statistic     Probability
------------------------------------------------------------------------------------
       CONSTANT       0.8965615       5.7234031       0.1566483       0.8755220
          NROOM       0.9025714       1.1030756       0.8182316       0.4132249
          NBATH       5.6027365       1.8055518       3.1030605       0.0019153
          PATIO       7.0068398       2.8343528       2.4721128       0.0134317
         FIREPL       7.0763557       2.5180454       2.8102574       0.0049502
             AC       6.4520788       2.4264263       2.6590871       0.0078353
            GAR       3.6412243       1.7757744       2.0504994       0.0403157
            AGE      -0.0919270       0.0543559      -1.6912033       0.0907980
          LOTSZ       0.0669372       0.0153583       4.3583650       0.0000131
           SQFT       0.0728409       0.1699806       0.4285248       0.6682691
        W_PRICE       0.4874444       0.0719813       6.7718234       0.0000000
------------------------------------------------------------------------------------
Instrumented: W_PRICE
Instruments: W2_AC, W2_AGE, W2_FIREPL, W2_GAR, W2_LOTSZ, W2_NBATH, W2_NROOM,
             W2_PATIO, W2_SQFT, W_AC, W_AGE, W_FIREPL, W_GAR, W_LOTSZ,
             W_NBATH, W_NROOM, W_PATIO, W_SQFT
================================ END OF REPORT =====================================
```

图 18.2　reg2 的标准结果输出图表

```
REGRESSION
----------
SUMMARY OF OUTPUT: SPATIAL TWO STAGE LEAST SQUARES
--------------------------------------------------
Data set            :     baltim
Weights matrix      :     baltim_k4
Dependent Variable  :        PRICE                Number of Observations:         211
Mean dependent var  :      44.3072                Number of Variables    :          11
S.D. dependent var  :      23.6061                Degrees of Freedom     :         200
Pseudo R-squared    :       0.7063
Spatial Pseudo R-squared:   0.6852

------------------------------------------------------------------------------------
       Variable     Coefficient       Std.Error     z-Statistic     Probability
------------------------------------------------------------------------------------
       CONSTANT       1.1925852       5.6945102       0.2094272       0.8341148
          NROOM       0.8935732       1.1024449       0.8105378       0.4176312
          NBATH       5.6033408       1.8047248       3.1048173       0.0019040
          PATIO       7.0508864       2.8318830       2.4898226       0.0127807
         FIREPL       7.1305549       2.5148945       2.8353296       0.0045778
             AC       6.4706298       2.4250725       2.6682212       0.0076254
            GAR       3.6645221       1.7744380       2.0651734       0.0389066
            AGE      -0.0935349       0.0542496      -1.7241593       0.0846791
          LOTSZ       0.0673072       0.0153360       4.3888340       0.0000114
           SQFT       0.0743614       0.1698795       0.4377300       0.6615820
        W_PRICE       0.4809951       0.0709521       6.7791488       0.0000000
------------------------------------------------------------------------------------
Instrumented: W_PRICE
Instruments: W2_AC, W2_AGE, W2_FIREPL, W2_GAR, W2_LOTSZ, W2_NBATH, W2_NROOM,
             W2_PATIO, W2_SQFT, W3_AC, W3_AGE, W3_FIREPL, W3_GAR, W3_LOTSZ,
             W3_NBATH, W3_NROOM, W3_PATIO, W3_SQFT, W_AC, W_AGE, W_FIREPL,
             W_GAR, W_LOTSZ, W_NBATH, W_NROOM, W_PATIO, W_SQFT
================================ END OF REPORT =====================================
```

图 18.3　w_lags＝3 时的标准结果输出图表

```
>>> b= reg1.betas[:-1]
```

我们再提取出空间自回归系数 rho：

```
>>> rho= reg1.betas[-1]
```

参照我们之前讨论的结果，一个解释变量的变化会对因变量造成的总体影响是 $\hat{\beta}/(1-\rho)$，我们用一个 numpy 数组来表示这个计算结果：

```
>>> btot= b/(1.0-rho)
```

从而，我们得出非直接影响是：

```
>>> bind= btot-b
```

我们通过 Python 的 for 循环语句来创建一个图表以更好地展示这个计算结果。首先，我们创建一个完整的变量名称列表，它需要整合常数项（'constant'）和 x_names 列表：

```
>>> varnames= ['constant']+ x_names
```

对于 varnames 中的每一个元素，我们将会循环调出并按预定格式打印出数组 b，bind，btot 中相对应的元素：

```
>>> print ('Variable Direct Indirect Total')
>>> for i in range(len(varnames)):
        print ('% 10s % 12.7f % 12.7f % 12.7f' %
        (varnames[i],b[i][0],bind[i][0],btot[i][0]))
```

结果如图 18.4 所示。

```
Variable      Direct      Indirect       Total
constant     1.3276578    1.2160026     2.5436604
   NROOM     0.8894675    0.8146638     1.7041313
   NBATH     5.6036165    5.1323558    10.7359723
   PATIO     7.0709845    6.4763190    13.5473035
  FIREPL     7.1552855    6.5535304    13.7088159
      AC     6.4790945    5.9342066    12.4133011
     GAR     3.6751527    3.3660746     7.0412273
     AGE    -0.0942686   -0.0863407    -0.1806092
   LOTSZ     0.0674761    0.0618014     0.1292775
    SQFT     0.0750551    0.0687430     0.1437982
```

图 18.4　各变量的直接效应、间接效应与总效应比较

在这个例子中，由空间乘子所造成的总体影响几乎是它们所造成的直接影响的两倍。

18.4 GM_Lag 与空间相关性检验

与 GeoDaSpace 不同，空间相关性检验在 spreg.GM_Lag 命令中并不是默认会计算的。为了获得 A-K 统计量，参数 spat_diag 必须被明确地赋值为 True，且由于 GM_Lag 本身就要求空间邻接权重对象为强制必需参数，所以不再需要明确一个空间权重对象。相应的命令如下：

> > > reg4= pysal.spreg.GM_Lag(y,x,w= w,spat_diag= True,name_y= y_name, name_x= x_names,name_w= 'baltim_k4',name_ds= 'baltim')

结果如图 18.5 所示。

```
REGRESSION
----------
SUMMARY OF OUTPUT: SPATIAL TWO STAGE LEAST SQUARES
--------------------------------------------------
Data set            :      baltim
Weights matrix      :   baltim_k4
Dependent Variable  :       PRICE     Number of Observations:        211
Mean dependent var  :     44.3072     Number of Variables   :         11
S.D. dependent var  :     23.6061     Degrees of Freedom    :        200
Pseudo R-squared    :      0.7064
Spatial Pseudo R-squared:   0.6856

------------------------------------------------------------------------
      Variable     Coefficient       Std.Error     z-Statistic   Probability
------------------------------------------------------------------------
      CONSTANT       1.3276578       5.7718694       0.2300222     0.8180746
         NROOM       0.8894675       1.1026083       0.8066940     0.4198428
         NBATH       5.6036165       1.8043761       3.1055700     0.0018991
         PATIO       7.0709845       2.8348494       2.4943069     0.0126203
        FIREPL       7.1552855       2.5203968       2.8389519     0.0045262
            AC       6.4790945       2.4253311       2.6714268     0.0075530
           GAR       3.6751527       1.7756639       2.0697344     0.0384772
           AGE      -0.0942686       0.0544832      -1.7302327     0.0835887
         LOTSZ       0.0674761       0.0153788       4.3875982     0.0000115
          SQFT       0.0750551       0.1699164       0.4417178     0.6586934
       W_PRICE       0.4780523       0.0738868       6.4700639     0.0000000
------------------------------------------------------------------------
Instrumented: W_PRICE
Instruments: W_AC, W_AGE, W_FIREPL, W_GAR, W_LOTSZ, W_NBATH, W_NROOM,
             W_PATIO, W_SQFT

DIAGNOSTICS FOR SPATIAL DEPENDENCE
TEST                         MI/DF      VALUE         PROB
Anselin-Kelejian Test            1      3.390         0.0656
================================ END OF REPORT ========================
```

图 18.5 reg4 的标准结果输出图表

18.5 GM_Lag 与怀特标准误

如果要获得对回归标准误的在异方差条件下的强估计,那么我们需要把参数 robust 从默认值重新明确设置为非默认值'white'。在我们的例子中,我们是这样设置参数的(其余参数不变):

```
>>> reg5=pysal.spreg.GM_Lag(y,x,w=w,robust='white',spat_diag=True,
        name_y=y_name,name_x=x_names,name_w='baltim_k4',name_ds='baltim')
```

结果如图 18.6 所示。

```
REGRESSION
----------
SUMMARY OF OUTPUT: SPATIAL TWO STAGE LEAST SQUARES
----------------------------------------
Data set            :      baltim
Weights matrix      :   baltim_k4
Dependent Variable  :       PRICE                Number of Observations:         211
Mean dependent var  :     44.3072                Number of Variables   :          11
S.D. dependent var  :     23.6061                Degrees of Freedom    :         200
Pseudo R-squared    :      0.7064
Spatial Pseudo R-squared:   0.6856

White Standard Errors
------------------------------------------------------------------------
       Variable     Coefficient       Std.Error     z-Statistic     Probability
------------------------------------------------------------------------
       CONSTANT       1.3276578       7.0498787       0.1883235       0.8506231
          NROOM       0.8894675       1.3949334       0.6376415       0.5237071
          NBATH       5.6036165       2.1970447       2.5505246       0.0107561
          PATIO       7.0709845       3.1925381       2.2148473       0.0267705
         FIREPL       7.1552855       2.4338903       2.9398554       0.0032837
             AC       6.4790945       2.6957981       2.4034050       0.0162432
            GAR       3.6751527       2.3904033       1.5374614       0.1241804
            AGE      -0.0942686       0.0985737      -0.9563261       0.3389075
          LOTSZ       0.0674761       0.0251552       2.6823926       0.0073098
           SQFT       0.0750551       0.2227874       0.3368913       0.7361989
        W_PRICE       0.4780523       0.1265144       3.7786378       0.0001577
------------------------------------------------------------------------
Instrumented: W_PRICE
Instruments: W_AC, W_AGE, W_FIREPL, W_GAR, W_LOTSZ, W_NBATH, W_NROOM,
             W_PATIO, W_SQFT

DIAGNOSTICS FOR SPATIAL DEPENDENCE
TEST                         MI/DF       VALUE          PROB
Anselin-Kelejian Test            1       3.390         0.0656
================================ END OF REPORT ================================
```

图 18.6 reg5 的标准结果输出图表

18.6 GM_Lag 与 HAC 标准误

为了获得 HAC 标准误的估计结果，我们需要把参数 robust 设置为 'hac'。这需要我们明确地给定一个空间核权重对象 gwk（并可选择地在 name_gwk 处附有名称，baltim_tri_k12）。我们利用在 18.1 节中已经定义好的空间核权重对象 kw12，键入完整的命令如下：

```
>>> reg6= pysal.spreg.GM_Lag(y,x,w= w,robust= 'hac',gwk= kw12,spat_diag
= True,name_y= y_name,name_x= x_names,name_w= 'baltim_k4',name_gwk=
'baltim_tri_k12',name_ds= 'baltim')
```

结果如图 18.7 所示。

```
REGRESSION
----------
SUMMARY OF OUTPUT: SPATIAL TWO STAGE LEAST SQUARES
--------------------------------------------------
Data set            :       baltim
Weights matrix      :    baltim_k4
Dependent Variable  :        PRICE    Number of Observations:         211
Mean dependent var  :      44.3072    Number of Variables   :          11
S.D. dependent var  :      23.6061    Degrees of Freedom    :         200
Pseudo R-squared    :       0.7064
Spatial Pseudo R-squared:   0.6856

HAC Standard Errors; Kernel Weights: baltim_tri_k12
---------------------------------------------------------------------
       Variable     Coefficient       Std.Error     z-Statistic     Probability
---------------------------------------------------------------------
       CONSTANT       1.3276578       7.3836487       0.1798105       0.8573013
          NROOM       0.8894675       1.4151498       0.6285324       0.5296552
          NBATH       5.6036165       2.1947207       2.5532253       0.0106730
          PATIO       7.0709845       3.1710956       2.2298238       0.0257591
         FIREPL       7.1552855       2.3991793       2.9823888       0.0028601
             AC       6.4790945       2.9269975       2.2135633       0.0268588
            GAR       3.6751527       2.4484638       1.5010035       0.1333547
            AGE      -0.0942686       0.0965855      -0.9760116       0.3290587
          LOTSZ       0.0674761       0.0229780       2.9365495       0.0033189
           SQFT       0.0750551       0.1979195       0.3792205       0.7045241
        W_PRICE       0.4780523       0.1140101       4.1930676       0.0000275
---------------------------------------------------------------------
Instrumented: W_PRICE
Instruments: W_AC, W_AGE, W_FIREPL, W_GAR, W_LOTSZ, W_NBATH, W_NROOM,
             W_PATIO, W_SQFT

DIAGNOSTICS FOR SPATIAL DEPENDENCE
TEST                          MI/DF       VALUE         PROB
Anselin-Kelejian Test             1       3.390       0.0656
================================ END OF REPORT =====================
```

图 18.7 reg6 的标准结果输出图表

18.7 含有内生解释变量的 GM_Lag 运算

当我们处理存在内生解释变量(及其相关工具变量)的回归问题时,需要在 GM_Lag 命令中添加 numpy 数组 yend 和 q(分别是内生解释变量数组和工具变量数组),当然可以选择性地确定它们的名称列表。

为了举例说明这种情况,我们使用第 17 章中的例子,读者可以参考其中所选择的因变量、解释变量以及空间权重对象。

我们设置参数 spat_diag 为 True,并给空间权重对象附加名称 nat_queen,其余参数保持为默认值,命令如下:

>>> reg7= pysal.spreg.GM_Lag(y,x,yend,q,w= w,spat_diag= True,name_y= y_name,name_x= x_names,name_yend= yend_names,name_q= q_names,name_w= 'nat_queen',name_ds= 'nat')
>>> print reg7.summary

结果如图 18.8 所示。

我们也可以使得工具变量不再做空间滞后的处理,这需要设置参数 lag_q 为 False,例如:

>>> reg8= pysal.spreg.GM_Lag(y,x,yend,q,w= w,lag_q= False,spat_diag= True,name_y= y_name,name_x= x_names,name_yend= yend_names,name_q= q_names,name_w= "nat_queen",name_ds= "nat")
>>> print reg8.summary

结果如图 18.9 所示。当然我们也可以通过改变 robust 参数的赋值来获得 white 或者是 HAC 强标准误,但是与 GeoDaSpace 不同的是,我们不能一次性地获得三种标准误的结果,为了获得某种标准误的值,必须设置相应的参数,而不能像在 GeoDaSpace 中一样,只要在相应的选项框中打钩,点击"运行"便可以一次获得若干种不同的标准误结果。

```
REGRESSION
----------
SUMMARY OF OUTPUT: SPATIAL TWO STAGE LEAST SQUARES
--------------------------------------------------
Data set            :          nat
Weights matrix      :     nat_queen
Dependent Variable  :         HR90                Number of Observations:        3085
Mean dependent var  :       6.1829                Number of Variables   :           6
S.D. dependent var  :       6.6414                Degrees of Freedom    :        3079
Pseudo R-squared    :       0.4186
Spatial Pseudo R-squared:   0.3914

------------------------------------------------------------------------------------
         Variable       Coefficient        Std.Error       z-Statistic     Probability
------------------------------------------------------------------------------------
         CONSTANT        10.0338240        1.3616383         7.3689349       0.0000000
             RD90         4.4092974        0.2400482        18.3683863       0.0000000
             MA90        -0.0500990        0.0286025        -1.7515613       0.0798493
             PS90         1.5813070        0.1084249        14.5843567       0.0000000
             UE90        -0.5182722        0.0882736        -5.8712062       0.0000000
           W_HR90         0.2123364        0.0371805         5.7109639       0.0000000
------------------------------------------------------------------------------------
Instrumented: UE90, W_HR90
Instruments: FH90, FP89, GI89, W_FH90, W_FP89, W_GI89, W_MA90, W_PS90,
             W_RD90

DIAGNOSTICS FOR SPATIAL DEPENDENCE
TEST                     MI/DF        VALUE           PROB
Anselin-Kelejian Test        1        2.517         0.1127
================================ END OF REPORT ====================================
```

图 18.8　reg7 的标准结果输出图表

```
REGRESSION
----------
SUMMARY OF OUTPUT: SPATIAL TWO STAGE LEAST SQUARES
--------------------------------------------------
Data set            :          nat
Weights matrix      :     nat_queen
Dependent Variable  :         HR90                Number of Observations:        3085
Mean dependent var  :       6.1829                Number of Variables   :           6
S.D. dependent var  :       6.6414                Degrees of Freedom    :        3079
Pseudo R-squared    :       0.4076
Spatial Pseudo R-squared:   0.3802

------------------------------------------------------------------------------------
         Variable       Coefficient        Std.Error       z-Statistic     Probability
------------------------------------------------------------------------------------
         CONSTANT        11.2850228        1.4177538         7.9597903       0.0000000
             RD90         4.6642007        0.2537771        18.3791221       0.0000000
             MA90        -0.0601927        0.0290474        -2.0722259       0.0382444
             PS90         1.6149324        0.1105060        14.6139849       0.0000000
             UE90        -0.6580528        0.0951942        -6.9127375       0.0000000
           W_HR90         0.2163835        0.0389967         5.5487653       0.0000000
------------------------------------------------------------------------------------
Instrumented: UE90, W_HR90
Instruments: FH90, FP89, GI89, W_MA90, W_PS90, W_RD90

DIAGNOSTICS FOR SPATIAL DEPENDENCE
TEST                     MI/DF        VALUE           PROB
Anselin-Kelejian Test        1        2.442         0.1182
================================ END OF REPORT ====================================
```

图 18.9　reg8 的标准结果输出图表

第 19 章 PySAL spreg 中的空间滞后模型的最大似然估计

19.1 回归运算的准备

我们继续使用与第 16 章相同的样本数据库(baltim.dbf)和模型。由于我们选取的因变量、解释变量、空间权重对象以及空间核权重对象都和第 16 章、第 18 章中的例子完全相同,因此建立因变量 numpy 数组、解释变量 numpy 数组等命令也是完全一致的,请读者参见第 16 章的准备工作,在此不再重复。

在完成类似上一章的准备工作后,我们应该有一个因变量 numpy 数组 y、一个解释变量 numpy 数组 x、一个空间权重对象 w(直接选择上一章的空间权重对象 baltim_k4.gal 以方便对照)和一个空间核权重对象 kw12。同时,我们还应该有一个因变量字符串列表 y_name、一个解释变量字符串列表 x_names、一个空间权重对象名称 name_w=baltim_k4 和数据库描述 name_ds=baltim。

19.2 ML_Lag 命令

我们用 ML 来估计空间滞后模型的 PySAL 用户类是 spreg.ML_Lag,它的三个强制必需参数包括因变量 numpy 数组 y 和解释变量 numpy 数组 x 以及一个空间权重对象 w。一个完整的 spreg.ML_Lag 命令如下:

```
>>> ml_lag= pysal.spreg.ML_Lag(y,x,w,method= 'full',epsilon= 0.0000001,
```

```
spat_diag= False,vm= False,name_y= None,name_x= None,name_w= None,name_ds
= None)
```

其他可选参数及其默认值如下：

- method：一个决定优化过程计算方法的选项，默认值是'full'，另一个是'ord'，是指最原始的 brutal force 算法；
- epsilon：在非线性优化步骤中的收敛判定标准，默认值是 0.000 000 1；
- spat_diag：空间相关性检验，这是一个为将来可能的新功能所准备的占位符，默认值是 False；
- vm：这个选项决定是否在正常回归结果的输出中附加整个系数方差-协方差矩阵，默认是不附加这个矩阵的（这个矩阵是一定会计算的，选项只是决定是否在结果中直接输出这个矩阵）；
- name_y：一个字符串，包含因变量 y 的名称，默认是没有明确的名称；
- name_x：一组字符串变量，包含所有解释变量 x 的名称，用户必须自己确保名称顺序和 x 数组的顺序对应正确，默认是没有明确的名称序列；
- name_w：空间权重对象的名称，默认是无名称；
- name_ds：数据库的描述，默认是没有数据库的描述。

19.3　ML_Lag 对象

与其他回归模型一样，spreg.ML_Lag 命令会运算生成一个回归对象。这个对象具有包括估计结果、标准误在内的许多属性，这其中也包括一些对后续计算或有帮助的中间结果。

同样地，我们在这里用最简单的命令生成一个回归对象：利用最开始所做的准备工作，y 和 x 分别为因变量和解释变量，邻接权重对象 w 为空间权重对象，除对变量、权重对象、数据库附加名称外，其他参数均取默认值。相应的命令如下：

```
>>> reg1= pysal.spreg.ML_Lag(y,x,w,name_y= y_name,name_x= x_names,name_w
```

```
= 'baltim_k4',name_ds= 'baltim')
```

计算结果被附加在了 reg1 这个回归对象上,其属性我们可以用 Python 的 dir 命令来查看:

```
>>> dir(reg1)
['_doc_', '_init_', '_module_', '_summary', '_cache', 'aic', 'betas',
'e_pred', 'epsilon', 'k', 'logll', 'mean_y', 'method', 'n', 'name_ds',
'name_w', 'name_x', 'name_y', 'pr2', 'pr2_e', 'predy', 'predy_e', 'rho',
'schwarz', 'sig2', 'sig2n', 'sig2n_k', 'std_err', 'std_y', 'summary',
'title', 'u', 'utu', 'vm', 'vm1', 'x', 'y', 'z_stat']
```

这其中大部分比较普遍的属性与第16章 OLS 回归对象的属性相同,请读者自行参见第16章的描述;两个有关模型契合程度的属性(pr2 和 pr2_e)与之前空间滞后模型 GM_Lag 回归对象的属性相同,这在第18章也有相关的说明。在这里我们着重强调一下 ML_Lag 回归对象特有的几个属性:

- k:解释变量的个数,这并不包括空间自回归系数;
- betas:一个$(k+1)\times 1$数组,回归系数的估计值,这个向量的最后一位是空间自回归系数;
- rho:空间自回归系数,与 betas[-1] 相同;
- vm:一个$(k+1)\times(k+1)$阶回归系数方差-协方差矩阵,最后一个元素是空间自回归系数 rho;
- vm1:一个$(k+2)\times(k+2)$阶回归系数方差-协方差矩阵,最后两个元素分别是空间自回归系数 rho 和 σ^2。

与之前的情况完全相同,我们可以单独地提取这些属性,比如可以获得回归系数的估计:

```
>>> reg1.betas
array([[ 7.44436176],
       [ 0.70354005],
       [ 5.61610186],
       [ 7.98111406],
```

```
[ 8.27519822],
[ 6.8624124 ],
[ 4.15655226],
[- 0.1274933 ],
[ 0.07512264],
[ 0.10647197],
[ 0.34478915]])
```

空间自回归系数是这个数组的最后一位：

```
>>> reg1.betas[-1][0]
0.34478915444092334
```

也可以通过属性 rho 单独获取：

```
>>> reg1.rho
0.34478915444092334
```

19.4　ML_Lag 估计中的选项

在 PySAL spreg 中，对空间滞后模型做 ML 的用户类 ML_Lag 只有仅有的几个选项。在这些选项当中，最重要的一个是 method，我们会在下面略加说明。另一个是 epsilon，收敛判定标准的精确度。这个参数最好保持为默认值，除非你需要更加精确的估计结果（赋较小的值），或者你需要提高运算速度（赋较大的值）。

参数 method 的默认值是'full'，类似地，我们可以通过 print reg1.summary 获得回归的标准结果输出图表，除在最上面一行出现了 METHOD=FULL 之外，其他都和 Geoda 中生成的结果完全一样，如图 19.1 所示。

当我们对参数 method 赋值（ord）时，优化过程会使用 Ord 方法，如：

```
>>> reg2= pysal.spreg.ML_Lag(y,x,w,method= 'ord',name_y= y_name,name_x=
x_names,name_w= 'baltim_k4',name_ds= 'baltim')
```

```
>>> print reg2.summary
```

回归的结果与使用 Full 方法所得的结果除抬头之外（METHOD=ORD），其他都是一模一样的，如图 19.2 所示。

```
REGRESSION
----------
SUMMARY OF OUTPUT: MAXIMUM LIKELIHOOD SPATIAL LAG (METHOD = FULL)
-----------------------------------------------------------------
Data set            :       baltim
Weights matrix      :    baltim_k4
Dependent Variable  :        PRICE      Number of Observations:       211
Mean dependent var  :      44.3072      Number of Variables   :        11
S.D. dependent var  :      23.6061      Degrees of Freedom    :       200
Pseudo R-squared    :       0.7057
Spatial Pseudo R-squared:   0.6913
Sigma-square ML     :      163.292      Log likelihood        :  -839.774
S.E of regression   :       12.779      Akaike info criterion :  1701.547
                                        Schwarz criterion     :  1738.418

------------------------------------------------------------------------
     Variable    Coefficient      Std.Error    z-Statistic   Probability
------------------------------------------------------------------------
     CONSTANT      7.4443618      5.0835158      1.4644120     0.1430814
        NROOM      0.7035401      1.0995064      0.6398690     0.5222578
        NBATH      5.6161019      1.8094350      3.1037876     0.0019106
        PATIO      7.9811141      2.8080688      2.8422074     0.0044802
       FIREPL      8.2751982      2.4891073      3.3245647     0.0008856
           AC      6.8624124      2.4216910      2.8337275     0.0046009
          GAR      4.1565523      1.7614609      2.3597187     0.0182888
          AGE     -0.1274933      0.0527665     -2.4161810     0.0156843
        LOTSZ      0.0751226      0.0150624      4.9874297     0.0000006
         SQFT      0.1064720      0.1694196      0.6284513     0.5297084
      W_PRICE      0.3447892      0.0555589      6.2058284     0.0000000
------------------------------------------------------------------------
============================== END OF REPORT ===========================
```

图 19.1　reg1 的标准结果输出图表

```
REGRESSION
----------
SUMMARY OF OUTPUT: MAXIMUM LIKELIHOOD SPATIAL LAG (METHOD = ORD)
----------------------------------------------------------------
Data set            :       baltim
Weights matrix      :    baltim_k4
Dependent Variable  :        PRICE      Number of Observations:       211
Mean dependent var  :      44.3072      Number of Variables   :        11
S.D. dependent var  :      23.6061      Degrees of Freedom    :       200
Pseudo R-squared    :       0.7057
Spatial Pseudo R-squared:   0.6913
Sigma-square ML     :      163.292      Log likelihood        :  -839.774
S.E of regression   :       12.779      Akaike info criterion :  1701.547
                                        Schwarz criterion     :  1738.418

------------------------------------------------------------------------
     Variable    Coefficient      Std.Error    z-Statistic   Probability
------------------------------------------------------------------------
     CONSTANT      7.4443618      5.0835158      1.4644120     0.1430814
        NROOM      0.7035401      1.0995064      0.6398690     0.5222578
        NBATH      5.6161019      1.8094350      3.1037876     0.0019106
        PATIO      7.9811141      2.8080688      2.8422074     0.0044802
       FIREPL      8.2751982      2.4891073      3.3245647     0.0008856
           AC      6.8624124      2.4216910      2.8337275     0.0046009
          GAR      4.1565523      1.7614609      2.3597187     0.0182888
          AGE     -0.1274933      0.0527665     -2.4161810     0.0156843
        LOTSZ      0.0751226      0.0150624      4.9874297     0.0000006
         SQFT      0.1064720      0.1694196      0.6284513     0.5297084
      W_PRICE      0.3447892      0.0555589      6.2058284     0.0000000
------------------------------------------------------------------------
============================== END OF REPORT ===========================
```

图 19.2　reg2 的标准结果输出图表

第 20 章 PySAL spreg 中的空间误差模型的广义矩估计

我们使用样本数据库 south.dbf 讨论美国南方自杀率问题。空间权重对象为 south_q.gal 文件（当然也可以从 shape 文件中重新生成），涉及的变量有 HR90、DV90、PS90、RD90、UE90、FH90、FP89、GI89。

在 PySAL 中，利用广义矩方法（GM/GMM）对空间误差模型进行估计的用户类共有六个，它们可以分为三类：GM 估计（在本方法中，λ 被视为一个多余参数），异方差情形下的 GMM 估计，同方差情形下的 GMM 估计。在上述每一类中，分别有一个解决含有内生解释变量的用户类和一个解决不含有内生解释变量的用户类。

20.1 回归运算的准备

我们再次详细地介绍一遍进行回归运算之前必要的准备工作，如何提取数据库文件，如何提取变量数据为 numpy 数组，以及如何生成空间权重对象。我们区分两种情况：一种是不含有内生解释变量的情况，另一种是含有内生解释变量的情况。与之前相同，我们首先应该输入 numpy 和 pysal 两个模块：

>>> import numpy as np

>>> import pysal

当只有外生解释变量时，我们只需要满足 spreg 命令所需的最基本的两个 numpy 数组 y 和 x，这里为了方便查看结果，仍然以 Python 列表的形式给出变量的名称：

```
>>> db= pysal.open(pysal.examples.get_path('south.dbf'),'r')
>>> y_name= "HR90"
>>> y= np.array([db.by_col(y_name)]).T
>>> x_names= ['RD90','PS90','UE90','DV90']
>>> x= np.array([db.by_col(var) for var in x_names]).T
```

当解释变量不仅有外生解释变量，还包含内生解释变量时，我们就需要多给出两个 numpy 数组，一个是内生解释变量数组 yend，另一个是工具变量数组 q，我们还需要重新定义 numpy 数组 x，使其只包含外生解释变量，我们重新定义它为 xe（为了区分于仅有外生解释变量情况时给出的 x）。下面的命令在之前的基础上完成了上述变量数组的提取与创建：

```
>>> yend_names= ['UE90']
>>> yend= np.array([db.by_col(var) for var in yend_names]).T
>>> q_names= ['FH90','FP89','GI89']
>>> q= np.array([db.by_col(var) for var in q_names]).T
>>> xe_names= ['RD90','PS90','DV90']
>>> xe= np.array([db.by_col(var) for var in xe_names]).T
```

最后，我们还需要确定一个空间权重对象，这可以通过读取已经存在的文件 south_q.gal 实现，我们提醒读者注意检查权重矩阵是否进行了行标准化，命令如下：

```
>>> galw= pysal.open(pysal.examples.get_path('south_q.gal'),'r')
>>> w1= galw.read()
>>> galw.close()
>>> w1.transform= 'r'
```

也可以通过 shape 文件生成相同的空间权重对象，命令为：

```
>>> w= pysal.queen_from_shapefile(pysal.examples.get_path('south.shp'),
    idVariable= 'FIPSNO')
```

```
>>> w.transform= 'r'
```

20.2 GM_Error 命令

在 PySAL spreg 中,运用广义矩来估计不含有内生解释变量的空间误差模型的用户类是 spreg.GM_Error,它有三个强制必需参数:因变量 numpy 数组 y 和解释变量 numpy 数组 x 以及一个空间权重对象 w。一个完整的 spreg.GM_Error 命令包含下列元素:

```
>>> gmError= pysal.spreg.GM_Error(y,x,w,vm= False,name_y= None,name_x= None,name_w= None,name_ds= None)
```

可选参数及其默认值为:

- vm:这个选项决定是否在正常回归计算结果的输出中附加整个系数方差-协方差矩阵,默认是不附加这个矩阵的(这个矩阵是一定会计算的,选项只是决定是否在结果中直接输出这个矩阵);
- name_y:一个字符串,包含因变量 y 的名称,默认是没有明确的名称;
- name_x:一组字符串变量,包含所有解释变量 x 的名称,用户必须自己确保名称顺序和 x 数组的顺序对应正确,默认是没有明确的名称序列;
- name_w:空间权重对象的名称,默认是无名称;
- name_ds:数据库的描述,默认是没有数据库的描述。

一个有效的 spreg.GM_Error 命令会生成一个回归对象,它具有包括估计结果、标准误在内的许多属性,其中也会包括一些对后续计算或有帮助的中间结果。我们利用之前做的准备工作进行一个回归计算来更详细地说明 GM_Error 回归对象,利用之前生成的数组 y 和 x 以及空间权重对象 south_q.gal,命令如下:

```
>>> gm1= pysal.spreg.GM_Error(y,x,w,name_y= y_name,name_x= x_names,name_
```

```
w= 'south_q',name_ds= 'south.dbf')
```

我们用 Python 的 dir 命令查看回归对象 gm1 的各个属性：

```
>>> dir(gm1)
['_doc_', '_init_', '_module_', '_summary', '_cache', 'betas', 'e_filtered',
'k', 'mean_y', 'n', 'name_ds', 'name_w', 'name_x', 'name_y', 'pr2', 'predy',
'sig2', 'std_err', 'std_y', 'summary', 'title', 'u', 'vm', 'x', 'y',
'z_stat']
```

大部分属性与 OLS 回归对象相同，只有两个不尽相同，列出如下：

- pr2：伪 R^2；
- e_filtered：除掉空间相关性后的残差。

像之前一样，每一个属性都可以被独立地提取调用。例如，估计系数数组（betas）可以像下面这样单独地提取出来：

```
>>> gm1.betas
array([[ 6.33865368],
       [ 4.43265183],
       [ 1.81335314],
       [-0.3985616 ],
       [ 0.47772164],
       [ 0.26040896]])
```

空间自回归系数是 betas 的最后一个数字：

```
>>> gm1.betas[-1][0]
0.2604089568850787
```

回归对象 gm1 的 summary 属性仍然包含了所有主要的回归结果，可以通过 print gm1.summary 得到，如图 20.1 所示。

```
REGRESSION
----------
SUMMARY OF OUTPUT: SPATIALLY WEIGHTED LEAST SQUARES
---------------------------------------------------
Data set            :       south.dbf
Weights matrix      :       south_q
Dependent Variable  :            HR90     Number of Observations:       1412
Mean dependent var  :          9.5493     Number of Variables    :          5
S.D. dependent var  :          7.0389     Degrees of Freedom     :       1407
Pseudo R-squared    :          0.3066

-----------------------------------------------------------------------------
       Variable     Coefficient       Std.Error     z-Statistic     Probability
-----------------------------------------------------------------------------
       CONSTANT       6.3386537       1.0155422       6.2416446       0.0000000
           RD90       4.4326518       0.2318185      19.1212180       0.0000000
           PS90       1.8133531       0.2105237       8.6135328       0.0000000
           UE90      -0.3985616       0.0772012      -5.1626346       0.0000002
           DV90       0.4777216       0.1203677       3.9688512       0.0000722
         lambda       0.2604090
-----------------------------------------------------------------------------
============================ END OF REPORT =================================
```

图 20.1　gm1 的标准结果输出图表

20.3　GM_Endog_Error 命令

当我们的回归模型中存在内生解释变量时，我们必须使用 GM_Endog_Error 命令来进行广义矩估计。这个用户类的强制参数包括 numpy 数组 y, x，yend, q 和 w，也就是因变量、外生解释变量、内生解释变量、工具变量和一个空间权重对象，完整的 spreg.GM_Endog_Error 命令如下：

\>>> gmEndogError= pysal.spreg.GM_Endog_Error(y, x, yend, q, w, vm= False, name_y= None, name_x= None, name_yend= None, name_q= q_names, name_w= None, name_ds= None)

可选参数及其默认值为：

• vm：这个选项决定是否在正常回归计算结果的输出中附加整个系数方差-协方差矩阵，默认是不附加这个矩阵的（这个矩阵是一定会计算的，选项只是决定是否在结果中直接输出这个矩阵）；

• name_y：一个字符串，包含因变量 y 的名称，默认是没有明确的名称；

- name_x：一组字符串变量，包含所有解释变量 x 的名称，用户必须自己确保名称顺序和 x 数组的顺序对应正确，默认是没有明确的名称序列；
- name_yend：一组字符串变量，包含所有内生解释变量 yend 的名称，用户必须自己确保名称顺序和 yend 数组的顺序对应正确，默认是没有明确的名称序列；
- name_q：一组字符串变量，包含所有工具变量 q 的名称，用户必须自己确保名称顺序和 q 数组的顺序对应正确，默认是没有明确的名称序列；
- name_w：空间权重对象的名称，默认是无名称；
- name_ds：数据库的描述，默认是无数据库的描述。

一个有效的 spreg.GM_Endog_Error 命令会生成一个回归对象，它具有包括估计结果、标准误在内的许多属性，其中也会包括一些对后续计算或有帮助的中间结果。我们利用之前做的准备工作进行一个回归计算来更详细地说明 GM_Endog_Error 回归对象，利用之前生成的四个 numpy 数组 y、xe、yend、q 以及空间权重对象 south_q.gal，命令如下：

```
>>> gm2= pysal.spreg.GM_Endog_Error(y,xe,yend,q,w,name_y= y_name,name_x = xe_names,name_q= q_names,name_yend= yend_names,name_w= 'south_q',name_ds= 'south.dbf')
```

我们用 Python 的 dir 命令查看回归对象 gm2 的各个属性：

```
>>> dir (gm2)
['_class_', '_delattr_', '_dict_', '_dir_', '_doc_', '_eq_', '_format_',
'_ge_', '_getattribute_', '_gt_', '_hash_', '_init_', '_init_subclass_',
'_le_', '_lt_', '_module_', '_ne_', '_new_', '_reduce_', '_reduce_ex_',
'_repr_', '_setattr_', '_sizeof_', '_str_', '_subclasshook_', '_summary',
'_weakref_', '_cache', 'betas', 'e_filtered', 'k', 'mean_y', 'n', 'name_ds',
'name_h', 'name_q', 'name_w', 'name_x', 'name_y','name_yend', 'name_z',
'pr2', 'predy', 'sig2', 'std_err', 'std_y', 'summary', 'title', 'u', 'vm',
'x', 'y', 'yend', 'z', 'z_stat']
```

它的各个属性和 GM_Error 是完全一致的，我们也可以单独地调用一个估计系数数组 betas 作为示范：

```
>>> gm2.betas
array([[10.7717841 ],
       [ 5.90371303],
       [ 2.04553882],
       [ 0.49190638],
       [-1.14071221],
       [ 0.23609742]])
```

空间自回归系数是 betas 的最后一个数字：

```
>>> gm2.betas[-1][0]
0.23609741914940524
```

回归对象 gm2 的 summary 属性仍然包含了所有主要的回归结果，可以通过 print gm2.summary 获得如图 20.2 所示的结果图表。

```
REGRESSION
----------
SUMMARY OF OUTPUT: SPATIALLY WEIGHTED TWO STAGE LEAST SQUARES
-------------------------------------------------------------
Data set            :    south.dbf
Weights matrix      :      south_q
Dependent Variable  :         HR90                Number of Observations:        1412
Mean dependent var  :       9.5493                Number of Variables   :           5
S.D. dependent var  :       7.0389                Degrees of Freedom    :        1407
Pseudo R-squared    :       0.2818

------------------------------------------------------------------------------------
       Variable     Coefficient       Std.Error     z-Statistic     Probability
------------------------------------------------------------------------------------
       CONSTANT      10.7717841       1.2771988       8.4339137       0.0000000
           RD90       5.9037130       0.3473996      16.9940125       0.0000000
           PS90       2.0455388       0.2190619       9.3377222       0.0000000
           DV90       0.4919064       0.1246483       3.9463541       0.0000794
           UE90      -1.1407122       0.1483842      -7.6875610       0.0000000
         lambda       0.2360974
------------------------------------------------------------------------------------
Instrumented: UE90
Instruments: FH90, FP89, GI89
============================== END OF REPORT =======================================
```

图 20.2　gm2 的标准结果输出图表

20.4 GM_Error_Het 命令

我们介绍 GM 只是为了使讨论更加完备,因为它已经逐渐被更新、更好的 GMM 替代。在 PySAL 中,进行 GMM 估计时用到的用户类是 spreg.GM_Error_Het,它的三个强制必需参数与 GM_Error 相同:因变量 numpy 数组 y 和解释变量 numpy 数组 x 以及一个空间权重对象 w。完整的命令为:

>>> gmErrorHet = pysal.spreg.GM_Error_Het(y, x, w, max_iter= 1, epsilon= 1e-5, step1c= False,Vm= False, name_y= None, name_x= None, name_w= None, name_ds= None)

可选参数及其默认值为:

- max_iter:最大迭代次数,默认值是没有迭代,也就是迭代次数设置为 1;
- epsilon:在非线性优化步骤中的收敛判定标准,默认值是 0.000 000 1;
- step1c:一个选项,它决定了对 λ 进行初始估计时是否进行额外一步计算,默认值是 False;
- vm:这个选项决定是否在正常回归计算结果的输出中附加整个系数方差-协方差矩阵;默认是不附加这个矩阵的(这个矩阵是一定会计算的,选项只是决定是否在结果中直接输出这个矩阵);
- name_y:一个字符串,包含因变量 y 的名称,默认是没有明确的名称;
- name_x:一组字符串变量,包含所有解释变量 x 的名称,用户必须自己确保名称顺序和 x 数组的顺序对应正确,默认是没有明确的名称序列;
- name_w:空间权重对象的名称,默认是无名称;
- name_ds:数据库的描述,默认是没有数据库的描述。

一个有效的 spreg.GM_Error_Het 命令会生成一个回归对象,它具有包括估计结果、标准误在内的许多属性,其中也会包括一些对后续计算或有帮助的中间结果。我们利用之前做的准备工作进行一个回归计算来更详细地说明 GM_Error_Het 回归对象,利用与生成 GM_Error 回归对象时所采用的相同的数组 y 和 x 以及空间权重对象 south_q.gal,命令如下:

```
>>> gm3= pysal.spreg.GM_Error_Het(y,x,w,name_y= y_name,name_x= x_names,
name_w= 'south_q', name_ds= 'south.dbf')
```

我们用 Python 的 dir 命令查看回归对象 gm3 的各个属性:

```
>>> dir(gm3)
['_class_', '_delattr_', '_dict_', '_dir_', '_doc_', '_eq_', '_format_',
'_ge_', '_getattribute_', '_gt_', '_hash_', '_init_', '_init_subclass_',
'_le_', '_lt_', '_module_', '_ne_', '_new_', '_reduce_', '_reduce_ex_',
'_repr_', '_setattr_', '_sizeof_', '_str_', '_subclasshook_', '_summary',
'_weakref_', '_cache', 'betas', 'e_filtered', 'iter_stop', 'iteration', 'k',
'mean_y', 'n', 'name_ds', 'name_w', 'name_x', 'name_y', 'pr2', 'predy',
'std_err', 'std_y', 'step1c', 'summary', 'title', 'u', 'vm', 'x', 'xtx', 'y',
'z_stat']
```

大部分属性与 OLS 回归对象相同,只有四个不尽相同,列出如下:

- pr2:伪 R^2;
- e_filtered:除掉空间相关性后的残差;
- iter_stop:在迭代中达到的停止标准;
- iteration:进行迭代的次数。

像之前一样,每一个属性都可以被独立地提取调用。例如,估计系数数组 betas 可以像下面这样单独地提取出来:

```
>>> gm3.betas
array([[ 6.25760366],
       [ 4.41953589],
       [ 1.79832764],
       [- 0.38976971],
       [ 0.48116579],
       [ 0.31474155]])
```

空间自回归系数是 betas 的最后一个数字：

```
>>> gm3.betas[-1][0]
0.3147415545104512
```

回归对象 gm3 的 summary 属性仍然包含了所有主要的回归结果，可以通过 print gm3.summary 获得如图 20.3 所示的结果图表。

```
REGRESSION
----------
SUMMARY OF OUTPUT: SPATIALLY WEIGHTED LEAST SQUARES (HET)
---------------------------------------------------------
Data set            :    south.dbf
Weights matrix      :    south_q
Dependent Variable  :        HR90     Number of Observations:      1412
Mean dependent var  :      9.5493     Number of Variables   :         5
S.D. dependent var  :      7.0389     Degrees of Freedom    :      1407
Pseudo R-squared    :      0.3062
N. of iterations    :           1     Step1c computed       :        No

------------------------------------------------------------------------
    Variable       Coefficient       Std.Error     z-Statistic   Probability
------------------------------------------------------------------------
    CONSTANT         6.2576037       1.0821873       5.7823668     0.0000000
        RD90         4.4195359       0.3468537      12.7417874     0.0000000
        PS90         1.7983276       0.3359957       5.3522335     0.0000001
        UE90        -0.3897697       0.0985644      -3.9544664     0.0000767
        DV90         0.4811658       0.1198516       4.0146802     0.0000595
      lambda         0.3147416       0.0374883       8.3957227     0.0000000
------------------------------------------------------------------------
================================ END OF REPORT ================================
```

图 20.3 gm3 的标准结果输出图表

像在 GeoDaSpace 中所讨论的那样，我们可以在对 λ 进行初始估计时进行额外的计算，这需要我们把参数 step1c 赋值为 True，命令如下：

```
>>> gm4= pysal.spreg.GM_Error_Het(y,x,w,step1c= True,name_y= y_name,
name_x= x_names, name_w= 'south_q', name_ds= 'south.dbf')
```

结果如图 20.4 所示。

类似地，我们也可以对 GMM 估计进行迭代，我们需要把参数 max_iter 赋值为一个大于 1 的整数（我们需要注意到，这里所谓的"最大可能迭代数"并不一定是真正被执行的迭代的次数）。无论是 max_iter 还是 epsilon，当这两个参数中的任何一个达到我们所给定的标准时，都会停止迭代。我们在下面的例子中，把 max_iter 赋值为 10：

```
>>> gm5= pysal.spreg.GM_Error_Het(y,x,w,max_iter= 10,name_y= y_name,
```

```
name_x= x_names, name_w= 'south_q', name_ds= 'south.dbf')
```

结果如图 20.5 所示,这个运算的迭代次数仅为 5。

```
REGRESSION
----------
SUMMARY OF OUTPUT: SPATIALLY WEIGHTED LEAST SQUARES (HET)
---------------------------------------------------------
Data set            :    south.dbf
Weights matrix      :    south_q
Dependent Variable  :         HR90    Number of Observations:        1412
Mean dependent var  :       9.5493    Number of Variables   :           5
S.D. dependent var  :       7.0389    Degrees of Freedom    :        1407
Pseudo R-squared    :       0.3059
N. of iterations    :            1    Step1c computed       :         Yes

----------------------------------------------------------------------------
       Variable     Coefficient       Std.Error     z-Statistic     Probability
----------------------------------------------------------------------------
       CONSTANT       6.1903085       1.0826509       5.7177328       0.0000000
           RD90       4.4088516       0.3472585      12.6961665       0.0000000
           PS90       1.7859187       0.3361596       5.3127111       0.0000001
           UE90      -0.3824992       0.0986013      -3.8792513       0.0001048
           DV90       0.4840327       0.1199034       4.0368561       0.0000542
         lambda       0.3161445       0.0374169       8.4492406       0.0000000
----------------------------------------------------------------------------
============================== END OF REPORT =================================
```

图 20.4 gm4 的标准结果输出图表

```
REGRESSION
----------
SUMMARY OF OUTPUT: SPATIALLY WEIGHTED LEAST SQUARES (HET)
---------------------------------------------------------
Data set            :    south.dbf
Weights matrix      :    south_q
Dependent Variable  :         HR90    Number of Observations:        1412
Mean dependent var  :       9.5493    Number of Variables   :           5
S.D. dependent var  :       7.0389    Degrees of Freedom    :        1407
Pseudo R-squared    :       0.3053
N. of iterations    :            5    Step1c computed       :          No

----------------------------------------------------------------------------
       Variable     Coefficient       Std.Error     z-Statistic     Probability
----------------------------------------------------------------------------
       CONSTANT       6.0484442       1.0837030       5.5812749       0.0000000
           RD90       4.3869346       0.3481280      12.6014996       0.0000000
           PS90       1.7599431       0.3365045       5.2300726       0.0000002
           UE90      -0.3672549       0.0986888      -3.7213436       0.0001982
           DV90       0.4900931       0.1200190       4.0834631       0.0000444
         lambda       0.3191342       0.0372671       8.5634294       0.0000000
----------------------------------------------------------------------------
============================== END OF REPORT =================================
```

图 20.5 gm5 的标准结果输出图表

20.5 GM_Endog_Error_Het 命令

当我们的回归模型中存在内生解释变量时，我们必须使用 GM_Endog_Error_Het 命令来进行 GMM 估计。这个用户类的强制必需参数包括 numpy 数组 $y, x, yend, q$ 和 w，也就是因变量、外生解释变量、内生解释变量、工具变量和一个空间权重对象，完整的 spreg.GM_Endog_Error_Het 命令如下：

```
>>> gmEndogErrorHet = pysal.spreg.GM_Endog_Error_Het(y, x, yend, q, w,
max_iter= 1, epsilon= 1e-5, step1c= False, inv_method= 'power_exp', vm=
False,name_y= None, name_x= None, name_yend= None, name_q= None, Name_w=
None, name_ds= None)
```

可选参数及其默认值大部分与上一节无内生解释变量的 GM_Error_Het 用户类相同，但是由于又多了内生解释变量数组 yend 和工具变量数组 q，我们还多了对它们附加名称的两个选项(即 name_yend 和 name_q)，有一些矩方程中需要对矩阵($I - \lambda W$)求逆，这就带来了一个新的可选参数：

- inv_method：一个选项，它决定了具体计算矩阵逆的方法，默认值是'power_exp'，即做方幂展开；另一个选项是'true_inv'，也就是使用标准的求逆算法(当我们要估计的模型数据量较大时可能会出现问题)。

一个有效的 spreg.GM_Endog_Error_Het 命令会生成一个回归对象，它具有包括估计结果、标准误在内的许多属性，其中也会包括一些对后续计算或有帮助的中间结果。我们利用之前做的准备工作进行一个回归计算来更详细地说明 GM_Endog_Error_Het 回归对象，利用与生成 GM_Endog_Error 回归对象时所采用的相同的数组 $y, xe, yend, q$ 以及空间权重对象 south_q.gal，命令如下：

```
>>> gm6= pysal.spreg.GM_Endog_Error_Het(y, xe, yend, q, w, name_y= y_name,
name_x= xe_names, name_yend= yend_names, name_q= q_names, name_w= 'south_q',
name_ds= 'south.dbf')
```

我们用 Python 的 dir 命令查看回归对象 gm6 的各个属性：

```
>>> dir(gm6)
['_class_', '_delattr_', '_dict_', '_dir_', '_doc_', '_eq_', '_format_',
'_ge_', '_getattribute_', '_gt_', '_hash_', '_init_', '_init_subclass_',
'_le_', '_lt_', '_module_', '_ne_', '_new_', '_reduce_', '_reduce_ex_',
'_repr_', '_setattr_', '_sizeof_', '_str_', '_subclasshook_', '_summary',
'_weakref_', '_cache', 'betas', 'e_filtered', 'h', 'hth', 'iter_stop',
'iteration', 'k', 'mean_y', 'n', 'name_ds', 'name_h', 'name_q','name_w',
'name_x', 'name_y', 'name_yend', 'name_z', 'pr2', 'predy', 'q', 'std_err',
'std_y', 'step1c', 'summary', 'title', 'u', 'vm', 'x', 'y', 'yend', 'z',
'z_stat']
```

它的绝大部分属性与 GM_Error_Het 相同。回归对象 gm6 的 summary 属性仍然包含了所有主要的回归结果，可以通过 print gm6.summary 获得如图 20.6 所示的结果图表。与 GM_Error_Het 一样，这里也可以对可选参数（step1c 和 max_iter）赋值，从而完成对 λ 进行初始估值时进行额外计算以及迭代。

20.6 GM_Error_Hom 命令

与 GM_Error_Het 相对应，我们用 GMM 估计没有异方差性的空间误差模型的用户类是 GM_Error_Hom。像其他只处理外生解释变量的用户类一样，它也只有三个强制必需参数：因变量 numpy 数组 y 和解释变量 numpy 数组 x 以及一个空间权重对象 w。完整的命令为：

```
>>> gmErrorHom= pysal.spreg.GM_Error_Hom(y,x,w,max_iter= 1,epsilon=
1e-5,A1= 'hom_sc',vm= False,name_y= None,name_x= None, name_w= None, name_ds= None)
```

我们仔细观察这个完整的命令会发现，它与 GM_Error_Het 只有两个细小的不同。首先,它不包含参数 step1c;其次,它有一个决定矩阵 A_1 形式的选项,这个选项明确了回归计算中使用的矩阵 A_1 是下面哪一种:$A_1 = W'W - (n^{-1})\text{tr}(W'W)I$ (方程 1)以及是否有缩放因子 $v = 1/[1 + [(1/n)\text{tr}(W'W)]^2]$ 和 $A_1 = W'W - \text{diag}(w'_{,i}w_{,i})$ (方程 2)。

```
REGRESSION
----------
SUMMARY OF OUTPUT: SPATIALLY WEIGHTED TWO STAGE LEAST SQUARES (HET)
------------------------------------------------------------------
Data set            :       south.dbf
Weights matrix      :         south_q
Dependent Variable  :            HR90   Number of Observations:        1412
Mean dependent var  :          9.5493   Number of Variables   :           5
S.D. dependent var  :          7.0389   Degrees of Freedom    :        1407
Pseudo R-squared    :          0.2820
N. of iterations    :               1   Step1c computed       :          No

------------------------------------------------------------------
       Variable     Coefficient       Std.Error     z-Statistic     Probability
------------------------------------------------------------------
       CONSTANT      10.7456340       1.5222725       7.0589425       0.0000000
           RD90       5.8976659       0.5199311      11.3431685       0.0000000
           PS90       2.0357920       0.3491174       5.8312538       0.0000000
           DV90       0.4927888       0.1266845       3.8898895       0.0001003
           UE90      -1.1375011       0.2109871      -5.3913304       0.0000001
         lambda       0.2616248       0.0414083       6.3181770       0.0000000
------------------------------------------------------------------
Instrumented: UE90
Instruments: FH90, FP89, GI89
================================= END OF REPORT =================================
```

图 20.6 gm6 的标准结果输出图表

可选参数及其默认值大部分见 GM_Error_Het 命令节,这里额外指出:

• A_1:一个字符串,决定了哪一种 A_1 矩阵会被用在回归运算中,默认值是'hom_sc',即带有缩放因子 v 的方程 1;另外两个选项是'hom',即无缩放因子 v 的方程 1,以及'het',即取 A_1 为方程 2。

一个有效的 spreg.GM_Error_Hom 命令会生成一个回归对象。我们利用之前做的准备工作进行一个回归计算来更详细地说明 GM_Error_Hom 回归对象,利用与生成 GM_Error 回归对象时所采用的相同的数组 y 和 x 以及空间权重对象 south_q.gal,命令如下:

```
>>> gm7= pysal.spreg.GM_Error_Hom(y,x,w,name_y= y_name,name_x= x_names,
    name_w= 'south_q', name_ds= 'south.dbf')
```

它的绝大部分属性与 GM_Error_Het 相同。回归对象 gm7 的 summary 属性仍然包含了所有主要的回归结果,可以通过 print gm7.summary 获得如图 20.7 所示的结果图表。

```
REGRESSION
----------
SUMMARY OF OUTPUT: SPATIALLY WEIGHTED LEAST SQUARES (HOM)
----------------------------------------
Data set            :    south.dbf
Weights matrix      :    south_q
Dependent Variable  :    HR90           Number of Observations:     1412
Mean dependent var  :    9.5493         Number of Variables   :        5
S.D. dependent var  :    7.0389         Degrees of Freedom    :     1407
Pseudo R-squared    :    0.3066
N. of iterations    :    1

------------------------------------------------------------------------
       Variable     Coefficient       Std.Error     z-Statistic    Probability
------------------------------------------------------------------------
       CONSTANT       6.3380348       1.0237066       6.1912612      0.0000000
           RD90       4.4325506       0.2336868      18.9679144      0.0000000
           PS90       1.8132381       0.2118595       8.5586829      0.0000000
           UE90      -0.3984943       0.0777957      -5.1223182      0.0000003
           DV90       0.4777479       0.1210440       3.9468939      0.0000792
         lambda       0.2798572       0.0355242       7.8779334      0.0000000
------------------------------------------------------------------------

================================ END OF REPORT ========================
```

图 20.7 gm7 的标准结果输出图表

我们也可以通过给选项 A_1 赋值来决定回归运算中使用的矩阵 A_1 的形式,默认值是'hom_sc',也就是带有缩放因子 v 的方程 1,可以对选项 A_1 赋值'hom'来去掉缩放因子 v,命令如下:

>>> gm8a= pysal.spreg.GM_Error_Hom(y, x, w, A_1 = 'hom', name_y= y_name, name_x= x_names, name_w= 'south_q', name_ds= 'south.dbf')

使用命令 print gm8a.summary 可以得到如图 20.8 所示的结果图表。我们需注意到,GeoDaSpace 中没有与 A_1 = 'hom' 相对应的选项,而且结果图表中也没有标识出我们使用了这个选项。与我们基本的例子相对照,这个改动对 λ 的影响是很小的,也就是说缩放因子 v 对 λ 的影响可以忽略。

从默认的 A_1 矩阵得到的渐近协方差矩阵并不一定是分块对角化的,对 OLS 回归来说这是一个潜在的问题。选项 A_1 = 'het' 可以确保渐近协方差矩阵是分块对角化的,命令如下:

>>> gm8a= pysal.spreg.GM_Error_Hom(y, x, w, A_1 = 'het', name_y= y_name,

```
           name_x= x_names, name_w= 'south_q', name_ds= 'south.dbf')

REGRESSION
----------
SUMMARY OF OUTPUT: SPATIALLY WEIGHTED LEAST SQUARES (HOM)
Data set            :       south.dbf
Weights matrix      :         south_q
Dependent Variable  :            HR90       Number of Observations:        1412
Mean dependent var  :          9.5493       Number of Variables   :           5
S.D. dependent var  :          7.0389       Degrees of Freedom    :        1407
Pseudo R-squared    :          0.3066
N. of iterations    :               1

------------------------------------------------------------------------------------
       Variable         Coefficient       Std.Error     z-Statistic     Probability
------------------------------------------------------------------------------------
       CONSTANT           6.3392818       1.0236978       6.1925324       0.0000000
           RD90           4.4327545       0.2336848      18.9689495       0.0000000
           PS90           1.8134699       0.2118581       8.5598346       0.0000000
           UE90          -0.3986299       0.0777951      -5.1241028       0.0000003
           DV90           0.4776919       0.1210433       3.9464801       0.0000793
         lambda           0.2798359       0.0355255       7.8770510       0.0000000
------------------------------------------------------------------------------------
================================ END OF REPORT ====================================
```

图 20.8　gm8a 的标准结果输出图表

使用命令 print gm8b.summary 可以得到如图 20.9 所示的结果图表。在这个图表中，我们可以看到，λ 的值出现了一点变化，但是其他系数和标准误所受到的影响是很小的。这样的结果说明，对于我们现在的样本数据而言，三种选择都给出了一致估计，它们在有限的样本数的情况下差异微乎其微，并没有显著地影响整体的分析结果。

20.7　GM_Endog_Error_Hom 命令

最后一个用户类 GM_Endog_Error_Hom 用来估计含有内生解释变量的空间误差模型，且它有一个同方差的误差项。它基本综合了 20.5 和 20.6 两节的内容，首先它额外要求了与内生解释变量有关的两个 numpy 数组作为强制必需参数 yend 和 q，其次它没有了 step1c 选项，反而多了一个关于矩阵 A_1 形式的可选参数。完整的命令为：

```
REGRESSION
----------
SUMMARY OF OUTPUT: SPATIALLY WEIGHTED LEAST SQUARES (HOM)
---------------------------------------------------------
Data set            :    south.dbf
Weights matrix      :    south_q
Dependent Variable  :    HR90          Number of Observations:    1412
Mean dependent var  :    9.5493        Number of Variables   :       5
S.D. dependent var  :    7.0389        Degrees of Freedom    :    1407
Pseudo R-squared    :    0.3062
N. of iterations    :    1

      Variable     Coefficient      Std.Error     z-Statistic    Probability
      CONSTANT       6.2576037      1.0361188      6.0394656      0.0000000
          RD90       4.4195359      0.2365100     18.6864665      0.0000000
          PS90       1.7983276      0.2138587      8.4089517      0.0000000
          UE90      -0.3897697      0.0786895     -4.9532615      0.0000007
          DV90       0.4811658      0.1220549      3.9422070      0.0000807
        lambda       0.3088889      0.0349241      8.8445872      0.0000000
---------------------------------------------------------
============================ END OF REPORT =============================
```

图 20.9 gm8b 的标准结果输出图表

>>> gmEndogErrorHom = pysal.spreg.GM_Endog_Error_Hom(y, x, yend, q, w, max_iter= 1, epsilon= 1e-5, A_1= 'hom_sc', vm= False, name_y= None, name_x= None, name_yend= None, name_q= None, name_w= None, name_ds= None)

一个有效的 spreg.GM_Endog_Error_Hom 命令会生成一个回归对象。我们利用之前做的准备工作进行一个回归计算来更详细地说明 GM_Endog_Error_Hom 回归对象,利用与生成 GM_Endog_Error 回归对象时所采用的相同的数组 $y, xe, yend, q$ 以及空间权重对象 south_q.gal,命令如下：

>>> gm9= pysal.spreg.GM_Endog_Error_Hom(y, xe, yend, q, w, name_y= y_name, name_x= xe_names, name_yend= yend_names, name_q= q_names, name_w= 'south_q', name_ds= 'south.dbf')

回归对象 gm9 的 summary 属性仍然包含了所有主要的回归结果,可以通过 print gm9.summary 获得如图 20.10 所示的结果图表。

与仅有外生解释变量的情况相同,我们也可以明确地对选项 A_1 赋值,首先令 A_1 = 'hom':

>>> gm10a = pysal.spreg.GM_Endog_Error_Hom(y, xe, yend, q, w, A_1= 'hom', name_y= y_name, name_x= xe_names, name_yend= yend_names, name_q= q_names,

```
          name_w= 'south_q', name_ds= 'south.dbf')
REGRESSION
----------
SUMMARY OF OUTPUT: SPATIALLY WEIGHTED TWO STAGE LEAST SQUARES (HOM)
------------------------------------------------------------------
Data set            :     south.dbf
Weights matrix      :       south_q
Dependent Variable  :          HR90    Number of Observations:        1412
Mean dependent var  :        9.5493    Number of Variables   :           5
S.D. dependent var  :        7.0389    Degrees of Freedom    :        1407
Pseudo R-squared    :        0.2818
N. of iterations    :             1
------------------------------------------------------------------
       Variable      Coefficient       Std.Error     z-Statistic     Probability
------------------------------------------------------------------
       CONSTANT       10.7713463       1.2834619       8.3924158       0.0000000
           RD90        5.9036116       0.3489835      16.9165947       0.0000000
           PS90        2.0453736       0.2197377       9.3082522       0.0000000
           DV90        0.4919212       0.1249985       3.9354165       0.0000831
           UE90       -1.1406585       0.1491507      -7.6476928       0.0000000
         lambda        0.2431636       0.0389702       6.2397251       0.0000000
------------------------------------------------------------------
Instrumented: UE90
Instruments: FH90, FP89, GI89
================================ END OF REPORT ====================================
```

图 20.10　gm9 的标准结果输出图表

使用命令 print gm10a.summary 可以得到如图 20.11 所示的结果图表。与仅有外生解释变量的情况相同，这个改动对 λ 的影响是很小的，也就是说缩放因子 v 对 λ 的影响可以忽略。

第二个选项的非默认值我们设置为'het'，相应的命令如下：

>>> gm10b = pysal.spreg.GM_Endog_Error_Hom(y, xe, yend, q, w, A_1= 'het', name_y= y_name,name_x= xe_names,name_yend= yend_names, name_q= q_names, name_w= 'south_q', name_ds= 'south.dbf')

使用命令 print gm10b.summary 可以得到如图 20.12 所示的结果图表。同样地，这个改动对 λ 的影响是很小的，并且对整个回归分析结果的影响也是可以忽略的。

```
REGRESSION
----------
SUMMARY OF OUTPUT: SPATIALLY WEIGHTED TWO STAGE LEAST SQUARES (HOM)
-----------------------------------------------------------------
Data set            :    south.dbf
Weights matrix      :    south_q
Dependent Variable  :       HR90         Number of Observations:     1412
Mean dependent var  :     9.5493         Number of Variables    :        5
S.D. dependent var  :     7.0389         Degrees of Freedom     :     1407
Pseudo R-squared    :     0.2818
N. of iterations    :          1

-----------------------------------------------------------------
       Variable     Coefficient     Std.Error     z-Statistic     Probability
-----------------------------------------------------------------
       CONSTANT      10.7722363     1.2834693       8.3930611       0.0000000
           RD90       5.9038177     0.3489855      16.9170837       0.0000000
           PS90       2.0457096     0.2197392       9.3097152       0.0000000
           DV90       0.4918910     0.1249994       3.9351462       0.0000831
           UE90      -1.1407677     0.1491515      -7.6483826       0.0000000
         lambda       0.2431583     0.0389707       6.2395091       0.0000000
-----------------------------------------------------------------
Instrumented: UE90
Instruments: FH90, FP89, GI89
============================== END OF REPORT ==============================
```

图 20.11　gm10a 的标准结果输出图表

```
REGRESSION
----------
SUMMARY OF OUTPUT: SPATIALLY WEIGHTED TWO STAGE LEAST SQUARES (HOM)
-----------------------------------------------------------------
Data set            :    south.dbf
Weights matrix      :    south_q
Dependent Variable  :       HR90         Number of Observations:     1412
Mean dependent var  :     9.5493         Number of Variables    :        5
S.D. dependent var  :     7.0389         Degrees of Freedom     :     1407
Pseudo R-squared    :     0.2820
N. of iterations    :          1

-----------------------------------------------------------------
       Variable     Coefficient     Std.Error     z-Statistic     Probability
-----------------------------------------------------------------
       CONSTANT      10.7456340     1.2965714       8.2877305       0.0000000
           RD90       5.8976659     0.3522831      16.7412669       0.0000000
           PS90       2.0357920     0.2211232       9.2065972       0.0000000
           DV90       0.4927888     0.1257156       3.9198710       0.0000886
           UE90      -1.1375011     0.1507539      -7.5454198       0.0000000
         lambda       0.2580216     0.0387024       6.6668084       0.0000000
-----------------------------------------------------------------
Instrumented: UE90
Instruments: FH90, FP89, GI89
============================== END OF REPORT ==============================
```

图 20.12　gm10b 的标准结果输出图表

第 21 章　PySAL spreg 中的空间误差模型的最大似然估计

21.1　回归运算的准备

我们继续使用第 20 章的讨论中所使用的样本数据库 south.dbf 及相同的模型,要使用的空间权重对象依然是小镇之间的 Queen 邻接权重对象,所以仍然使用现有的权重对象文件 south_q.gal。在这里,最初建立因变量 numpy 数组、解释变量 numpy 数组等命令也是完全一致的,读者如有疑问,请参见第 16 章中所做的类似准备工作。在完成准备工作后,我们应该有一个因变量 numpy 数组 y、一个解释变量 numpy 数组 x、一个空间权重对象 w。同时,我们还应该有一个因变量字符串列表 y_name、一个解释变量字符串列表 x_names、一个空间权重对象名称 name_w=south_q 以及数据库描述 name_ds=south。

21.2　ML_Error 命令

我们用 ML 来估计空间误差模型的 PySAL 用户类是 spreg.ML_Error,它和第 19 章中 spreg.ML_Lag 的结构非常相似。它有三个强制必需参数,分别是因变量 numpy 数组 y 和解释变量 numpy 数组 x 以及一个空间权重对象 w。一个完整的 spreg.ML_Error 命令如下:

```
>>> ml_error = pysal.spreg.ML_Error(y, x, w, method = 'full', epsilon =
```

```
0.0000001,spat_diag= False,vm= False,name_y= None,name_x= None,name_w=
None,name_ds= None)
```

其他可选参数及其默认值如下：

- method：一个决定优化过程计算方法的选项，默认值是'full'，另一个是'ord'；
- epsilon：在非线性优化步骤中的收敛判定标准，默认值是 0.000 000 1；
- spat_diag：空间相关性检验，这是一个为将来可能的新功能所准备的占位符，默认值是 False；
- vm：这个选项决定是否在正常回归计算结果的输出中附加整个系数方差-协方差矩阵，默认是不附加这个矩阵的（这个矩阵是一定会计算的，选项只是决定是否在结果中直接输出这个矩阵）；
- name_y：一个字符串，包含因变量 y 的名称，默认是没有明确的名称；
- name_x：一组字符串变量，包含所有解释变量 x 的名称，用户必须自己确保名称顺序和 x 数组的顺序对应正确，默认是没有明确的名称序列；
- name_w：空间权重对象的名称，默认是无名称；
- name_ds：数据库的描述，默认是没有数据库的描述。

21.3　ML_Error 对象

与其他回归模型一样，spreg.ML_Error 命令会运算生成一个回归对象。这个对象具有包括估计结果、标准误在内的许多属性，其中也会包括一些对后续计算或有帮助的中间结果。

同样地，在这里用最简单的命令生成一个回归对象：利用最开始所做的准备工作，y 和 x 分别为因变量和解释变量，邻接权重对象 w 为空间权重对象，除对变量、权重对象、数据库附加名称外，其他参数均取默认值。相应的命令如下：

```
>>> reg1= pysal.spreg.ML_Error(y,x,w,name_y= y_name,name_x= x_names,name
```

```
_w= 'south_q',name_ds= 'south')
```

计算结果被附加在了 reg1 这个回归对象上,我们可以用 Python 的 dir 命令来查看其属性:

```
>>> dir(reg1)
['_doc_', '_init_', '_module_', '_summary', '_cache', 'aic', 'betas',
'e_filtered', 'epsilon', 'get_x_lag', 'k', 'lam', 'logll', 'mean_y',
'method', 'n', 'name_ds', 'name_w', 'name_x', 'name_y', 'pr2', 'predy',
'schwarz', 'sig2', 'sig2n', 'sig2n_k', 'std_err', 'std_y', 'summary',
'title', 'u', 'utu', 'vm', 'vm1', 'x', 'y', 'z_stat']
```

这其中大部分比较普遍的属性与第 16 章 OLS 回归对象的属性相同,请读者参见第 16 章对它们的描述。在这里我们着重强调一下 ML_Lag 回归对象特有(ML 方法所特有的)的几个属性:

- k:解释变量的个数,这并不包括空间自回归系数;
- betas:一个$(k+1)\times 1$ 数组,回归系数的估计值,这个向量的最后一位是空间自回归系数;
- lam:空间自回归系数,与 betas[-1]相同;
- vm:一个$(k+1)\times(k+1)$阶回归系数方差-协方差矩阵,最后一个元素是空间自回归系数 lam;
- vm1:一个$(k+2)\times(k+2)$阶回归系数方差-协方差矩阵,最后两个元素分别是空间自回归系数 lam 和 σ^2;
- e_filtered:除掉空间相关性后的残差;
- get_x_lag:为空间体系设计的帮助功能。

类似地,我们可以单独地提取这些属性,比如可以获得回归系数(betas)的估计:

```
>>> reg1.betas
array([[ 6.14922448],
       [ 4.40242008],
       [ 1.77837119],
```

```
       [- 0.37807309],
       [ 0.48578577],
       [ 0.29907789]])
```

空间自回归系数是这个数组的最后一位：

```
>>> reg1.betas[-1][0]
0.29907789381940336
```

也可以通过属性 lam 单独地获取：

```
>>> reg1.lam
0.29907789381940336
```

21.4 ML_Error 估计中的选项

在 PySAL spreg 中,对空间误差模型做 ML 的用户类 ML_Error 只有仅有的几个选项,这和空间滞后模型所对应的 ML 用户类 ML_Lag 非常类似。在这些选项当中,最重要的一个是 method,我们会在下文略加说明。另一个是 epsilon,收敛判定标准的精确度。这个参数最好保持为默认值,除非你需要更加精确的估计结果(赋较小的值),或者你需要提高运算速度(赋较大的值)。

参数 method 的默认值是'full',类似地,我们可以通过 print reg1.summary 获得回归的标准结果图表,如图 21.1 所示,除在最上面一行出现了 METHOD=FULL 之外,其他都和 GeoDa 给出的结果完全一样。

当我们对参数 method 赋值'ord'时,优化过程会使用 Ord 方法,如：

```
>>> reg2= pysal.spreg.ML_Error(y,x,w,method='ord',name_y=y_name,name_x
= x_names,name_w='south_q',name_ds='south')
>>> print reg2.summary
```

回归的结果与使用 Full 方法所得的结果除抬头之外(METHOD=ORD),其他都是一模一样的,如图 21.2 所示。

```
REGRESSION
----------
SUMMARY OF OUTPUT: MAXIMUM LIKELIHOOD SPATIAL ERROR (METHOD = FULL)
------------------------------------------------------------------
Data set            :       south
Weights matrix      :     south_q
Dependent Variable  :        HR90        Number of Observations:      1412
Mean dependent var  :      9.5493        Number of Variables   :         5
S.D. dependent var  :      7.0389        Degrees of Freedom    :      1407
Pseudo R-squared    :      0.3058
Sigma-square ML     :      32.407        Log likelihood        :  -4471.407
S.E of regression   :       5.693        Akaike info criterion :   8952.814
                                         Schwarz criterion     :   8979.078

       Variable     Coefficient       Std.Error     z-Statistic     Probability
-------------------------------------------------------------------------------
       CONSTANT       6.1492248       1.0318746       5.9592751       0.0000000
           RD90       4.4024201       0.2355472      18.6901829       0.0000000
           PS90       1.7783713       0.2131787       8.3421633       0.0000000
           UE90      -0.3780731       0.0783853      -4.8232686       0.0000014
           DV90       0.4857858       0.1217110       3.9913061       0.0000657
         lambda       0.2990778       0.0378155       7.9088781       0.0000000
-------------------------------------------------------------------------------
============================ END OF REPORT =================================
```

图 21.1 reg1 的标准结果输出图表

```
REGRESSION
----------
SUMMARY OF OUTPUT: MAXIMUM LIKELIHOOD SPATIAL ERROR (METHOD = ORD)
------------------------------------------------------------------
Data set            :       south
Weights matrix      :     south_q
Dependent Variable  :        HR90        Number of Observations:      1412
Mean dependent var  :      9.5493        Number of Variables   :         5
S.D. dependent var  :      7.0389        Degrees of Freedom    :      1407
Pseudo R-squared    :      0.3058
Sigma-square ML     :      32.407        Log likelihood        :  -4471.407
S.E of regression   :       5.693        Akaike info criterion :   8952.814
                                         Schwarz criterion     :   8979.078

       Variable     Coefficient       Std.Error     z-Statistic     Probability
-------------------------------------------------------------------------------
       CONSTANT       6.1492248       1.0318746       5.9592751       0.0000000
           RD90       4.4024201       0.2355472      18.6901829       0.0000000
           PS90       1.7783713       0.2131787       8.3421633       0.0000000
           UE90      -0.3780731       0.0783853      -4.8232686       0.0000014
           DV90       0.4857858       0.1217110       3.9913061       0.0000657
         lambda       0.2990778       0.0387445       7.7192378       0.0000000
-------------------------------------------------------------------------------
============================ END OF REPORT =================================
```

图 21.2 reg2 的标准结果输出图表

最后，为了展示出 Full 和 Ord 两种优化方法的不同，我们使用 IPython ％ timeit 命令获得一些运算时间上的结果：

```
Full: 2.32 s ± 16 ms per loop (mean ± std. dev. of 7 runs, 1 loop each)
Ord: 1.51 s ± 24.1 ms per loop (mean ± std. dev. of 7 runs, 1 loop each)
```

我们可以看到，在这样的情况下，Ord 优化方法会比默认的 Full 方法节约一些时间。但是，这两种方法都会在数据量较大时（$n > 6000$）出现数值计算的不稳定性（这个阈值取决于计算机的硬件）。

第 22 章 PySAL spreg 中的滞后与误差共存的广义空间两阶段最小二乘估计

为了在 spreg 中演示如何进行对既有空间滞后又有空间误差的模型的回归估计，我们利用样本数据库 NAT.dbf，空间权重对象为 nat_queen.gal，因变量为 HR60，外生解释变量为 BLK60、DV60、PS60、RD60，内生解释变量为 UE60，选取的工具变量为 FH60、FP59 和 GI59。

这样的滞后与误差共存的组合模型（以下简称"组合模型"，即 GS2SLS）在回归时，综合了空间滞后模型中的空间两阶段最小二乘法（S2SLS）与空间误差模型中的广义矩方法（GM/GMM）两种估计方法；在本质上，这样的组合模型问题被化归成为一种带有内生解释变量的空间误差模型。因此，与第 9 章的 GM/GMM 估计法不同，这里的用户类不会再区分有无内生解释变量的模型了。相应的，本章将要讲解和演示使用的是如下三个用户类：GM 估计法对应的 GM_Combo（虽然它基本上被淘汰了，但是为了使我们的讨论更加完整，所以对它也加以说明）、异方差情形下 GMM 估计法对应的 GM_Combo_Het 和同方差情形下 GMM 估计法对应的 GM_Combo_Hom。

22.1 回归运算的准备

我们再次详细地介绍一遍进行回归运算之前必要的准备工作，如何提取数据库文件，如何提取变量数据为 numpy 数组，以及如何生成空间权重对象。我们区分两种情况:一种是不含有内生解释变量的情况,另一种是含有内生解释变量的情况。与之前相同,我们首先应该输入 numpy 和 pysal 两个模块:

```
>>> import numpy as np
>>> import pysal
```

当只有外生解释变量时,我们只需要满足 spreg 命令所需的最基本的两个 numpy 数组 y 和 x,这里为了方便查看结果,我们仍然以 Python 列表的形式给出变量的名称:

```
>>> db= pysal.open(pysal.examples.get_path('NAT.dbf'),'r')
>>> y_name= "HR60"
>>> y= np.array([db.by_col(y_name)]).T
>>> x_names= ["RD60","PS60","UE60","DV60","BLK60"]
>>> x= np.array([db.by_col(var) for var in x_names]).T
```

当解释变量不仅有外生解释变量,还包含内生解释变量时,我们就需要多给出两个 numpy 数组,一个是内生解释变量数组 yend,另一个是工具变量数组 q,我们还需要重新定义 numpy 数组 x,使其只包含外生解释变量,我们重新定义它为 xe(为了区分于仅有外生解释变量情况时给出的 x)。下面的命令在之前的基础上完成了上述变量数组的提取与创建:

```
>>> yend_names= ['UE60']
>>> yend= np.array([db.by_col(var) for var in yend_names]).T
>>> q_names= ['FH60','FP59','GI59']
>>> q= np.array([db.by_col(var) for var in q_names]).T
>>> xe_names= ['RD60','PS60','DV60','BLK60']
>>> xe= np.array([db.by_col(var) for var in xe_names]).T
```

最后,我们还需要确定一个空间权重对象,这可以通过读取已经存在的文件 nat_queen.gal 实现,我们提醒读者注意检查权重矩阵是否进行了行标准化,命令如下:

```
>>> galw= pysal.open(pysal.examples.get_path('nat_queen.gal'),'r')
>>> w= galw.read()
>>> galw.close()
```

```
>>> w.transform='r'
```

也可以通过 shape 文件生成相同的空间权重对象,命令为:

```
>>> w= pysal.queen_from_shapefile(pysal.examples.get_path('nat.shp'),
idVariable= "FIPSNO")
>>> w.transform='r'
```

22.2 GM_Combo 命令

解决组合模型回归问题的"古老"的 GM 估计法在 PySAL spreg 中相应的用户类是 spreg.GM_Combo,它有三个强制必需参数:因变量 numpy 数组 y 和外生解释变量 numpy 数组 x 以及一个空间权重对象 w。我们必须注意,在这里空间权重对象必须以赋值形式输入,即 $w=$ weightsobject,而不能像之前那样只输入 w;实际操作中最简便的方法就是 $w=$ w。当我们还需要处理内生解释变量时,除了之前必需的 y 和 x,我们还需要以赋值形式给出 yend=endogenousarray 和 $q=$ instrumentarray;最简便的方法同样是 yend=yend,$q=$ q。一个完整的 spreg.GM_Combo 命令如下:

```
>>> gmCombo= pysal.spreg.GM_Combo(y,x,yend= None,q= None,w= None,w_lags
= 1,lag_q= True,vm= False,name_y= None,name_x= None,name_yend= None,name_
q= None,name_w= None,name_ds= None)
```

其他可选参数及其默认值为:

- yend:一个内生解释变量 numpy 数组,默认值是无内生解释变量;
- q:一个工具变量 numpy 数组,默认值是无工具变量;
- w:空间权重对象,尽管由于 Python 自身的原因其默认值被设置为了无空间权重对象,但是它必须被明确地赋值,最简便的方法是 $w=$ w;
- w_lags:在创建空间滞后解释变量(WX)作为工具变量时,所取的邻接矩阵的阶数,默认值是 1,也就是取 WX(若赋值为 2,则取 WX 与 W2X 为工具变量);

- lag_q:是一个决定空间滞后变量(Wq)是否包含于整体的工具变量 q 中的选项,默认值是 True,也就是包含;
- vm:这个选项决定是否在正常回归计算结果的输出中附加整个系数方差-协方差矩阵,默认是不附加这个矩阵的(这个矩阵是一定会计算的,选项只是决定是否在结果中直接输出这个矩阵);
- name_y:一个字符串,包含因变量 y 的名称,默认是没有明确的名称;
- name_x:一组字符串变量,包含所有解释变量 x 的名称,用户必须自己确保名称顺序和 x 数组的顺序对应正确,默认是没有明确的名称序列;
- name_yend:一组字符串变量,包含所有内生解释变量 yend 的名称,用户必须自己确保名称顺序和 yend 数组的顺序对应正确,默认是没有明确的名称序列;
- name_q:一组字符串变量,包含所有工具变量 q 的名称,用户必须自己确保名称顺序和 q 数组的顺序对应正确,默认是没有明确的名称序列;
- name_w:空间权重对象的名称,默认是无名称;
- name_ds:数据库的描述,默认是没有数据库的描述。

一个有效的 spreg.GM_Combo 命令会生成一个回归对象,它具有包括估计结果、标准误在内的许多属性,其中也会包括一些对后续计算或有帮助的中间结果。我们利用之前做的准备工作进行一个回归计算来更详细地说明 spreg.GM_Combo 回归对象,命令如下:

```
>>> combo1= pysal.spreg.GM_Combo(y,x,w= w,name_y= y_name,name_x= x_names,name_w= 'nat_queen',name_ds= 'NAT')
```

我们用 Python 的 dir 命令查看回归对象 combo1 的各个属性:

```
>>> dir(combo1)
['_class_', '_delattr_', '_dict_', '_dir_', '_doc_', '_eq_', '_format_', '_ge_', '_getattribute_', '_gt_', '_hash_', '_init_', '_init_subclass_', '_le_', '_lt_', '_module_', '_ne_', '_new_', '_reduce_', '_reduce_ex_', '_repr_', '_setattr_', '_sizeof_', '_str_', '_subclasshook_', '_summary_', '_weakref_', '_cache', 'betas', 'e_filtered', 'e_pred', 'k', 'mean_y', 'n',
```

```
'name_ds', 'name_h', 'name_q', 'name_w', 'name_x', 'name_y', 'name_yend',
'name_z', 'pr2', 'pr2_e', 'predy', 'predy_e', 'rho', 'sig2', 'std_err',
'std_y', 'summary', 'title', 'u', 'vm', 'x', 'y', 'yend', 'z', 'z_stat']
```

大部分属性与OLS回归对象、空间滞后模型和GM空间误差模型相同，列出一部分较为特殊的属性如下：

- k：参数的个数，它包括回归的系数、空间滞后的自回归系数，但是不包括空间误差的自回归系数；
- betas：一个$(k+1)\times 1$的估计系数向量，空间滞后的自回归系数ρ是倒数第二项，空间误差的自回归系数λ是最后一项；
- rho：空间滞后项的自回归系数；
- vm：$k\times k$的估计系数的方差-协方差矩阵，注意GM空间误差模型对λ没有方差估计；
- predy_e：一个$n\times 1$向量，包含化简形式的预测值；
- e_pred：一个$n\times 1$向量，包含化简形式下的误差；
- e_filtered：除掉空间相关性后的残差；
- pr2_e：基于化简形式的预测值的空间伪R^2。

这样的每个属性均可以被单独地提取。例如，我们可以单独地提取估计系数列向量 betas：

```
>>> combo1.betas
array([[ 0.32411091],
       [ 0.80866252],
       [ 0.1056478 ],
       [ 0.05279337],
       [ 0.61577086],
       [ 0.07096489],
       [ 0.44950309],
       [-0.1884266 ]])
```

空间滞后的自回归系数可以从倒数第二项提取出来：

```
>>> combo1.betas[-2][0]
```
0.449503091444976

也可以通过 rho 属性提取调用：

```
>>> combo1.rho
```
array([0.44950309])

空间误差的自回归系数可以从最后一项提取出来：

```
>>> combo1.betas[-1][0]
```
- 0.18842659944632473

组合模型回归对象 combo1 的完整结果图表如图 22.1 所示。

```
REGRESSION
----------
SUMMARY OF OUTPUT: SPATIALLY WEIGHTED TWO STAGE LEAST SQUARES
-------------------------------------------------------------
Data set            :       NAT
Weights matrix      :  nat_queen
Dependent Variable  :      HR60      Number of Observations:    3085
Mean dependent var  :    4.5041      Number of Variables    :       7
S.D. dependent var  :    5.6497      Degrees of Freedom     :    3078
Pseudo R-squared    :    0.3333
Spatial Pseudo R-squared:  0.2854

------------------------------------------------------------------------------------
       Variable     Coefficient       Std.Error     z-Statistic     Probability
------------------------------------------------------------------------------------
       CONSTANT       0.3241109       0.2492294       1.3004522       0.1934460
           RD60       0.8086625       0.1400977       5.7721323       0.0000000
           PS60       0.1056478       0.0843697       1.2522008       0.2104967
           UE60       0.0527934       0.0308956       1.7087671       0.0874941
           DV60       0.6157709       0.0980317       6.2813471       0.0000000
          BLK60       0.0709649       0.0105437       6.7305432       0.0000000
         W_HR60       0.4495031       0.0652376       6.8902409       0.0000000
         lambda      -0.1884266
------------------------------------------------------------------------------------
Instrumented: W_HR60
Instruments: W_BLK60, W_DV60, W_PS60, W_RD60, W_UE60
================================ END OF REPORT ======================================
```

图 22.1 combo1 的标准结果输出图表

当我们要处理含有内生解释变量的情况时，我们就需要对 yend 和 q 赋值。我们利用之前所做的准备工作，利用 numpy 数组 y, xe, yend 和 q，执行如下命令：

```
>>> combo2= pysal.spreg.GM_Combo(y,xe,yend= yend,q= q,w= w,name_y= y_name,name_x= xe_names,name_yend= yend_names,name_q= q_names,name_w= 'nat_queen',name_ds= 'NAT')
```

结果如图 22.2 所示。

```
REGRESSION
----------
SUMMARY OF OUTPUT: SPATIALLY WEIGHTED TWO STAGE LEAST SQUARES
-------------------------------------------------------------
Data set            :        NAT
Weights matrix      :   nat_queen
Dependent Variable  :       HR60        Number of Observations:       3085
Mean dependent var  :     4.5041        Number of Variables   :          7
S.D. dependent var  :     5.6497        Degrees of Freedom    :       3078
Pseudo R-squared    :     0.3328
Spatial Pseudo R-squared:  0.2812

-------------------------------------------------------------------------------
      Variable       Coefficient        Std.Error       z-Statistic   Probability
-------------------------------------------------------------------------------
      CONSTANT        -0.0618162        0.3505032        -0.1763642     0.8600079
          RD60         0.6903681        0.1485215         4.6482704     0.0000033
          PS60         0.0636171        0.0911780         0.6977245     0.4853495
          DV60         0.5411868        0.1009337         5.3618036     0.0000001
         BLK60         0.0703360        0.0108268         6.4964399     0.0000000
          UE60         0.1276860        0.0688647         1.8541563     0.0637168
        W_HR60         0.4818021        0.0610440         7.8926964     0.0000000
        lambda        -0.1901571
-------------------------------------------------------------------------------
Instrumented: UE60, W_HR60
Instruments: FH60, FP59, GI59, W_BLK60, W_DV60, W_FH60, W_FP59, W_GI59,
             W_PS60, W_RD60
================================ END OF REPORT ================================
```

图 22.2　combo2 的标准结果输出图表

22.3　GM_Combo_Hom 命令

最适合估计误差项的空间自回归系数的方法是 GMM 估计方法而不是"古老"的 GM 估计方法,就像我们在第 20 章中处理空间误差模型时所做的一样,这里我们把情况也分为两种:有异方差的情况和没有异方差的情况。由于在 GeoDaSpace 中,默认设置是同方差的情况,我们先来考虑同方差的用户类 GM_Combo_Hom。但在实际应用中,异方差的方法是最合适的。GM_Combo_Hom 用户类的三个强制必需参数和 GM_Combo 相同,numpy 数组 y 和 x 以及一个要被明确赋值的空间权重对象($w=w$),完整的命令如下:

>>> gmComboHom= pysal.spreg.GM_Combo_Hom(y, x, yend= None, q= None, w=

None,w_lags= 1,lag_q= True,max_iter= 1,eosilon= 1e-5,A_1= 'hom_sc',vm= False,name_y= None,name_x= None,name_yend= None,name_q= None,name_w= None,name_ds= None)

可选参数及其默认值为：

- yend：一个内生解释变量 numpy 数组，默认值是无内生解释变量；
- q：一个工具变量 numpy 数组，默认值是无工具变量；
- w：空间权重对象，尽管由于 Python 自身的原因其默认值被设置为了无空间权重对象，但是它必须被明确地赋值，最简单的方法是 $w=w$；
- w_lags：在创建空间滞后解释变量（WX）作为工具变量时，所取的邻接矩阵的阶数，默认值是 1，也就是取 WX（若赋值为 2，则取 WX 与 W2X 为工具变量）；
- lag_q：是一个决定空间滞后变量（Wq）是否包含于整体的工具 q 中的选项，默认值是 True，也就是包含；
- max_iter：最大迭代次数，默认值是没有迭代，也就是迭代次数设置为 1；
- epsilon：在非线性优化步骤中的收敛判定标准，默认值是 0.000 000 1；
- A_1：它的值是一个字符串，决定了哪一种 A_1 矩阵会被用在回归运算中；默认值是'hom_sc'，即带有缩放因子 v 的方程 1；另外两个选项是'hom'，即无缩放因子 v 的方程 1，以及'het'，即取 A_1 为方程 2（具体的方程请参见第 9 章的 GM_Error_Hom 用户类）；
- vm：这个选项决定是否在正常回归计算结果的输出中附加整个系数方差-协方差矩阵，默认是不附加这个矩阵的（这个矩阵是一定会计算的，选项只是决定是否在结果中直接输出这个矩阵）；
- name_y：一个字符串，包含因变量 y 的名称，默认是没有明确的名称；
- name_x：一组字符串变量，包含所有解释变量 x 的名称，用户必须自己确保名称顺序和 x 数组的顺序对应正确，默认是没有明确的名称序列；
- name_yend：一组字符串变量，包含所有内生解释变量 yend 的名称，用

户必须自己确保名称顺序和 yend 数组的顺序对应正确,默认是没有明确的名称序列;

- name_q:一组字符串变量,包含所有工具变量 q 的名称,用户必须自己确保自己的名称顺序和 q 数组的顺序对应正确,默认是没有明确的名称序列;
- name_w:空间权重对象的名称;默认是无名称;
- name_ds:数据库的描述;默认是没有数据库的描述。

一个有效的 spreg.GM_Combo_Hom 命令会生成一个回归对象,它具有包括估计结果、标准误在内的许多属性,其中也会包括一些对后续计算或有帮助的中间结果。我们利用之前做的准备工作进行一个仅有外生解释变量的回归计算来更详细地说明 spreg.GM_Combo_Hom 回归对象,命令如下:

```
>>> combo3= pysal.spreg.GM_Combo_Hom(y,x,w=w,name_y=y_name,name_x=x_names,name_w='nat_queen',name_ds='NAT')
```

我们用 Python 的 dir 命令查看回归对象 combo3 的各个属性:

```
>>> dir(combo3)
['_class_', '_delattr_', '_dict_', '_dir_', '_doc_', '_eq_', '_format_',
'_ge_', '_getattribute_', '_gt_', '_hash_', '_init_', '_init_subclass_',
'_le_', '_lt_', '_module_', '_ne_', '_new_', '_reduce_', '_reduce_ex_',
'_repr_', '_setattr_', '_sizeof_', '_str_', '_subclasshook_', '_summary',
'_weakref_', '_cache', 'betas', 'e_filtered', 'e_pred', 'h', 'hth',
'iter_stop', 'iteration', 'k', 'mean_y', 'n', 'name_ds', 'name_h', 'name_q',
'name_w', 'name_x', 'name_y', 'name_yend', 'name_z', 'pr2', 'pr2_e', 'predy',
'predy_e', 'q', 'rho', 'sig2', 'std_err', 'std_y', 'summary', 'title', 'u',
'vm', 'x', 'y', 'yend', 'z', 'z_stat']
```

这些属性基本上是由 GM_Lag 对象和 GM_Endog_Error_Hom 对象的属性组成的。像上一个模型一样,k 并不包括空间误差的自回归系数。然后由于 GMM 估计方法给出了标准误的估计值 λ,方差-协方差矩阵 vm 的维数变成了 $(k+1)\times(k+1)$,这与 GM_Combo 对象的 $k \times k$ 阶是不同的;其他属性和 GM_Combo 对象的属性一致。结果如图 22.3 所示。

```
REGRESSION
----------
SUMMARY OF OUTPUT: SPATIALLY WEIGHTED TWO STAGE LEAST SQUARES (HOM)
-------------------------------------------------------------------
Data set              :        NAT
Weights matrix        :  nat_queen
Dependent Variable    :       HR60    Number of Observations:    3085
Mean dependent var    :     4.5041    Number of Variables    :       7
S.D. dependent var    :     5.6497    Degrees of Freedom     :    3078
Pseudo R-squared      :     0.3333
Spatial Pseudo R-squared:   0.2854
N. of iterations      :          1
-------------------------------------------------------------------
     Variable     Coefficient     Std.Error     z-Statistic    Probability
-------------------------------------------------------------------
     CONSTANT      0.3239850      0.2364887      1.3699807      0.1706929
         RD60      0.8086410      0.1364000      5.9284534      0.0000000
         PS60      0.1056035      0.0804090      1.3133301      0.1890717
         UE60      0.0527400      0.0295573      1.7843270      0.0743705
         DV60      0.6158838      0.0969425      6.3530825      0.0000000
        BLK60      0.0709563      0.0103216      6.8745561      0.0000000
       W_HR60      0.4495694      0.0652271      6.8923719      0.0000000
       lambda     -0.2729182      0.1021516     -2.6716980      0.0075469
-------------------------------------------------------------------
Instrumented: W_HR60
Instruments: W_BLK60, W_DV60, W_PS60, W_RD60, W_UE60
============================= END OF REPORT =============================
```

图 22.3　combo3 的标准结果输出图表

当我们要处理含有内生解释变量的情况时，我们就需要对 yend 和 q 赋值。我们利用之前所做的准备工作，利用 numpy 数组 y, xe, yend 和 q, 执行如下命令：

>>> combo4= pysal.spreg.GM_Combo_Hom(y,xe,yend= yend,q= q,w= w,name_y= y_name,name_x= xe_names,name_yend= yend_names,name_q= q_names,name_w= 'nat_queen',name_ds= 'NAT')

结果如图 22.4 所示。

22.4　GM_Combo_Het 命令

我们使用 PySAL 用户类 spreg.GM_Combo_Het 对有异方差情况的组合模型进行 GMM 估计，它的强制必需参数和 GM_Combo_Hom 是一样的，只有在可选参数中有一点细微的变化，完整的命令如下：

```
REGRESSION
----------
SUMMARY OF OUTPUT: SPATIALLY WEIGHTED TWO STAGE LEAST SQUARES (HOM)
-----------------------------------------------------------------
Data set            :         NAT
Weights matrix      :    nat_queen
Dependent Variable  :        HR60         Number of Observations:       3085
Mean dependent var  :      4.5041         Number of Variables   :          7
S.D. dependent var  :      5.6497         Degrees of Freedom    :       3078
Pseudo R-squared    :      0.3328
Spatial Pseudo R-squared:  0.2812
N. of iterations    :           1

------------------------------------------------------------------
      Variable     Coefficient       Std.Error     z-Statistic    Probability
------------------------------------------------------------------
      CONSTANT      -0.0617938       0.3188267      -0.1938164      0.8463197
          RD60       0.6902893       0.1403672       4.9177379      0.0000009
          PS60       0.0635952       0.0851447       0.7469065      0.4551200
          DV60       0.5412369       0.0977580       5.5365000      0.0000000
          BLK60      0.0703134       0.0103875       6.7690271      0.0000000
          UE60       0.1275722       0.0631550       2.0199859      0.0433848
        W_HR60       0.4819608       0.0602250       8.0026721      0.0000000
        lambda      -0.3104618       0.0989503      -3.1375537      0.0017036
------------------------------------------------------------------
Instrumented: UE60, W_HR60
Instruments: FH60, FP59, GI59, W_BLK60, W_DV60, W_FH60, W_FP59, W_GI59,
             W_PS60, W_RD60
============================== END OF REPORT ==========================
```

图 22.4 combo4 的标准结果输出图表

> > > gmComboHet= pysal.spreg.GM_Combo_Het(y, x, yend= None, q= None, w= None, w_lags= 1, lag_q= True, max_iter= 1, epsilon= 1e-5, step1c= False, inv_method= 'power_exp', vm= False, name_y= None, name_x= None, name_yend= None, name_q= None, name_w= None, name_ds= None)

大体来说,其可选参数与 GM_Combo_Hom 用户类是相同的,但是对于异方差的情况,我们不再有可选参数 A_1,反而出现了之前 GM_Error_Het 用户类中的两个可选参数:

• step1c:一个选项,它决定了对 λ 进行初始估计时是否进行额外一步计算,默认值是 False;

• inv_method:一个选项,它决定了具体计算矩阵逆的方法,默认值是'power_exp',即做方幂展开,另一个选项是'true_inv',也就是使用标准的求逆算法(当我们要估计的模型数据量较大时可能会出现问题)。

举例说明这个方法,我们将之前只有外生解释变量的数据运用到这个用户类中去运算,需要给出 numpy 数组 y 和 x 以及赋值 $w=$ w。依据我们最开始进行的准备工作,并且附加上对因变量、解释变量和空间权重对象的名称,命令如下:

> > > combo5= pysal.spreg.GM_Combo_Het(y,x,w= w,name_y= y_name,name_x= x_names,name_w= 'nat_queen',name_ds= 'NAT')

这个回归对象的属性和 GM_Combo_Hom 对象的属性基本相同,但是它没有对残差的方差的估计。结果如图 22.5 所示。

```
REGRESSION
----------
SUMMARY OF OUTPUT: SPATIALLY WEIGHTED TWO STAGE LEAST SQUARES (HET)
------------------------------------------------------------------
Data set            :       NAT
Weights matrix      :  nat_queen
Dependent Variable  :      HR60                Number of Observations:        3085
Mean dependent var  :    4.5041                Number of Variables   :           7
S.D. dependent var  :    5.6497                Degrees of Freedom    :        3078
Pseudo R-squared    :    0.3333
Spatial Pseudo R-squared:    0.2853
N. of iterations    :         1                Step1c computed       :          No

------------------------------------------------------------------------------
     Variable      Coefficient       Std.Error     z-Statistic     Probability
------------------------------------------------------------------------------
     CONSTANT        0.3264431       0.2256289       1.4468142       0.1479490
         RD60        0.8090534       0.1532549       5.2791308       0.0000001
         PS60        0.1064660       0.1016379       1.0475035       0.2948674
         UE60        0.0537745       0.0287134       1.8728001       0.0610960
         DV60        0.6136830       0.1071702       5.7262456       0.0000000
         BLK60       0.0711234       0.0122398       5.8108400       0.0000000
         W_HR60      0.4482870       0.0719587       6.2297823       0.0000000
         lambda     -0.4383045       0.0979689      -4.4739149       0.0000077
------------------------------------------------------------------------------
Instrumented: W_HR60
Instruments: W_BLK60, W_DV60, W_PS60, W_RD60, W_UE60
================================ END OF REPORT ================================
```

图 22.5　combo5 的标准结果输出图表

然而运用一开始所做的准备工作,我们也可以给出与上述相对应的包含外生解释变量和内生解释变量的例子,命令如下:

> > > combo6= pysal.spreg.GM_Combo_Het(y,xe,yend= yend,q= q,w= w,name_y= y_name,name_x= xe_names,name_yend= yend_names,name_q= q_names,name_w= 'nat_queen',name_ds= 'NAT')

结果如图 22.6 所示。

```
REGRESSION
----------
SUMMARY OF OUTPUT: SPATIALLY WEIGHTED TWO STAGE LEAST SQUARES (HET)
-------------------------------------------------------------------
Data set              :       NAT
Weights matrix        :       nat_queen
Dependent Variable    :       HR60         Number of Observations:        3085
Mean dependent var    :       4.5041       Number of Variables    :           7
S.D. dependent var    :       5.6497       Degrees of Freedom     :        3078
Pseudo R-squared      :       0.3328
Spatial Pseudo R-squared:     0.2810
N. of iterations      :            1       Step1c computed        :          No
-------------------------------------------------------------------
       Variable      Coefficient      Std.Error     z-Statistic     Probability
-------------------------------------------------------------------
       CONSTANT      -0.0622402       0.3447555     -0.1805344       0.8567330
           RD60       0.6916849       0.1395608      4.9561544       0.0000007
           PS60       0.0639946       0.0894662      0.7152939       0.4744275
           DV60       0.5402806       0.1044551      5.1723732       0.0000002
          BLK60       0.0707237       0.0111402      6.3485286       0.0000000
           UE60       0.1296600       0.0692818      1.8714876       0.0612775
         W_HR60       0.4790831       0.0645823      7.4181827       0.0000000
         lambda      -0.4644452       0.0926202     -5.0145115       0.0000005
-------------------------------------------------------------------
Instrumented: UE60, W_HR60
Instruments: FH60, FP59, GI59, W_BLK60, W_DV60, W_FH60, W_FP59, W_GI59,
     W_PS60, W_RD60
================================ END OF REPORT ====================================
```

图 22.6　combo6 的标准结果输出图表

参考文献

[1] Anselin, L. (1980). Estimation methods for spatial autoregressive structures. Regional Science Dissertation & Monograph Series, Program in Urban and Regional Studies, Cornell University, 8, 273.

[2] Anselin, L. (1986). Non-nested tests on the weight structure in spatial autoregressive models: Some Monte Carlo results. Journal of Regional Science, 26(2), 267-284.

[3] Anselin, L. (1988). A test for spatial autocorrelation in seemingly unrelated regressions. Economics Letters, 28(4), 335-341.

[4] Anselin, L. (1988). Lagrange multiplier test diagnostics for spatial dependence and spatial heterogeneity. Geographical Analysis, 20(1), 1-17.

[5] Anselin, L. (1988). Model validation in spatial econometrics: A review and evaluation of alternative approaches. International Regional Science Review, 11(3), 279-316.

[6] Anselin, L. (1988). Spatial Econometrics: Methods and Models. Dordrecht: Kluwer Academic Publishers.

[7] Anselin, L. (1990). Some robust approaches to testing and estimation in spatial econometrics. Regional Science and Urban Economics, 20(2), 141-163.

[8] Anselin, L. (1990). Spatial dependence and spatial structural instability in applied regression analysis. Journal of Regional Science, 30(2), 185-207.

[9] Anselin, L. (1992). Space and applied econometrics: Introduction. Regional Science and Urban Economics, 22(3), 307-316.

[10]Anselin, L. (1995). Local indicators of spatial association-LISA. Geographical Analysis, 27(2), 93-115.

[11]Anselin, L. (1998). GIS research infrastructure for spatial analysis of real estate markets. Journal of Housing Research, 9(1), 113-133.

[12] Anselin, L. (2000). Computing environments for spatial data analysis. Journal of Geographical Systems, 2(3), 201-220.

[13]Anselin, L. (2001). Rao's score test in spatial econometrics. Journal of Statistical Planning and Inference, 97(1), 113-139.

[14]Anselin, L. (2003). Spatial externalities, spatial multipliers, and spatial econometrics. International Regional Science Review, 26(2), 153-166.

[15] Anselin, L. (2006). Spatial econometrics. In: Mills, T., & K. Patterson (Eds.), Palgrave Handbook of Econometrics: Volume 1, Econometric Theory. Basingstoke: Palgrave Macmillan.

[16]Anselin, L. (2010). Thirty years of spatial econometrics. Regional Science, 89(1), 3-25.

[17]Anselin, L., & Griffith, D. A. (1988). Do spatial effecfs really matter in regression analysis? Papers in Regional Science, 65(1), 11-34.

[18]Anselin, L., & Hudak, S. (1992). Spatial econometrics in practice: A review of software options. Regional Science and Urban Economics, 22(3), 509-536.

[19]Anselin, L., & Kelejian, H. H. (1997). Testing for spatial error autocorrelation in the presence of endogenous regressors. International Regional Science Review, 20(1-2), 153-182.

[20]Anselin, L., & Rey, S. (1991). Properties of tests for spatial dependence in linear regression models. Geographical Analysis, 23(2), 112-131.

[21]Anselin, L., & Rey, S. J. (1997). Introduction to the special issue on spatial econometrics. International Regional Science Review, 20(1-2), 1-7.

[22]Anselin, L., & Rey, S. J. (2014). Modern spatial econometrics in practice: A guide to GeoDa, GeoDaSpace and PySAL. GeoDa Press LLC, Chicago.

[23]Anselin, L., & Smirnov, O. (1996). Efficient algorithms for constructing proper higher order spatial lag operators. Journal of Regional Science, 36(1), 67-89.

[24]Anselin, L., Bera, A. K., Florax, R., & Yoon, M. J. (1996). Simple diagnostic tests for spatial dependence. Regional Science and Urban Economics, 26(1), 77-104.

[25]Arraiz, I., et al. (2010). A spatial cliff-ord-type model with heteroskedastic innovations: Small and large sample results. Journal of Regional Science 50 (2), 592-614.

[26]Baller, R. D., Anselin, L., Messner, S. F., & Deane, G. (2010). Structural covariates of U.S. county homicide rates: Incorporating spatial effects. Criminology, 39(3), 561-588.

[27]CliffA., & Ord J. K. (1973). Spatial Autocorrelation. London: Pion.

[28]CliffA., & Ord J. K. (1981). Spatial Processes: Models and Applications. London: Pion.

[29]Drukker, D. M., Egger, P., & Prucha, I. R. (2013). On two-step estimation of a spatial autoregressive model with autoregressive disturbances and endogenous regressors. Econometric Reviews, 32(5-6), 686-733.

[30]Dubin, R. A. (1992). Spatial autocorrelation and neighborhood quality. Regional Science and Urban Economics, 22(3), 433-452.

[31]Goodchild, M. F., Anselin, L., Appelbaum, R. P., & Harthorn, B. H. (2000). Toward spatially integrated social science. International Regional Science Review, 23(2), 139-159.

[32]Goodchild, M., Haining, R., & Wise, S. (1992). Integrating GIS

and spatial data analysis: Problems and possibilities. International Journal of Geographical Information Systems, 6(5), 407-423.

[33]Goodman, A. C. (1978). Hedonic prices, price indices and housing markets. Journal of Urban Economics, 5(4), 471-484.

[34]Isard, W. (1956). Location and Space-Economy. Cambridge: MIT Press.

[35] Isard, W. (1975). Introduction to Regional Science. Englewood Cliffs, NJ: Prentice-Hall.

[36]Isard, W., et al. (1960). Methods of Regional Analysis: An Introduction to Regional Science. Cambridge: MIT Press.

[37]Kelejian, H. H., & Prucha, I. R. (1997). Estimation of spatial regression models with autoregressive errors by two-stage least squares procedures: A serious problem. International Regional Science Review, 20(1-2), 103-111.

[38]Kelejian, H. H., & Prucha, I. R. (1998). A generalized spatial two-stage least squares procedure for estimating a spatial autoregressive model with autoregressive disturbances. The Journal of Real Estate Finance and Economics, 17(1), 99-121.

[39]Kelejian, H. H., & Prucha, I. R. (1999). A generalized moments estimator for the autoregressive parameter in a spatial model. International Economic Review, 40(2), 509-533.

[40]Kelejian, H. H., & Robinson, D. P. (1993). A suggested method of estimation for spatial interdependent models with autocorrelated errors, and an application to a county expenditure model. Papers in Regional Science, 72(3), 297-312.

[41]Messner, S., Anselin, L., Hawkins, D., Deane, G., Tolnay, S., & Baller R. (2000). An Atlas of the Spatial Patterning of County-Level

Homicide, 1960-1990. Pittsburgh: National Consortium on Violence Research (NCOVR).

[42] Pace, R. K., & Barry, R. (1998). Spatial Statistics Toolbox 1.0. Real Estate Research Institute, Louisiana State University, Baton Rouge, LA.

[43] Paelinck, J., & Klaassen, L. (1979). Spatial Econometrics. Farnborough: Saxon House.

[44] 沈体雁,于瀚辰. 空间计量经济学(第二版). 北京:北京大学出版社,2019.

[45] 沈体雁等. 空间计量经济学. 北京:北京大学出版社,2010.

[46] 汤国安,杨昕. Arcgis 地理信息系统空间分析实验教程. 北京:科学出版社,2006.